Deep Learning Technologies for Social Impact

Online at: https://doi.org/10.1088/978-0-7503-4024-3

IOP Series in Next Generation Computing

Series editors

Prateek Agrawal

University of Klagenfurt, Austria and Lovely Professional University, India

Anand Sharma

Mody University of Science and Technology, India

Vishu Madaan

Lovely Professional University, India

About the series

The motivation for this series is to develop a trusted library on advanced computational methods, technologies, and their applications.

This series focuses on the latest developments in next generation computing, and in particular on the synergy between computer science and other disciplines. Books in the series will explore new developments in various disciplines that are relevant for computational perspective including foundations, systems, innovative applications, and other research contributions related to the overall design of computational tools, models, and algorithms that are relevant for the respective domain. It encompasses research and development in artificial intelligence, machine learning, block chain technology, quantum cryptography, quantum computing, nanoscience, bioscience-based sensors, IoT applications, nature inspired algorithms, computer vision, bioinformatics, etc. and their applications in the areas of science, engineering, business, and the social sciences. It covers a broad spectrum of applications in the community, including those in industry, government, and academia.

The aim of the series is to provide an opportunity for prospective researchers and experts to publish works based on next generation computing and its diverse applications. It also provides a data-sharing platform that will bring together international researchers, professionals, and academics. This series brings together thought leaders, researchers, industry practitioners, and potential users of different disciplines to develop new trends and opportunities, exchange ideas and practices related to advanced computational methods, and promote interdisciplinary knowledge.

A full list of titles published in this series can be found here: https://iopscience.iop.org/bookListInfo/iop-series-in-next-generation-computing.

Deep Learning Technologies for Social Impact

Shajulin Benedict
Indian Institute of Information Technology Kottayam,
Valavoor P.O. Kottayam District, Kerala, India

IOP Publishing, Bristol, UK

ISBN   978-0-7503-4024-3 (ebook)
ISBN   978-0-7503-4022-9 (print)
ISBN   978-0-7503-4025-0 (myPrint)
ISBN   978-0-7503-4023-6 (mobi)

DOI   10.1088/978-0-7503-4024-3

Version: 20221001

IOP ebooks

British Library Cataloguing-in-Publication Data: A catalogue record for this book is available from the British Library.

Published by IOP Publishing, wholly owned by The Institute of Physics, London

IOP Publishing, Temple Circus, Temple Way, Bristol, BS1 6HG, UK

US Office: IOP Publishing, Inc., 190 North Independence Mall West, Suite 601, Philadelphia, PA 19106, USA

To my father C Benedict, mother J Mary Alphonsal, wife Rejitha R S, son Shaun Benedict, and daughter Sharlina R S.

Contents

Part III Security, performance, and future directions

11 Data security and platforms

Preface

'Never worry about numbers. Help one person at a time, and start with the person nearest you.'—Mother Teresa.

'The best way to find yourself is to lose yourself in the service of others.'—Mahatma Gandhi.

In the modern era, social problems and allied impacts are increasing daily. Technological growth and associated gadgets have raised the importance of the emotional quotient among people so that it is equivalent to that of the increasing intelligence quotient. Some important questions that we need to ask ourselves are as follows:

- How good are we?
- How much can we give to society?
- Can we be people who work for social good?
- Do we have the technological strength to address societal problems?

In fact, addressing the existing challenges of societal problems using traditional approaches remains ineffective—i.e. it becomes crucial to practice specific methods and procedures, such as adopting deep-learning approaches, in order to address societal challenges such as water quality, air quality, women's empowerment, and so forth.

Smart cities are increasingly promoting innovative solutions for social good, with the intention of enhancing self-sustainability and addressing societal problems using novel technologies, including deep learning and IoT solutions.

This book presents the application of deep-learning technologies to increasing near-future innovation in society. It motivates students, entrepreneurs, readers, and practitioners, to develop novel ideas while incorporating deep-learning techniques into their existing problem domains. It improves the thought processes used to examine modern societal problems and suggests procedures with which to address them.

I dedicate this book to my loving parents (Mr C Benedict and Mrs J Mary Alphonsal), my wife (Rejitha R S), and children. I acknowledge the tireless support provided by Prof. Michael Gerndt in mentoring me throughout my career. In addition, I thank Prof. Schrier for patiently proof-reading a few pages of this book. I extend my gratitude to TUM-Germany, AIC/IIIT-Kottayam, and the editors and reviewers of IOP Publishing.

—Dr Shajulin Benedict
(http://www.sbenedictglobal.com)

Acknowledgement

I acknowledge the support provided by Professor Michael Gerndt of TUM, Professor Tina Schrier of TUM, IIIT-Kottayam officials (Director and Registrar), AIM officials, Government of India, and my PhD scholars for supporting this work.

Author biography

Shajulin Benedict

Shajulin Benedict graduated with Distinction in 2001 from Manonmaniam Sunderanar University, India. In 2004, he received an ME Degree in Digital Communication and Computer Networking from Arulmigu Kalasalingam College of Engineering (AKCE), Anna University, Chennai. His master's degree was ranked second in the University. He did his PhD degree on the topic of grid scheduling at Anna University, Chennai (Supervisor—Dr V Vasudevan, Director, Software Technologies Group of the Technology Information Forecasting and Assessment Council (TIFAC) CORE in Network Engineering). He was affiliated to the same group and has published further papers in international journals.

After his PhD award, he joined a research team in Germany to pursue a postdoctorate career under the guidance of Prof. Gerndt. He served as Professor at St. Xavier's Catholic College of Engineering (SXCCE), a research centre of Anna University-Chennai. Later, he visited the Technical University of Munich (TUM), Germany, to teach Cloud Computing as a Guest Professor of the TUM.

Currently, he works at the Indian Institute of Information Technology (IIIT) Kottayam, Kerala, India, an institute of national importance in India, and as Guest Professor of TUM. Additionally, he serves as Director/PI/Representative Officer of Atal Innovation Mission, IIIT (AIC-IIIT) Kottayam (Sec.8 Company) an incubation centre for young entrepreneurs of India. His research interests include deep learning, high-performance computing (HPC)/cloud/grid scheduling, performance analysis of parallel applications (including exascale), IoT cloud, etc.

Part I

Introduction

Chapter 1

Deep learning for social good—an introduction

Deep learning is a subset of the machine learning domain that has created a sharp rise in applications, more specifically, applications for social good. Such applications are used in combination with multiple technologies, such as the Internet of things (IoT), 5G, the blockchain, the cloud, edge computing, and so forth. Deep learning is an incredibly powerful learning mechanism based on the functioning of neural networks which mimic the neurons of the human brain.

This chapter introduces deep learning and its applications; in addition, it emphasises the applications that benefit a large number of people in society.

1.1 Deep learning—a subset of AI

Deep learning is not a competitive technology with respect to machine learning and artificial intelligence (AI). It is a subset of the other traditional learning systems. It is based on functional layers that utilize raw input data to automatically create abstract features and perform learning tasks such as regression, classification, or ranking. There are several misconceptions about the differences between deep learning and AI or machine learning. Figure 1.1 pictorially clarifies where the deep learning domain resides in relation to these other technologies.

Generally, intelligence is based on acquiring knowledge from the past and processing it to provide new insights into data. Obviously, human intelligence requires a lot of time to obtain the information required to take decisive actions—i.e. a human being might need several months in infancy to identify a pen or other objects.

Artificial intelligence utilizes algorithms and techniques to mimic human-like behavior—i.e. to take correct decisions, such as quickly classifying objects based on previous observations. AI corresponds to digital systems, whereas the human brain resembles an analog system.

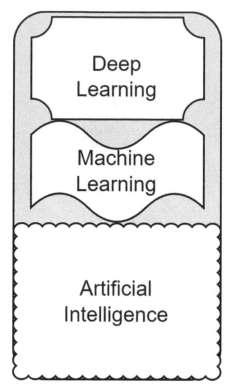

Figure 1.1. Deep learning—a subset of AI.

As can be observed in figure 1.2, AI is a basic technique for other techniques such as machine learning and deep learning. Machine learning remains a subset of artificial intelligence. It aims to develop algorithms/programs and insert them into machines to take decisions based on the input data. The decisions can be either regression or classification performed using smaller or larger volumes of input data.

Deep learning evolved as a subset of machine learning. It attempts to identify specific patterns or features in data. Utilizing these patterns, deep learning algorithms perform novel inferences and pursue actions. Deep learning models structure algorithms to create layers of algorithms used to learn data and take decisions in an automated fashion.

Deep learning has found many uses in several domains such as voice synthesis, vehicle automation, image classification, intelligent transportation systems, forensics, energy analysis, economy forecasting, and so forth, which promote social goodness. Notably, there are several applications that directly influence the well-being of a large number of people. For instance, chatbot applications assist survivors of sexual harassment, security applications improve privacy and fairness while sharing data, healthcare applications assist medical practitioners, financial applications guide investors/consumers, opinion-related applications enhance the visibility of people in society, and so forth.

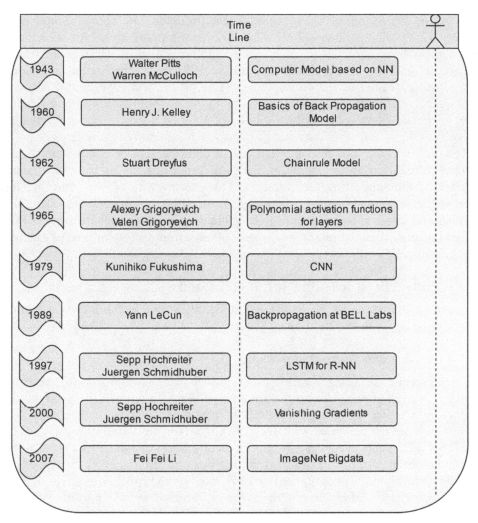

Figure 1.2. History of deep learning.

1.2 History of deep learning

Traditionally, AI was often implemented using rule-based reasoning engines [2]. However, the surge in multidimensional data obtained from a large array of problem domains, including varying application sectors, has given birth to deep learning.

Initially, in 1943, Walter Pitts and Warren McCulloch designed a computer model based on neural networks. This theoretical model gave confidence to their peer designers and scientists. Later, in the 1960s, Henry J. Kelley disclosed the basics of the backpropagation model. As discussed later in this book, backpropagation [8] remains an important technique for developing deep learning algorithms. In 1962, Stuart Dreyfus designed the chain rule model; in 1965, Alexey Grigoryevich and Valen Grigoryevich designed activation functions [1] for neural network layers.

Later, in 1979, Kunihiko Fukushima developed the first convolutional neural network [7] for image analysis. This became the stepping stone for speeding up neural network solutions. In 1989, Yann LeCun implemented the backpropagation concept at Bell Labs. After much research, in 1997, Sepp Hochreiter and Juergen Schmidhuber developed the concept of LSTM [9] for recursive neural networks. Subsequently, in 2000, the vanishing gradient problem was discussed and solutions were proposed by several authors; and, in 2007, Fei-Fei Li designed the first ImageNet [10] to solve big data image processing and analysis problems.

Recently, several years of continued research into, and the development of, deep learning innovations have resulted in the growth not only of algorithmic efficiency but also of the supporting architectures. The practitioners of deep learning have investigated the use of central processing units (CPUs), graphical processing units (GPUs), and tensor processing units (TPUs)/field-programmable gate array (FPGA) devices made available through inexpensive cloud computing solutions for executing deep learning algorithms.

1.3 Trends—deep learning for social good

This section showcases the current trends of deep learning technology which enable other technologies to promote social values.

1.3.1 Increasing data; increasing machines

The intersection of deep learning with industry [5], healthcare [6], consumer products, and so forth, has promoted a large array of innovative products that process data either from large numbers of participants or from machines. Most newer machines are equipped with deep learning algorithms and sensor devices that collect big data either periodically or aperiodically. The emergence of a large volume of data has improved the accuracy of predictions and strengthened the rise of deep learning techniques. For instance, sensor data periodically submitted to cloud infrastructures to predict the health status of a motor vehicle can provide more accurate results if deep learning algorithms are utilized.

Figure 1.3 reveals the importance of deep learning neural networks in big data applications. Traditional machine learning algorithms, such as support vector

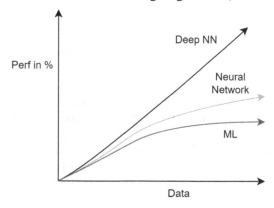

Figure 1.3. Performance curve indicating the relationship between performance and data.

machines, random forests, k-nearest neighbors (KNN), and so forth, report better prediction accuracy when the input data is small. However, the performance and accuracy of applications are improved by increasing the volume of data when we experiment with deeper neural networks or their corresponding algorithms.

1.3.2 Increasing publications

The number of published articles and citations related to deep learning for social-good applications has increased tremendously in recent years. The DBLP indexing engine reveals the increasing trend of deep learning interest among researchers, as shown in figure 1.4.

As can be observed, the number of published articles has drastically increased between 2016 and today. This is evidence of the boom in deep learning and allied concepts in the research literature.

Similarly, a few leading international conferences/workshops have recently established a platform on which deep learning scientists can work and innovate. For instance, the Workshop on Deep Learning on Supercomputers (DLS @ SC), the International Conference on Learning Representations (ICLR), and the International Conference on Medical Imaging with Deep Learning (MIDL) have helped various researchers to develop innovations based on deep learning.

In addition, a few very influential conferences bring together researchers, academics, and practitioners to discus innovations for social-good applications. Conferences such as Association for the Advancement of Artificial Intelligence, International Joint Conference on Artificial Intelligence, Innovative Applications of Artificial Intelligence, International Conference on Autonomous Agents and Multiagent Systems, International Conference on Knowledge Discovery and Data Mining and ACM SIGCAS/SIGCHI Conference on Computing and Sustainable Societies (COMPASS) have striking initiatives to improve innovations that support societal benefits.

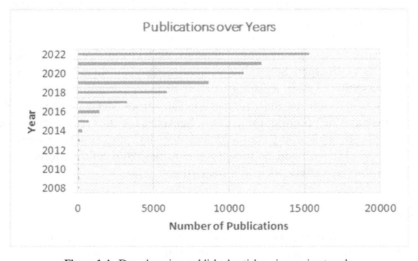

Figure 1.4. Deep learning published articles—increasing trend.

Figure 1.5. Google Trends analysis—region-wise reports [3]. Data source: Google Trends (https://www.google.com/trends).

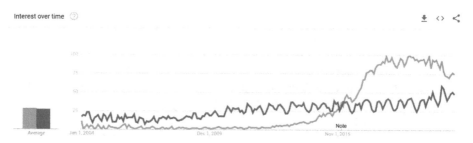

Figure 1.6. Deep learning versus social good [3]. Data source: Google Trends (https://www.google.com/trends).

1.3.3 International trends

The increasing interest in deep learning and its applications has been constant for the past few years across the globe. A Google trend analysis illustrates that requests per region for the search term 'deep learning' are growing for several continents (see figure 1.5).

Notably, China has become the leader in this topic [4], compared to several other countries, and has utilized deep learning for multiple innovations/purposes. Following China, the UK, India, South Korea, and Singapore have attempted to apply deep learning in solutions.

The most influential authors in the field of deep learning, namely, Geoffrey Hinton (Japan), Ian GoodFellow, Ruslan Salakhutdinov (Carnegie Mellon University, USA), Juergen Schmidhuber (Switzerland), and so forth, have widely spread novel aspects of deep learning to their broader communities.

In figure 1.6, we observe that queries for the topics 'deep learning' and 'social good' demonstrate the potential for growth. Searches for the term 'social good' have remained constant, while the term 'deep learning' has seen drastic growth over the past few years. This obviously reflects the anticipated innovations due to the marriage of these two concepts in the near future.

1.4 Motivations

I wrote this book to cover as many social-good solutions as possible in order to increase the goodness of societies. Environmental issues, such as air pollution, water pollution, waste disposal, forest fires, emotional failures, and so forth must be efficiently handled in the future.

In general, several technologies could be integrated with existing gadgets or societal instruments. However, the majority of these developments are organized by high-end industries that do not share sufficient knowledge for mass innovation. With the evolution of startups and entrepreneurial interests in several countries, the number of innovations has increased.

We need to drive innovation for social-good purposes not only at the industrial level but also at the graduate, school, or public levels.

1.5 Deep learning for social good—a need

This book can enlighten readers who are interested in developing social-good applications or people willing to understand possible approaches to handling social-good situations while applying deep learning techniques.

Accordingly, this book takes the reader in the following directions:

1. This book delivers a few techniques involved in deep learning, such as image classification, image enhancement, word analysis, human–machine emotional interfaces, and so forth, that can be applied for social-good applications.
2. This book covers a few applications related to smart cities and societal problems.
3. This book explains code snippets from a few social-good applications implemented using TensorFlow to motivate readers to develop similar applications.
4. It also describes enough of the fundamental technologies, such as the IoT, the cloud, Docker, programming topics, and so forth to engage readers while reading this book.

1.6 Intended audience

In general, I wrote the book for various readers who are interested in applying deep learning techniques to enhance the social-good applications of their regions. The potential readers of the book are categorized in the following sections.

1.6.1 Students

I focused on introductory-level interdisciplinary students of Computer Science, Electronics, Communications, and other subjects while writing this book. The book is written for students who wish to incorporate deep learning techniques into their projects. In addition, it will motivate students to develop social-good applications. In fact, students may want to understand the inner details of deep learning techniques that could be adopted for smart cities and similar application domains. From this book, they will get an understanding of deep learning techniques and the associated ideas used to develop social-good applications.

1.6.2 Researchers

The number of researchers, particularly interdisciplinary ones, is increasing daily all over the globe. The majority of these researchers are interested in applying deep learning techniques to their research problems. For instance, researchers working in the HPC domain try to apply deep learning to predict the performance of applications using sophisticated tools rather than executing them. Obviously, the energy consumed by searching for the best HPC application performance increases during the search process.

In addition, researchers may read this book to learn about the existing techniques used by many researchers and industrialists in the past. The book provides a more profound knowledge and insight that will help researchers to undertake future research in their fields based on deep learning techniques.

1.6.3 Practitioners/startup entrepreneurs

Practitioners reading this book may have more innovative ideas. In fact, this book highlights several examples that touch upon newer ideas and solutions. By reading this book, practitioners from industry can understand the innovations created in the past so that the birth of innovations in other directions becomes possible.

1.6.4 Government/smart city officials

The techniques provided in the book could become a guideline for best practices for smart city officials. For instance, the situations in which a residual neural network (e.g. ResNet-50) or a convolutional neural network (CNN) are applicable will become clear when implementing the techniques discussed in this book. In addition, the application of generative adversarial network (GAN) methods or similar algorithms will become more precise after reading the book.

1.7 Chapters and descriptions

Overall, I have tried to include many thoughts/notions that can increase social awareness. The proposed ideas may highlight the crucial techniques that can be applied for social goodness. For instance, the application of deep learning techniques and algorithms for emotional-intelligence-related social-good applications could increase interest among readers.

The chapters are organized as described below to engage readers during the process of reading the book.

1.7.1 About deep learning

This chapter provides a brief introduction to deep learning techniques. More importantly, it motivates readers to look at future chapters, and it help them to understand the necessity of reading the book. It also highlights the past trends of applying deep learning techniques to different problem domains. In this way, the readers get some additional solid points that encourage them to continue reading the book.

1.7.2 Social-good applications

The implementation of social-good applications relating to air quality, water quality, energy reduction, and so forth has tremendously increased in recent years. This chapter lists the most commonly utilized social-good applications which can be studied/practiced in smart cities or similar domains.

In order for deep learning techniques to be incorporated into applications, there is a need to understand the related techniques. A few of the most important technologies discussed in this chapter include the following:

- clouds for scalable infrastructures;
- the use of the IoT to sense data and communicate the resulting data to connected services/machines;
- blockchain technologies for protecting data, when experimented on societies;
- computing infrastructures that are utilized for deep learning techniques, and so forth.

This chapter delves into the required base technologies used to develop deep-learning-related applications for the benefit of society.

1.7.3 Computing architectures—base technologies

Deep learning scientists or practitioners have to appropriately choose the architectures, computing machines, IoT components, deep learning libraries, and so forth, in order to obtain better performance from algorithms.

This chapter describes the existing computing architectures that are used for the inner functionalities of deep learning algorithms. It extends the previous chapter, placing more emphasis on the associated technologies while developing deep learning algorithms.

Additionally, the focus of the chapter is to explain the availability of IoT-enabled systems and connectivity procedures that submit relevant sensor data for processing via deep learning intelligence by cloud services or computing infrastructures. This chapter underlines the relevant communication protocols and connectivity service-level protocols of IoT systems in detail.

As a result of understanding the details of the underlying computing architectures, including IoT-enabled infrastructures, readers should be comfortable choosing the right computing infrastructure when developing or executing deep-learning-based social-good applications.

Additionally, a few programming models, libraries such as Tensorflow and PyTorch, relevant datasets, and applications are described in this chapter.

1.7.4 Convolutional neural network techniques

Image processing and computer vision applications can generally implement CNN techniques. This chapter reveals the CNN techniques and the inner details of developing applications using CNN-based algorithms. An analogous example of how CNNs are related to the human brain is discussed in this chapter. In addition, the building blocks of CNNs, such as convolutions, activation layers, pooling layers, and connected layers, are discussed.

This chapter highlights a few social-good applications that apply CNN-based deep learning techniques. These applications are combined with CNN implementation steps using Tensorflow libraries.

Finally, the chapter explains the evolving challenges and future directions for researchers working in areas based on CNN techniques.

1.7.5 Object detection techniques and algorithms

This chapter explains the most popular algorithms, such as YOLOv3, YOLOv5, R-CNN, Fast R-CNN, and so forth. These algorithms are used to solve object-detection-related problems. The major objectives of object detection are discussed in this chapter. It also describes algorithms that can be applied for e-learning applications, one of the social-good applications, using PyTorch implementations.

1.7.6 Sentiment analysis—algorithms and frameworks

Personal branding is becoming popular in the modern era. Social media sites such as Twitter, LinkedIn, personal pages, and so forth, suggest textual content. This information has to be analyzed using specific deep learning algorithms such as LSTM.

This chapter explains the concepts of sentiment analysis, such as the data-processing stages, learning and classification stages, and so forth. It delves into the implementation aspects of a recommendation system using sentiment analysis techniques, specifically, a movie recommendation system. In addition it describes a few of the available tools and frameworks that can be utilized to perform sentiment analysis.

1.7.7 Autoencoders and variational autoencoders

Autoencoders and variational autoencoders can be utilized for delving into the latent space of data. This chapter explains the theory behind implementing autoencoders and variational autoencoders while modifying the datasets that are specific to societal applications.

To this end, a few types of autoencoder, such as convolutional autoencoders, sparse autoencoders, deep autoencoders, contractive autoencoders, denoising autoencoders, under-complete autoencoders, and variational autoencoders are studied in this chapter.

In addition, the most commonly found applications of autoencoders, such as image-reconstruction applications, image colorization, high-resolution image generation, image compression, and so forth, are discussed based on autoencoders. Finally, the chapter explains procedures used to generate handwritten numbers from Modified National Institute of Standards and Technology datasets using an autoencoder implementation—i.e. one based on TensorFlow libraries.

1.7.8 Generative adversarial networks and disentangled mechanisms

GANs apply to a specific subset of societal applications. The importance of GANs and disentanglement in choosing datasets are discussed in this chapter. In general, GANs utilize generative and discriminative models. The basic architecture required to use these models in order to generate images or datasets is studied. The chapter explains the concepts of GANs using a bare minimum of implementation steps and TensorFlow libraries.

Additionally, this chapter throws light on the different types of GAN, such as Deep Convolutional Generative Adversarial Networks, CycleGANs, Enhanced Super-Resolution Generative Adversarial Networks, Generative Facial Prior Generative Adversarial Networks, and StyleGANs, helping them to be used in social-good applications by future innovators.

1.7.9 Deep reinforcement learning architectures

Industrial IoT-based applications assist the improvement of societies in smart cities. Reinforcement learning (RL) is well suited to such environments. This chapter showcases the basic principles of utilizing reinforcement agents in environments such as industries. The differences between deep reinforcement learning mechanisms and other techniques, such as machine learning and deep learning, are described. In addition, the major components of RL frameworks, such as policy-related components, value functions, and model-based components that are crucial for building reinforcement learning systems are discussed in this chapter. Finally, the chapter presents a taxonomy for reinforcement learning algorithms and the procedures used to integrate these algorithms with computing systems.

1.7.10 Facial recognition and applications

Facial-recognition-related applications, such as identity management, home automation, passport verification, and so forth, can utilize deep learning models and architectures. This chapter explains the utility of deep learning models for recognizing facial expressions and emotions. It showcases the processes involved in the facial recognition processes, such as the face detection, analysis, feature extraction, data conversion, and classification processes. The chapter highlights a few applications in which social goodness can be retained. Additionally, it illustrates innovations for future researchers, practitioners, or students.

1.7.11 Data security and platforms

Although various social-good applications can be oriented toward deep learning concepts and algorithms, the evolving architectures must contain sophisticated security features. Overlooking security components in applications might lead to detrimental effects. This chapter highlights the possible data security features that can be used to strengthen deep learning applications so that they can be applied in society.

The first part of the chapter explains all the possible security attacks in the modern computing world, such as malware attacks, phishing attacks, DoS attacks, rootkit attacks, integrity attacks, authentication attacks, authorization attacks, availability attacks, and data tampering cases. Also, deep-learning-related attacks, such as model invasion attacks, inference hacking issues, and privacy attacks are described. The chapter next describes deep learning adversarial problems, such as perturbation issues, issues related to patch application, challenging probability distributions, evasion attacks, GAN attacks, and hosted model attacks.

In the second part of this chapter, the utilization of deep learning algorithms to enhance the security features of the existing computing infrastructures is discussed. This approach is considered to be a serious social problem that needs to be addressed at minimal cost. In this context, this chapter covers the application of deep learning algorithms to the improvement of security features.

1.7.12 Performance monitoring and analysis

Monitoring deep learning algorithms and measuring the performances of societal applications are crucial for the improving the development of deep learning architectures. This chapter discloses the most commonly available performance monitoring tools and associated architectures that automatically improve the performance of applications in various dimensions.

The chapter highlights the need for performance monitoring tools rather than urging application developers or users to tune their applications based on underlying computing infrastructures. The most commonly applied performance monitoring mechanisms, such as the expert opinion approach, characterization of workload approach, benchmarking approach, top-down analysis approach, bottom-up analysis approach, tool-based monitoring approach, and prediction/modeling approach are discussed in detail. Additionally, the commonly chosen performance metrics used to assess the performances of deep learning algorithms, such as hardware utilization, scalability feature, Floating Point OPerations per Second (FLOPs), throughput, energy consumption, network buffers, time accuracy, communication overheads, tool overheads, information density, transfer size, prediction accuracy, and so forth, are studied. Finally, the evaluation platforms and the associated metrics that are suitable for applications are illustrated in this chapter.

1.7.13 Deep learning—future perspectives

The last chapter of this book lists the potential future directions for developing societal applications based on deep learning architectures. This chapter suggests how researchers or practitioners can delve into deep learning techniques in near future by offering ideas that pinpoint the problems of societies.

1.8 Reading flow

To help the reader to navigate this book with ease, the book is subdivided into three major parts, as shown below:
1. Part I: Introduction
2. Part II: Techniques
3. Part III: Security, performance, and future directions

The purpose of having these three major parts is to encourage readers interested in the preliminary level to stick to the introductory part of the book. This part of the book covers chapters 1–3, which include several social-good applications and ideas that could be incorporated into deep learning techniques. However, a few preliminary details of the underlying computing architectures are described in chapter 3. This chapter may be excluded by time-pressed readers at the introductory level before they proceed with the other parts of the book.

Part II starts with CNN techniques and object detection algorithms in chapters 4 and 5. These chapters are crucial for deep learning practitioners and academics if they want to develop a few ideas for targeting societal problems. Chapters 7–9 describe a few advanced topics of deep learning techniques, such as autoencoders, GANs, and deep reinforcement learning methods. Authors who are familiar with CNNs and object detection may proceed with these chapters.

Additionally, chapters 6 and 10 focus on certain applications related to deep learning algorithms. Notably, chapter 6 explains the application of LSTM-related deep learning models for predicting sentiments, and chapter 10 focuses on facial emotion detection approaches and analysis methods. Readers can directly jump to one of these chapters after reading chapters 4 and 5. Obviously, chapters 1 and 2 are crucial for all the remaining chapters.

Part III of the book focuses on auxiliary topics that highlight the necessity for more reasonable learning algorithms for applications. For instance, improving security components or the performance aspects of implementing deep learning algorithms are essential topics for advanced developers or application users. This part of the book covers the essentials of security features and performance analysis steps. Additionally, the future directions of the use of deep learning algorithms for social-good applications are covered in this part of the book.

References

[1] Activation functions, May 2022 Page Version ID: 1088786364
[2] Deep learning, May 2022 Page Version ID: 1088786364
[3] Google trends—region wise report, May 2022 Page Version ID: 1088786364
[4] Trends, May 2022
[5] Chen J and Xu S 2022 Research on the development of digital creative sports industry based on deep learning *Comput. Intell. Neurosci.* **2022** 7760263
[6] Esteva A, Robicquet A, Ramsundar B, Kuleshov V, DePristo M, Chou K, Cui C, Corrado G, Thrun S and Dean J 2019 A guide to deep learning in healthcare *Nat. Med.* **25** 24–9
[7] Fukushima K 2014 One-shot learning with feedback for multi-layered convolutional network *Artificial Neural Networks and Machine Learning—ICANN 2014—24th International Conference on Artificial Neural Networks* (Lecture Notes in Computer Science vol 8681) (Berlin: Springer) pp 291–8
[8] Grubb A and Bagnell J A 2010 Boosted backpropagation learning for training deep modular networks *27th International Conference on Machine Learning (ICML-10)* ed J Fürnkranz and T Joachims (Madison, WI: Omnipress) pp 407–14

[9] Hochreiter S and Schmidhuber J 1996 LSTM can solve hard long time lag problems *Advances in Neural Information Processing Systems 9, NIPS, Denver, CO, USA, December 2–5, 1996* ed M Mozer, M I Jordan and T Petsche (Cambridge, MA: MIT Press) pp 473–9

[10] Russakovsky O 2015 ImageNet large scale visual recognition challenge *Int. J. Comput. Vis.* **115** 211–52

Chapter 2

Applications for social good

A massive victory of citizens and living beings in the world will materialize if they are aided by appropriate applications and sophisticated gadgets. Applications require precise learning assistance based on robust algorithms or methods, including deep learning. Deep learning applications for social good have gradually gained momentum over the years [24]. This chapter reflects on the repeated forecasts of evolving applications that will improve the fortunes of society at large.

2.1 Characteristics of social-good applications

Applications for social good [10] are a type of software combined with hardware platforms and sensor nodes [5] that performs actions that benefit people's lives and society.

Several features characterize applications that are societal applications, as given below:

1. Participation—while the debate on possibilities, alternatives, challenges, and deficiencies posed by evolving technologies, such as the cloud or the block-chain, is bound to continue, participants and contributors will inevitably be involved. More participants are required for the success of the applications belonging to this category. The participation could be direct, for example, if citizens or machines/robots represent a society.
2. Prediction—the comprehensive nature of applications for social good high-lights the involvement of predictions or machine-level analysis using robust algorithms, including deep learning. In most cases, waiting for new infor-mation or future information could hamper the functioning of systems. Predictions have to be straightforward and automatic based on the input provided by algorithms or machines.
3. Decision-makers—societal applications preferably involve decision-makers or officials in order to quickly deliver authenticated information.

Stakeholders such as citizens, smart city officials, government authorities, and so forth, are involved in a machine-authenticated solution that provides data or its associated visualizations to a public audience.

4. Infrastructures—typically, societal applications involve robust infrastructures to process big data. For instance, sensors, edge computing, and clouds are established to deliver the required information for applications. Renowned organizations, including Google LLC, provide their infrastructure and mobile connections to deliver the information relevant to applications in the right form.

2.2 Generic architecture—entities

Considering the crucial features that are unique to social-good applications, this section explains the important entities involved in formulating societal applications and their functionalities in detail. Figure 2.1 illustrates the components used in the generic architecture of a social-good application.

2.2.1 User interface

Users connect to social-good applications through specifically designed frameworks or connection modules. These users are represented as clients of the system. The clients have the options to connect to the applications from mobile nodes, such as smartphones or standalone machines. Typically, these users have the opportunity to connect with associated services, including deep learning services, that are hosted in edge, fog, or cloud environments. The most common programming languages utilized to design such interfaces are Django, Nodejs, Reactjs, AngularJs, and so forth.

2.2.2 Sensor connectivity

Data needs to be assessed and formatted before analyses are performed. In fact, the data are collected from distributed sources available from heterogeneous nodes,

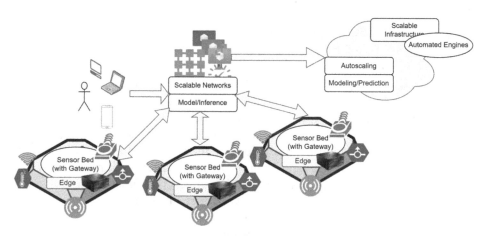

Figure 2.1. The generic architecture of social-good applications.

including sensor nodes [4]. The sensor nodes belong to different proprietors or industries that may follow different communication protocols or connectivity standards. A detailed description of the different communication protocols and standards that are utilized to collect sensor data is discussed in the latter part of this chapter.

The sensor data are transported through gateways to connected services or machines available in cloud environments.

2.2.3 Hierarchical intelligence

Considering the large volume of sensor nodes and the availability of sources, learning should happen from the edge level. Obviously, this could improve the latency and privacy of learning inferences in a social-good application. In lieu of this, several techniques that offer hierarchical intelligence to a framework are commonly employed in such applications.

Scalable infrastructures, in the form of services that enhance databases, scalability, modeling support, and so forth, are used in associated frameworks that enable social-good applications.

2.2.4 Data security—immutability

To secure the models and corresponding data, architectures that provide social-good applications involve secured environments. The security features are implemented starting from the location where the data sources are found. Several security breaches have occurred [9], especially when sensor-enabled data are utilized in the model. Obviously, one of the crucial design objectives of developing an architecture for social-good applications is to provide robust security.

2.2.5 Notification/visualization

Users must be notified about the findings or forecasted situations produced by deep learning models in a user-friendly manner. In some cases, the notification needs to take the form of an instant message. Otherwise, it should be in the form of a visual representation. This part of the architecture should be able to notify users (typically in the tens of thousands) in real time, while consuming limited bandwidth and energy.

2.3 Applications for social good

The role of practitioners/researchers has become clear, because a surge in social-good applications have been recorded in the recent past. The taxonomy of these applications is shown in figure 2.2. This section provides a synopsis of these applications.

2.3.1 Economic forecasting

Forecasting sales and business traction are quite important for the economic improvement of society. After predicting the costs involved in selling goods, the

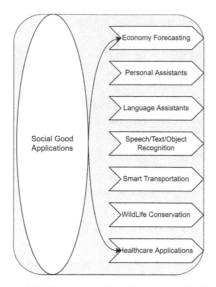

Figure 2.2. Taxonomy of social-good applications.

required amount of production or raw materials can be justified [17]. Accordingly, industries and production sectors can efficiently plan for the manpower or raw materials required. In contrast, in recent decades, owners and production managers have either purchased additional components or wasted a large volume of raw materials.

In some situations, the availability of raw materials is very limited. For instance, producing gold-related aesthetic products requires skilled procurement of raw materials such as gold. In such cases, purchasing too much or too little gold could lead to inefficiency.

Deep learning or similar machine learning techniques are necessary in order to reduce the costs involved in production [26]. Consequently, the economy, including people who purchase goods, would benefit.

2.3.2 Personal assistants

In the modern world, applications that assist people [3] help to improve their productivity and connections. A few devices are particularly beneficial to blind people. For instance, voice assistant applications have traditionally been utilized by the visually impaired to safely live and travel in unknown locations.

In recent years, cities have mandated appropriate tools that help visually impaired people to walk along the sidewalk and enter shared vehicles using personal assistance devices. For instance, most smart cities have incorporated announcement media into public transport vehicles, including buses and trains. In this way, blind people and inattentive passengers can easily be notified about upcoming stops.

Personal assistants have been devised in order to increase attention, encourage caution, and entertain users, as discussed in the following subsections.

2.3.2.1 Attention boosters

The productivity of people has dropped due to distractions from synchronized and asynchronous electronic gadgets. Too much data is produced by connected devices, and their applications are synchronized with social media sites such as Twitter, LinkedIn, and Facebook. However, the focus on being productive in nature is degraded in most cases. Specifically, students, including differently abled students [8], have to perform in exams, workers have to complete their assigned tasks, and researchers have to deeply dive into a topic without much distraction for a specified time. However, social media sites captivate their users, causing them to deviate from their skills and timely relationships. Consequently, the expected productivity of society dramatically declines—a societal problem.

Voice assistants [2] could remind them about their original activities in an automatic fashion by learning about human features. In doing so, the productivity curve of society could be improved.

In addition, personal assistance devices could suggest the best deals on products in markets or shops. As a result of this feature, the cost of purchasing goods could be minimized.

2.3.2.2 Intelligent reminders

Reminders keep people abreast of their 'to do' lists. In spite of several mechanisms offering them reminders, they keep failing to achieve the most basic tasks, due to manual interventions.

In fact, the reminders need to be prioritized by following the personal behaviors of users in an automated fashion. To do so, an appropriate learning approach will be one of the solutions. Deep learning has become the most utilized learning approach for setting up reminders and notifying citizens using voice assistants.

2.3.2.3 Chatbots—recreation and safety

Voice assistant solutions using chatbot applications have become more popular. Chatbots [6] were developed for several purposes: (i) recreation, (ii) product sales, and (iii) safety.

Several voice assistant solutions exist, including Amazon's Alexa and Apple's Siri [1]. These voice assistants befriend people for entertainment purposes. For instance, if a person needs to play their favorite music or a video, the voice assistant devices can accomplish it. Additionally, these devices can personalize users' interests in an automated fashion.

Voice assistants in the form of chatbots are quite popular on product sale websites. Typically, industries or companies release newer products and offer online assistance using chatbots. The responsibilities of the chatbots are to organize demonstrations or to trigger compliance/feedback actions related to the product installations.

A few researchers have applied chatbots to enrich citizen security. For instance, sexual harassment takes place in various workplaces and leading corporate communities. Chatbots, in many situations, were utilized by survivors to avoid wrong decisions such as committing suicide.

2.3.3 Language assistance

Over tens of thousands of languages are officially classed as means of communication. These languages are county-specific and community-specific, with various dialects spoken by geographically dispersed regions around the globe. Notably, languages such as English, Hindi, German, Chinese, Russian, and so forth, have attracted a remarkable number of speakers across the globe, in addition to those who use sign languages [25].

Tourists or residents traveling to different countries might not get prompt tourism information if they are unfamiliar with the locally spoken languages. Most countries display information and notice boards in their local languages. For instance, Germany, India, and China have travel information displayed in their regionally approved languages such as German, Hindi, and Chinese.

In recent years, deep-learning-enabled language-translation-related applications [23] have become much more popular for translating regional languages into the known language of the user. Typically, these applications are installed in various wearable devices such as mobile phones, tablets, or wristwatches. In these applications, videos are often captured and processed by edge devices such as mobile phones rather than being sent to cloud infrastructure.

Language assistance techniques are applied to read traffic information, street notices, product catalogs in malls, and so forth. These applications are soon expected to gain traction with the emergence of a large number of allied applications.

2.3.4 Speech, text, and object recognition

Recognizing objects, text, and speech is vital for the modern representation of the digital world. In fact, object recognition, speech recognition, and text recognition are not novel concepts; they have been in existence for decades. However, the implementation of these concepts using deep learning models has improved the accuracy of their applications.

For instance, the accuracy of classifying an apple from an orange, classifying potato blemishes [18], or detecting a human face from an input image has tremendously improved recently due to the application of increasingly sophisticated deep learning algorithms. Similarly, text prediction results have improved in mobile-based smartphone applications—i.e. the next sequence of words is almost accurately predicted based on the historical occurrences of texts.

In addition, speech recognition has been utilized to convert speech to text or speech to action, depending on the intended use of a given application. Several notable applications were developed in the past for the benefit of image detection users. Applications such as computer vision for self-driving cars, medical image analysis, drone-assisted city modeling, character recognition from number plates, visual grading and harvesting, the identification of ripe fruits, calculating the number of vegetables/fruits/objects, and so forth, have earned plaudits in the machine learning community groups.

2.3.5 Smart transportation

Smart transportation offers traffic management and planning [21], which improve the cost efficiency of traveling residents in smart cities. It increases road safety by avoiding accidents in the curves of roadways or hidden line-of-sight areas on highways; it promotes shared mobility by optimally allocating seats to travelers while considering several factors such as pollution-free locations, etc.

CNN models or similar modern learning models of deep learning have an inbuilt learning mechanism that studies parameters hierarchically so that higher-accuracy models can be developed and installed in smart transportation frameworks.

Researchers have characterized the performance of travelers and associated traffic routes while developing travel plans. For instance, the electric stations, gas stations, and workshop locations could be planned in advance with the optimal use of resources to avoid the over-utilization of travel resources. The optimal resources could be scheduled based on the learning inferences obtained from deep learning models.

Identifying vehicles and controlling the entrances to certain roads, including parking lots, have been widely applied in several countries. Automatic ticketing has diverted manpower utilization and improved security in various countries. This has happened due to the use of deep learning models that automatically capture license plate details using smart transportation frameworks.

The shared transport aspect of the intelligent transportation systems in smart cities is also gaining momentum [20]. The deployment of shared transport requires an expert skill set to allocate seats to appropriate communities to avoid risks and facilitate journeys. The automatic processes used to allocate seats in shared transport services need robust learning mechanisms in order to reduce discrimination— i.e. solutions that support social goodness.

2.3.6 Wildlife conservation

The conservation of rare species in wild habitats is considered to be a major task for countries [7]. Each country has been tasked to protect them by carefully monitoring them without any human intervention. After the animals are photographed using cameras in their natural habitats (mainly woods), the images must be analyzed and the animals' presence must be confirmed. In addition, the migratory patterns of animals (for example, while searching for prey) and the invasions of domestic areas by animals could be monitored.

In some cases, there is a need to protect wild animals from the relevant rare species. Animals such as tigers, leopards, and elephants can be easily tracked and characterized using highly sophisticated learning models.

2.3.7 Healthcare applications

Deep learning has magnified the utility of existing healthcare applications and provided new perspectives on health diagnosis. The impressive accuracy benefits of deep-learning-assisted healthcare applications have encouraged medical practitioners to use these solutions as assistance tools. Applications, for example, those that identify pneumonia in chest images or tumor cells in brain images, those that locate patterns in medical symptoms, diagnose skin diseases, etc. have been implemented in devices using deep learning algorithms to increase the lifespan of humans.

Often, medical practitioners are skeptical about the use of algorithms to detect diseases. However, the extremely accurate findings produced by deep learning algorithms have encouraged their adoption in modern medical systems.

In recent years, the concept of green gyms has attracted the healthcare community. Green gyms promote exercise in public locations, which keeps citizens healthy. In addition, these gyms contribute to generating green energy, which is scarce in most developing countries, including India. People are directly or indirectly engaged in these gyms for social good—i.e. generating renewable energy from exercise in public locations.

2.4 Technologies and techniques

The methods and techniques involved in developing social-good applications are not only limited to deep-learning-algorithm designs. Figure 2.3 illustrates the techniques/technologies most commonly utilized for building social-good applications.

A few notable techniques/technologies that coexist in the delivery of social-good applications are listed below:

1. Blockchain technology
2. AI/machine learning/deep learning
3. The Internet of things (IoT)/sensor technology
4. Robots
5. Computing infrastructures/architectures
6. Edge/fog/cloud environments
7. Security features

Brief notes on these technologies and their associations with social-good applications are discussed in the following subsections.

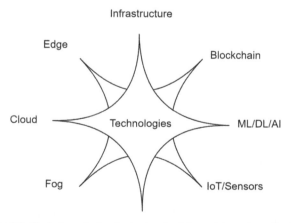

Figure 2.3. Techniques/technologies involved in social-good applications.

2.5 Technology—blockchain

The blockchain is a tamper-resistant shared ledger or storage unit that registers data in a public or private network. According to Marco Lansiti [13], the blockchain is defined as an open distributed ledger that can record transactions between two parties efficiently. These records are verifiable and permanent.

Blockchain technology is applied in situations where trust may be challenged [16]. For instance, social enterprises often fail due to trust failures among the promoters; businesses related to social improvements only scale up if a trusted mechanism is used by the participants. Typically, for any success in an endeavor, three elements need to be trusted:

1. the counterparty—the person to whom a transaction has to be transferred,
2. the intermediary—an organization or intermediate people who are involved in suggesting the counterparties for the business or transaction, and
3. the dispute-resolution mechanism—an organization or a community, such as the courts of law, which are responsible for looking into any issues caused during transactions.

In the modern era, there are situations in which people cannot trust the participants or organizations involved in transactions, including the government, banks, or other trusted parties.

Generally speaking, trust fails in one of the three ways discussed below:

1. Direct violations—knowledge of any trust violations in the past discourages the same participants from continuing the venture in the future. For instance, if a mechanic was not successful in repairing a taxi, the owner of the taxi might not turn to him for future repairs. The impact of direct violations on decisions is hard and fast.
2. Opportunistic behavior violations—trust in an organization or a team can be degraded if any anticipated opportunities are missed. Opportunistic behavior is an act that motivates a team or an individual to seek economic or similar benefits. If the opportunities are missed, the trust of the team or the individual in an organization is challenged.
3. Organizational failures—apart from direct or team-level trust violations, there are situations in which organizations fail. Such failures can damage the existing trust gained by the participants over a period of time.

2.5.1 Types of transaction

A true trustless transaction is considered to be a direct transaction in which a seller makes a direct deal with the consumer—see figure 2.4. Although this approach avoids double spending, it has poor scalability—i.e. such transactions are not possible for a large number of potential customers (which is the reality in the Internet world).

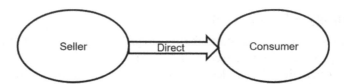

Figure 2.4. Pure trustless transaction.

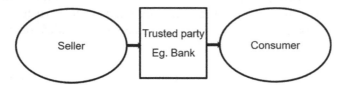

Figure 2.5. Trustful transactions.

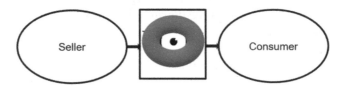

Figure 2.6. Trustless trust using a blockchain.

In contrast, a pure trustful transaction provides an intermediary system that connects sellers with consumers. For example, trusted parties, such as national banks, are involved in establishing money transfers between participants. In doing so, the seller does not need to have a direct connection to the consumer. Rather, all dealings related to the transactions are carried out through the trusted party. Various parties, such as online payment providers, remittance companies, credit card vendors, and so forth (which are similar to banks) can serve as third parties that facilitate transactions. Figure 2.5 illustrates the concept in a pictorial fashion.

Recently, trustless trust mechanisms have become crucial in blockchain-enabled systems. These systems offer a platform that establishes a trust mechanism among participants without their direct involvement or the inclusion of a third party. They are considered trustless trust environments, as the trust is provided through a network of intelligent systems rather than humans—i.e. a blockchain network is placed in between the seller and the consumer (see figure 2.6).

2.6 AI/machine learning/deep learning techniques

Advances in AI have enabled opportunities in several sectors due to its higher success rate in recent years. Upcoming advanced techniques, such as generative AI, federated learning, and AI-embedded brains could enrich the living standards of people in the near future. A detailed description of these techniques is provided in the forthcoming chapters of this book.

2.7 The Internet of things/sensor technology

The IoT is an extended network system where the Internet is connected to objects such as lights, fans, tables, and so forth. Extending the Internet to these objects enables a knowledgeable society in a short period. This is because the sensed data are processed, analyzed, and delivered to the users at large.

Sensor technologies are often applied in social-good applications. For instance, controlling the air pollution in a smart city requires the periodic measurement of the SO_2, NO_2, CO_2, and O_2 levels at various locations. In addition, these monitoring values have to be processed in decentralized locations, and control measures have to be implemented in a reasonably short time. Air quality monitoring sensors [19] are spread across streets to collect this information in order to ensure a pollution-free city.

The IoT is subdivided into five major domains based on its applications (see figure 2.7). A synopsis of these types is given in the following paragraphs:

2.7.1 The industrial IoT

Sensor technology, when applied in industries to assist business processes and enhance development efficiency, is classified as the industrial IoT (IIoT). The term 'IIoT' is commonly used in the USA, and the same concept is named Industry 4.0 in

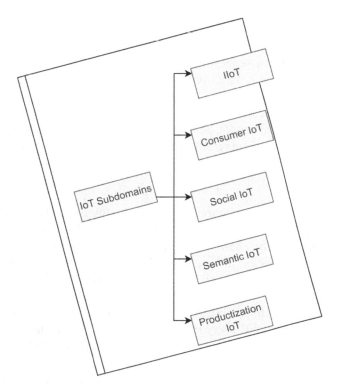

Figure 2.7. Subdomains of IoT technology.

Europe. It is the fourth industrial revolution. The first three revolutions were due to the invention of steam engines, electricity, and the Internet. Industry 4.0 extends the connectivity between cyber and physical systems to objects/things using the extended Internet.

Industry 4.0 has several use cases [22] that exemplify its proliferation in society. For instance, a car owner might not be careful to check the status of the tires or oil of a vehicle. Sensors installed in the vehicle could communicate with an associated workshop. As a result, machines in workshop centers could proactively search for tires or products that are cost-efficient. Searching for better priced products improves manufacturers' businesses—i.e. the mass manufacturing of products is possible because of requests made by multiple customers across the globe. Similarly, this approach benefits car owners by taking timely action at considerably cheaper prices. This is because quotes are automatically produced by machines that compare several manufacturers around the globe.

2.7.2 The consumer IoT

The consumer IoT is an IoT system that deals with sensors or devices that are often personal or attached to people. In the consumer IoT, wearables such as smart watches, gadgets, voice assistants, automatic reminders, camera devices, wallets, and so forth, are connected to networked devices. This type of IoT collects and shares data used to improve the wellbeing of people, including their healthcare conditions.

Applications such as fall identification, mental status monitoring, stress pattern analysis, regular hypertension checks, medical decision-making, physical exercise suggestions, weight control suggestions, and so forth, offer users remarkable value. Recently, a few industries have developed textiles that can warm up users during cold weather (e.g. Polar Seal).

These applications typically utilize edge devices such as mobile phones to process sensor data. The processed sensor data or a synopsis of sensor data over a period of time are submitted to cloud servers for further analysis and preventative action.

2.7.3 The social IoT

Today, most users and products are connected through social media sites, such as Facebook, Google+, LinkedIn, Twitter, WhatsApp, and so forth. Consumers and producers are connected by these social media—the former suggests recommendations in the form of likes or dislikes and the latter launches newer products. In addition, these social sites establish social relationships through devices among a group of people.

The social IoT [11] enables relationships among a group of people by sensing the basic information of each and every member of the group. For instance, a politician could utilize social IoT to obtain the numbers of likes and dislikes prompted by making a speech on large media such as LinkedIn or the newspapers. Based on inference, the social IoT system could suggest that the relevant community fine-tunes its stance in near-future decisions.

2.7.4 The semantic IoT

The semantic IoT is the subdivision of the IoT which handles the contextualized dealings of people. It applies Ontology Web Language (OWL) and semantic inference engines within connected devices to define, modify, or interpret the data sensed by the system. Semantic IoT systems are often tailor-made solutions developed for the semantic representations of inferences obtained from sensor devices.

2.7.5 The productization IoT

Modern manufacturing approaches have improved the techniques used to produce newer products. The inclusion of novelty in products has been enabled by the use of personal fabrication tools such as 3D printers. People are allowed to design their own products, and prototypes or products can be immediately produced. The productization IoT is a category of IoT systems in which sensors are used to collect novel designs and approaches to producing products using 3D printers. In fact, this productization approach is assisted by the use of distributed cloud systems to enable shared manufacturing based on designs suggested by the users.

2.8 Robotic technology

Robots and drones are utilized in a few social-good applications. Education-related applications, which train machines or organize exams, have become popular these days—e.g. robotic teachers. Additionally, robots have been applied in houses, especially in kitchens, to assist the inhabitants. A few robots have been employed in houses to prevent children from watching television too close to the screen.

Similarly to robots, drones, which are considered to be flying robots, have been applied in agricultural, educational [12], and smart city applications. Drones have been used to assess weeds in plantations, determine the productivity of crops on farms, gauge the maturity of fruits on farms, etc. Farmers and city dwellers have derived social benefits from this kind of application.

Likewise, there are tens of thousands of use cases that utilize robots for the benefit of society.

2.9 Computing infrastructures—a needy technology

The other most important technologies that remain crucial for the development of social-good applications are the underlying architectures and the associated computing infrastructures.

Social-good applications, due to the involvement of distributed computational units, require appropriate computing devices. These applications would ideally be able to access the nearest compute devices as well as geographically diverse compute devices. Generally, the nearest compute devices, which have minimal computational power, are termed edge devices. Devices such as personal mobile phones act as edge nodes for most social-good applications. For instance, collecting health-related information from patients and depicting it in a pictorial form could be carried out using edge nodes.

Edge nodes cannot carry out the majority of the computation, as a large volume of data is required for social-good applications. Hence, the infrastructures of these applications are structured hierarchically. Edge devices share filtered information with fog nodes or fog clusters. Fog nodes are organized in city centers or in farm locations where a cluster of compute nodes are interconnected to process data intelligence collected from multiple edge devices within a location. Fog nodes have comparatively more computational power than edge nodes. However, these nodes are not sufficiently geographically dispersed to perform gigantic tasks. Such tasks are performed by cloud nodes or cloud datacenters.

'Cloud computing' is the term used for platforms for distributed computing that provide a tremendous amount of computational capacity. Such platforms have significant industrial owners that can provide the processing capacity to launch socially beneficial applications. The ability to host computing infrastructure as a service has led to the adoption of cloud computing approaches by nearly all socially beneficial applications. These applications can be implemented using any of the four cloud deployment models: private, public, hybrid, and community.

2.10 Security-related techniques

Security features must be extended to social-good applications in a similar way to the approach used for other networked applications. Risk mitigation, data visibility challenges [14], configurational issues, the security of credentials, and so forth, need to be effectively handled to protect the devices and security of associated people.

Risk mitigation is the process of reducing the potential vulnerability to threats of any social-good application. The social good applications could involve several sensor-enabled heterogeneous devices in large networks. The potential threats due to these devices could be quickly identified using deep learning algorithms.

Devices, machines, or human beings involved in these applications require appropriate credentials to protect them from hackers. Attacks on computing machines can be prevented to some extent, as these devices have sufficient computing power available. However, the issue becomes an arduous task for sensor-connected social-good applications for the following reasons:

1. the devices are battery-operated [15];
2. counter-algorithms might not be executed on these devices;
3. the heterogeneity of the devices hampers connectivity with other networked devices, including cloud nodes.

References

[1] Apple's siri, May 2022 Page Version ID: 1088786364
[2] Acero A 2016 Siri's voice gets deep learning *The 9th ISCA Speech Synthesis Workshop, Sunnyvale, CA, USA, 13–15 September 2016* (Baixas, France: ISCA)
[3] Azaria A and Nivasch K 2020 SAIF: a correction-detection deep-learning architecture for personal assistants *Sensors* **20** 5577
[4] Behera T K, Bakshi S and Sa P K 2021 Aerial data aiding smart societal reformation: current applications and path ahead *IT Prof.* **23** 82–8

[5] Benedict S 2020 Serverless blockchain-enabled architecture for IoT societal applications *IEEE Trans. Comput. Soc. Syst.* **7** 1146–58

[6] Cuayáhuitl H, Lee D, Ryu S, Cho Y, Choi S, Indurthi S R, Yu S, Choi H, Hwang I and Kim J 2019 Ensemble-based deep reinforcement learning for chatbots *Neurocomputing* **366** 118–30

[7] Curran B, Nekooei S M and Chen G 2022 Accurate New Zealand wildlife image classification-deep learning approach *ppAI 2021: Advances in Artificial Intelligence—34th Australasian Joint Conference* vol 13151 ed G Long, X Yu and S Wang (Berlin: Springer) pp 632–44

[8] Dash S K, Biswal R M, Misra A, Swain R, Ray S and Mishra J 2021 Enhancing education and interaction for the visually impaired using deep learning and IoT *Int. J. Mob. Hum. Comput. Interact.* **13** 1–16

[9] de Carvalho V D H and Costa A P C 2021 Public security sentiment analysis on social web: a conceptual framework for the analytical process and a research agenda *Int. J. Decis. Support Syst. Technol.* **13** 1–20

[10] Duan H, Li J, Fan S, Lin Z, Wu X and Cai W 2021 Metaverse for social good: a university campus prototype *MM '21: Multimedia Conference, Virtual Event, China, October 20–24, 2021* ed H T Shen, Y Zhuang, J R Smith, Y Yang, P Cesar, F Metze and B Prabhakaran (New York: ACM) pp 153–61

[11] Floris A, Porcu S, Atzori L and Girau R 2022 A social IoT-based platform for the deployment of a smart parking solution *Comput. Netw.* **205** 108756

[12] Hoople G D 2020 *Drones for Good: How to Bring Sociotechnical Thinking into the Classroom* (Synthesis Lectures on Engineers, Technology and Society) (Cham: Springer)

[13] Iansiti M and Lakhani K 2017 The truth about blockchain *Harv. Bus. Rev.* **95** 118–27

[14] Ince M 2022 Automatic and intelligent content visualization system based on deep learning and genetic algorithm *Neural Comput. Appl.* **34** 2473–93

[15] Lee B M 2018 Improved energy efficiency of massive MIMO-OFDM in battery-limited IoT networks *IEEE Access* **6** 38147–60

[16] Liu L and Li Z 2022 Permissioned blockchain and deep reinforcement learning enabled security and energy efficient healthcare internet of things *IEEE Access* **10** 53640–51

[17] Livieris I E 2019 Forecasting economy-related data utilizing weight-constrained recurrent neural networks *Algorithms* **12** 85

[18] Marino S, Beauseroy P and Smolarz A 2019 Deep learning-based method for classifying and localizing potato blemishes *Proceedings of the 8th International Conference on Pattern Recognition Applications and Methods, ICPRAM 2019, Prague, Czech Republic, February 19–21, 2019* ed M De Marsico, G S di Baja and A L N Fred (Setúbal: SciTePress) pp 107–17

[19] Martín-Baos J Á, Rodriguez-Benitez L, García-Ródenas R and Liu J 2022 IoT based monitoring of air quality and traffic using regression analysis *Appl. Soft Comput.* **115** 108282

[20] Mauri A, Khemmar R, Decoux B, Haddad M and Boutteau R 2021 Real-time 3D multi-object detection and localization based on deep learning for road and railway smart mobility *J. Imaging* **7** 145

[21] Mushtaq A, Ul Haq I, Imtiaz M U, Khan A and Shafiq O 2021 Traffic flow management of autonomous vehicles using deep reinforcement learning and smart rerouting *IEEE Access* **9** 51005–19

[22] Salem R M M, Saraya M S and Ali-Eldin A M T 2022 An industrial cloud-based IoT system for real-time monitoring and controlling of wastewater *IEEE Access* **10** 6528–40

[23] Sharma S and Singh S 2022 Recognition of Indian Sign Language (ISL) using deep learning model *Wirel. Pers. Commun.* **123** 671–92

[24] Thomas C 2014 An open source perspective on innovative societal applications and policy making *IEEE 7th International Workshop on Requirements Engineering and Law, RELAW 2014, 26–26 August, 2014, Karlskrona, Sweden* ed D Amyot, A I Antón, T D Breaux, A K Massey and A Siena (Los Alamitos, CA: IEEE Computer Society Press)

[25] Wang W and Yang H 2021 Towards realizing sign language to emotional speech conversion by deep learning *12th International Symposium on Chinese Spoken Language Processing, ISCSLP 2021, Hong Kong, January 24–27* (Piscataway, NJ: IEEE) pp 1–5

[26] Yazici I, Beyca Ö F and Delen D 2022 Deep-learning-based short-term electricity load forecasting: a real case application *Eng. Appl. Artif. Intell.* **109** 104645

Chapter 3

Computing architectures—base technologies

Building deep learning algorithms for social-good applications or similar applications requires computing architectures, efficient libraries, and appropriate datasets. This chapter discusses the basics of the different computing architectures that are used to build deep learning algorithms. Additionally, a few relevant basics of the available libraries and datasets are discussed.

3.1 History of computing

In general, computing is a process that uses a computer architecture to execute some specified goals with achievable performance/cost. It mostly deals with the design aspects of these algorithmic processes and associated computational components. All types of counting or calculating process involve logic and hardware. For instance, when you count the number of sweets in a box, you must use the logic of counting one sweet after the other using brain/fingers. In this example, counting the sweets resembles the logic, the brain/fingers correspond to the hardware units.

The history of computing starts with the old abacus system and analog/digital computers. Charles Babbage, who is considered the father of computers, manifested his computing thoughts using a cowcatcher. He designed mechanical devices that automated several astronomy-related computations with ease. In the early 19th century, he was able to demonstrate an analytical engine which was particularly intended to be a general-purpose and automatic mechanical digital computing machine.

Computing systems were invented to improve calculations and reduce manual labor. A few polynomial calculations performed by automated machines or analytical engines encouraged several scholars to invest their time in creating many innovations and programming wonders.

3.2 Types of computing

Computing is often required to process deep learning tasks. Computing involves several components that effectively exchange information. If appropriate computing components are not used to solve deep learning problems, they are either unsuitable for their tasks or or offer poor performance.

In general, computing is performed in several ways, as shown in figure 3.1. More details about these computing techniques are given, together with their capabilities and scaling features, in the following:

1. Serial computing—traditionally, only serial computing was practiced before the evolution of parallelism. In serial computing, instructions were processed one after the other. Obviously, the computational time available for realizing real-world problems, including deep learning-based problems, was very limited.

2. Parallel computing—as a result of hardware-related technological advancements, various applications and compiler extensions became a reality. In parallel computing, most the instructions are executed by parallel computational units of the same machine. Typically, parallel computing represents the concept of splitting a bigger problem into smaller tasks and mapping the tasks to parallel computational units. These parallel computational units generally consist of shared-memory units, although distributed memory units are possible.

   The development of parallel computing led to the evolution of parallel compilers and programming languages or application programming interfaces (APIs) for shared-memory units, such as Open Multi-Processing (OpenMP), pThreads, Cilk, etc. Notably, a few Python packages have been implemented using OpenMP programming to support deep learning algorithms.

3. Distributed computing—distributed computing involves the use of multiple computers or nodes to process user requests. These requests to solve deep learning problems need to be combined with efficient programming models or libraries. Some of the most commonly available programming models used to implement distributed programming include Message Passing

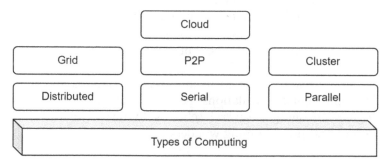

Figure 3.1. Major types of computing.

Interface (MPI), partitioned global address space (PGAS), MPI+OpenMP, and so forth. Distributed computing supports distributed memory-enabled devices that process instructions. It is worth noting that distributed memory-enabled devices have disjoint memory units—i.e. the memory units are not shared by user programs. Apparently, the memory access time for distributed nodes or computers can be significantly better than that of shared-memory programming models.

Deep learning algorithms that execute on multiple independent nodes using programming models such as MPI or Python packages fall under this category.

4. Cluster computing—in cluster computing, a set of computers or servers collaboratively works together on a task. These computers are often tightly coupled using high-speed networks such as Infiniband networks or gigabit-speed networks. A typical cluster environment consists of thousands of servers specifically dedicated to computation and a few nodes for storage purposes. Additionally, input/output (I/O) nodes are separately handled in clusters. Most datacenters are designed based on cluster computing concepts.

5. Peer-to-peer (P2P) computing—P2P computing distributes tasks among peer computing nodes without much hierarchy. It is a computational architecture based on networked nodes that have uniform permissions or policies to handle tasks, including routine tasks. In this way, affinity nodes are clustered based on overlay network constructions which improve application perform-ance. For instance, a deep learning application executed in a P2P computa-tional environment could combine the nodes that have the data relevant to specific applications using overlays.

6. Grid computing—grid computing is a computing environment in which several datacenters or computing centers are combined together to solve multiple tasks [12]. Grid computing is based on the power grid concept of electrical engineering in which the power source is placed in different locations from the utility zones. In fact, the same concept was transferred to computers—i.e. resources are shared across regions based on the demand for resources in areas where they are unavailable or scarcely available.

Grids are typically similar to clusters in distributing the tasks among nodes. However, in contrast to clusters, grids can include heterogeneous computing nodes with tightly coupled or loosely coupled networks across the globe.

7. Cloud computing—cloud computing is similar to the grid computing concept, in which resources are shared among multiple programs/tasks. The cloud, however, has a major attraction for a large number of users, namely, its pay-as-you-go model. The major objective of grid computing, which is to share resources, including computing and instruments, across geographical regions, is realized by the cloud with limited cost and utilization factors.

Additionally, grid computing environments expect project proposal submissions related to datacenters before they grant approval to utilize the devices.

Cloud computing is an attractive technology to startups and researchers who want to experiment with their algorithms in a scalable manner with fewer costs; it is similar to a market-oriented approach [7]. In fact, several deep learning algorithms have been implemented and tested on cloud services and scalable resources, as the workloads differ between the training and testing phases.

3.3 Hardware support for deep learning

Deep learning requires specific hardware for efficient programming. Traditionally, computing environments required central processing units (CPUs), I/O, and memory units. With the introduction of support for parallelism, the number of CPUs in professional computing machines has increased. Also, memory technologies have seen robust changes that have increased the speed of processing units.

In addition to the most common hardware support such as CPU, memory, etc. graphics processing unit (GPU) computing elements have frequently been applied in deep learning tasks [23]. GPU computing elements act as coprocessors that compute vector processing instructions with the assistance of CPUs—i.e. the information required to process instructions is provided by CPUs. Without CPUs, GPUs cannot process any instructions. However, GPU computations are very popular for processing large arrays of data using limited instructions—i.e. GPUs belong to the single instruction, multiple data (SIMD) category of Flynn's taxonomy [26].

GPU-level processing is good for applications, including deep learning applications. These applications include a large number of matrix calculations which can be processed by submitting single instructions with an array of data.

3.3.1 CPUs versus GPUs

Typically, GPUs are utilized by programmers who wish to harness the power of GPU threads or cores along with the power of CPU cores. GPU hardware units are utilized by programming models such as NVIDIA's Compute Unified Device Architecture (CUDA) programming or Open Computing Language (OpenCL) thread-based programming. GPU-based computing is very powerful for various applications related to deep learning, scientific simulation, matrix multiplication, linear algebra calculations, and so forth.

The major differences between CPUs and GPUs are as follows:

1. Concurrency level—the levels of concurrency provided by CPUs and GPUs have clear differences. For instance, a typical computing machine has only four to eight CPU cores. However, the number of GPU cores in a normal computing machine, such as a laptop, can easily reach 256 cores.
2. Instruction capabilities—the number of instructions provided by CPUs is typically higher than the number of instructions supported by GPUs.

Obviously, this restricts the utilization of GPUs to more general-purpose applications.

3. Processing capabilities—although more generic instructions can be executed by CPUs, the instruction throughput provided by GPUs is significantly higher. CPUs are known to offer a powerful instruction-processing capability. However, due to the unavailability of a large volume of CPUs, their parallelism is typically lower than that of GPUs.

3.3.2 CPUs versus TPUs

In addition to CPUs and GPUs, tensor processing units (TPUs) have recently evolved to support artificial intelligence (AI)-based applications. These hardware units are application-specific integrated circuits (ASICs) specially designed by Google LLC.

The main objective of designing TPUs is to offer higher-throughput output for deep-learning-related custom applications while supporting applications using Google resources.

Starting from 2016, Google constantly improved the development of the TPU hardware units. The chip developments improved from the first version to the fourth version—the first version described only an eight-bit matrix multiplication accelerator engine; the fourth version improved the performance of the accelerator by many times.

TPUs consist of tensors, bfloats, and systolic arrays. The tensors are considered to be the fundamental data-holding units of tasks. Tensors have several multi-dimensional arrays that hold data for processing applications. The bfloats describe the brain floating-point operations of processing elements. The systolic arrays are responsible for processing tasks. These arrays contain several processing elements to handle tasks in parallel. Typically, these arrays have networked architectures connected through the processing elements to execute tasks with a high degree of parallelism [21].

The TPU tasks are executed such that the required matrices of the adders and multipliers are selected; then, the data are transferred from the memory to the arrays; then, the computed values are transferred to the subsequent multipliers.

The major differences between CPUs and TPUs are as follows:

1. Generalization—TPUs are more focused on AI-based applications, compared to CPUs.
2. Processing speed—The processing speed for AI-based applications is very high for TPU-based architectures due to their custom designs. However, CPUs cannot cope with the massive parallelism requirement of deep learning algorithms.
3. Libraries—TPUs require custom libraries to support the hardware used to provide parallelism. For instance, the TensorFlow library is specifically designed for TPU-based AI problems, including deep learning applications.

3.4 Microcontrollers, microprocessors, and FPGAs

Deep-learning-based applications are often executed on microprocessor-based machines or in cloud environments. This is due to the fact that these learning algorithms are often computationally intensive or data-intensive, as opposed to network-intensive tasks. In most applications involving the IoT or edge nodes, it is preferable to use microcontrollers to perform processing in the computational layers of deep neural networks (DNNs). Hence, the importance of these hardware components must be studied.

The major differences between microcontrollers and microprocessors are as follows:

1. Chip design—in microcontrollers, all the important components of computing elements are present within one chip—i.e. the components such as the CPU, memory, I/O, and so forth, required to process applications are found in one chip; on contrary, the chips designed for microprocessors have CPU units, but the other components are external.
2. Control method—microcontrollers are designed to control connected devices, such as sensors or objects, whereas, microprocessors are used to control the crucial components of computers, such as memory or I/O.
3. Processing instructions—in microcontrollers, a limited number of instructions are executed. Accordingly, there is specific control for handling these devices. On the other hand, microcontrollers perform a large number of complex instructions to support a wide range of applications.
4. Application domain—most of the applications related to embedded domains use microcontrollers, but microprocessors are often utilized by general-purpose applications, including training algorithms or deep learning algorithm implementations.

The majority of edge-based application developments and deep learning implementations require microcontrollers rather than microprocessors. However, to handle the large computational requirement, the microcontrollers are interfaced with more robust computing systems that are often hosted by cloud or fog environments.

In addition to the hardware units commonly used to solve deep learning applications, such as microcontrollers and microprocessors, there is also the practice of designing custom hardware based on field programmable gate arrays (FPGAs).

FPGAs are specialized hardware units that can be configured using specialized software modules. These devices are designed without permanent etching principles, which allow programmers to frequently modify the hardware circuits. This leads to the modern concept of the hardware customization principle. It is a known fact that the performance of any application can be improved if it is designed at the hardware level. Here, FPGAs permit application developers to design custom applications that can be fine-tuned based on the requirements of customers/developers. In fact, researchers have applied FPGAs as accelerators to improve the performance of deep learning algorithms [15].

3.5 Cloud computing—an environment for deep learning

In general, cloud computing is defined as a computing technique that shares resources from a pool of reconfigurable machines/resources with minimal management overheads using a pay-as-you-go model. The term 'cloud computing' analogously refers to normal clouds, since the sky has tens of thousands of clouds that can combine to provide rain.

The terms used in the definition of cloud computing can be summarized as follows:

1. Shared resources—similarly to other modern computing techniques, such as grid or P2P computing techniques, the cloud provides an opportunity to use shared resources if the required resources are unavailable for computation. For instance, a deep learning task consisting of training and testing components will require different levels of computation. The amount of computation required for the training phase is comparatively larger than that required for the testing phase. In such cases, purchasing computers or servers to perform variable tasks is not a viable solution. Rather, the cloud offers a solution based on the use of shared resources, depending on the requirements.
2. A pool of reconfigurable resources—cloud resources are designed so that their configurations are easy to change. The configuration files not only alter the computation, but also other networking infrastructure, such as routers, gateways, firewalls, and so forth. As these devices can be adjusted on demand, the cloud has become a product of several organizations and applications.
3. Minimal management—most people would agree that configuring computing machines is not as easy as utilizing a preconfigured machine. For instance, many educated people would struggle to install an operating system on a machine. If so, the situation becomes more critical if one must handle tens of thousands of machines to hardwire them based on the needs of applications. Clouds provide an easy way of managing these resources.
4. Pay-as-you-go model—the pay-as-you-go model of computing has drawn the attention of several enterprises. This concept enables resources to be shared based on resource utilization; this is in contrast to grids, in which resources are reserved for the users.

Cloud computing is frequently utilized by deep learning experts and application developers. The major reasons for this include:

- Cost efficiency—due to the pay-as-you-go model of cloud computing, resources are scaled based on the workloads of deep learning applications. Such applications often experience bursty requirements, especially when training the models.
- Rapid provisioning—rapid provisioning, a cloud feature, enables deep learning experts to quickly launch their deep learning-enabled products into markets. This increases the revenue of connected businesses. For instance, the

DevOps feature of the cloud has tight integration between application developers and operational managers in the market.

- Geographical footprints—cloud environments are often geographically spread across the globe. Accordingly, the resources can be placed in affinity locations based on customer requirements. For instance, a few AWS and Google products have opinion collection features that use nearby customer regions for which learning inferences are required.
- Wider market—a large number of cloud platforms are suitable for machine-learning service models. These services could be plugged into applications or programmed via available APIs to benefit from cloud services.

3.6 Virtualization—a base for cloud computing

Virtualization is a computer architecture technology that enables the abstraction of resources and the utilization of multiple resources that are multiplexed to a limited number of resources. It is the concept of providing a virtual resource—i.e. something that is not real but emulates the real thing.

Imagine a scene in which there is a forest consisting of a few lions, i.e. real ones; and near these lions, there is a tree that appears to have an image of a lion. Thus, a normal person might immediately observe the scenery as having more lions, although there are only a few real lions. Similarly, a few virtual reality paintings resemble real sceneries. Virtualization resembles a similar concept in the context of computing resources. This technology remains a base technology for clouds.

The concept of virtualization is not a new one. It has a history dating back to the 1960s, when IBM introduced mainframes. Typically, mainframes are meant to have a large size with more computational capabilities and processing power. These devices shared resources among their users in a time-sharing fashion. The concept of mainframes did not significantly improve due to the advancement in processor technologies and hardware domain spaces. But, the idea of sharing compute resources was well-accepted among the cloud developers/users.

3.6.1 Virtualization—an analogous example

The concept of virtualization can be analogously explained. For instance, imagine that there is a bungalow with several rooms, kitchens, bedrooms, and so forth. Naturally, owning such a beautiful bungalow could typically cost around 10 crore rupees—i.e. 100 million rupees.

If a person claims that you could purchase this house for 10 lakh rupees, the average person would be happy to purchase it.

3.6.1.1 Utilization pattern

We need to observe that the rooms available in the bungalow are not often utilized by the owner. They are rarely utilized and they are not simultaneously utilized by a single owner—i.e. a person utilizing the bedroom is not utilizing the kitchen. Hence, the utilization is very low in such bungalows.

Similarly, in computing machines, most of the computers/servers are only five percent utilized. The remaining 95 percent of the time the resources are kept idle. Virtualization attempts to utilize the maximum possible resources efficiently.

3.6.1.2 Sharing method

To efficiently utilize the bungalow, imagine that a person is appointed to guide multiple owners who want to own the bungalow. The duty of this person is to help owners to reach rooms and toilets such that only one owner is present in a room at a time. By using this concept, known as a mapping process, multiple owners feel that they are the owner of the bungalow at a lower cost.

In the same way, the users of computers or servers are allowed to own resources such as memory, CPU, I/O, printers, and so forth, simultaneously. Typically, the operating system of a computer is responsible for controlling and managing all resources. In a virtualization environment, multiple operating systems are permitted to manage the resources—i.e. the hardware is multiplexed so that it can be used by multiple users/owners. The person appointed to guide multiple owners is analogously replaced with by software called a hypervisor.

3.6.2 Objectives of virtualization

A few of the major objectives of virtualization in cloud environments are as follows:

1. To allow resources to be shared by many users at a time
2. To allow hardware to be replaced and upgraded on the fly (a sort of isolation between guests)
3. To allow new devices, such as network cards, processors, and so forth, to be added without rebooting machines
4. To reduce the downtime of running applications
5. To carry out administrative tasks, such as installing software, planning new virtual machines (VMs), optimizing VMs, and so forth, at run time
6. To provision multiple machines in an agile way

3.6.3 VMs—comparison to physical machines

Virtual machines can be compared to physical machines which have operating systems (OSs) running in ring zero and applications running in rings one, two, or three. Operating systems function in layers, and the most privileged instructions are kept in ring zero. These instructions are often operated in kernel mode, whereas the instructions belonging to user applications are operated in user mode, which is considered less privileged.

In physical machines, the kernel instructions of the OS are executed in ring zero, which provides more control over the underlying hardware components of the machines. However, in virtual machines, as multiple owners are engaged in the operation, and multiple OSs are involved in the resource-sharing processes, the OSs are moved to ring one. Instead, the software that is responsible for guiding the guest operating systems is placed in ring zero. In short, only the hypervisor or virtual machine manager (VMM) has full control and the ability to utilize resources.

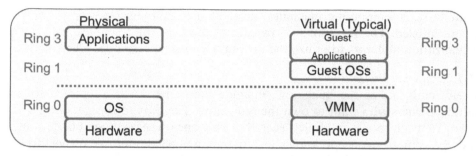

Figure 3.2. Comparison of a VM versus a physical machine.

A hypervisor is a piece of software that guides guest operating systems to utilize the resources. For instance, if four to six VMs are loaded on the physical hardware, the guest OSs of these VMs are operated in ring one, which is considered to be for less privileged instructions compared to the VMM. Figure 3.2 compares a physical machine and a virtual machine in a diagrammatic form.

3.6.4 VMs—case studies

VMs have a major attraction when a new OS is required for experimentation. They are also useful when a deep learning expert wants to develop applications using different Python packages and working environments. If the same installation were to be carried out on bare-metal machines, the reconfiguration and fault recovery options would be limited.

The application of VM technology is clearly visible in cases in which it is necessary to apply a patch. In general, a patch is a software update that addresses a security update or provides a performance update for an existing implementation. In particular, patching could be a harmful activity when graphics-card-related processing needs to be handled. It often ends in system crashes that cannot recovered from. Debugging these issues can be a particularly painful event, for most computing aspirants.

On contrary, VMs provide an opportunity to revert such an update using either snapshots or images. Snapshots are saved versions of VMs with the information about their states; images contain all the information, including the data, state, and installed software and can be saved in any location.

3.7 Hypervisors—impact on deep learning

Depending on the location of the hypervisor, virtual machines are classified as follows:
1. Bare-metal hypervisor
2. Hosted hypervisor

3.7.1 Bare-metal hypervisor

A bare-metal hypervisor uses the location of a VMM which is just above the hardware—i.e. the hypervisor software is directly installed on the machine, instead of an operating system. In some cases, this software is installed at the firmware level. This is often termed type-I virtualization.

A few examples of bare-metal hypervisors include Hyper-V, VMWare, ESXi, Xen, and so forth.

3.7.2 Hosted hypervisors

In hosted hypervisor, the software that guides guest operating systems is one level above the host operating system. This means that the host operating system needs to be loaded before executing the hypervisor. This type of hypervisor is known as a type-II hypervisor, and the virtualization belonging to this category is named type-II virtualization.

Hosted hypervisors pretend to be normal applications that combine a group of processes and computing machines. It can be seen in figure 3.3 that the OS of the host machine is located in ring zero and that the hypervisors operate in the higher rings. These hypervisors are developed to work along with the applications of the host machines. Accordingly, all other guest operating systems become another layer on top of these hypervisor layers.

A few examples of hosted hypervisors include VMWare workstation, VMware Fusion, Oracle VirtualBox, Parallels, Solaris, and so forth.

3.7.3 Full virtualization

Full virtualization ensures that the guest operating system is not modified while executed on machines. For instance, a type-1 virtualization environment with hypervisors hosted on a bare-metal device can load guest operating systems such as Ubuntu, Fedora, Windows, and so forth, that are available in the public domain without any modifications.

As can be observed, the operating systems assume full control over the associated hardware. Accordingly, all instructions attempt to directly utilize the hardware. However, these instructions, including privileged kernel instructions, operate in ring one. Only hypervisors operate in ring zero. Due to this phenomenon, applications that are executed by guest operating systems, except for user-mode instructions, are trapped by the hypervisors. Traps are typical software interrupts that are assumed to

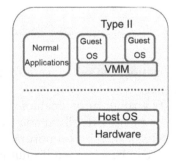

Figure 3.3. Hosted virtualization—type-II virtualization.

be caused by exceptional conditions, such as divide by zero, invalid memory access, and so forth.

Upon receipt of such traps, hypervisors attempt to intercept these instructions or system calls on the fly. As this processing happens during the run time of the guest operating systems' applications, the performance is comparatively lower than that of host machines.

Although this procedure was quite successful with many of the x86 instructions, a few instructions were not trapped by hypervisors. This setting meant that a complicated setup was required to handle full virtualization. However, in the meantime, VMware Inc. proposed the idea of binary translation.

3.7.3.1 VMware's binary translation

VMware introduced the concept of translating the privileged instructions of the guest OS on the fly at the binary level. Translation at the binary level requires parsing the binaries of instructions and identifying the privileged instructions that are not following the security principles; additionally, it must transform these instructions into another form of x86 instruction so the privileged instructions are driven to directly access the hypervisors instead of the hardware.

The binary translation of x86 privileged instructions to another x86 instruction set that is secured leads to the following challenges:

1. Delayed processing—clearly, the computation time increases for applications that are executed by a guest OS of a machine. The increase is profoundly higher if more system calls need to be processed by VMs.
2. Impacted system calls—in general, system calls are expensive in terms of execution time. A typical system call is propagated via the kernel of an OS— i.e. a system call without any virtualization would require around 242 clock cycles. This number often depends on the nature of the system call and ranges from 150 clock cycles to over 10K clock cycles, especially when context switching is involved. The most common system calls are related to process-management instructions, memory-management instructions, file-management instructions, and so forth. In x86_64 architectures, there are over 358 system calls. A few examples of system calls are given below:

```
sys_enter
sys_exit
```

With the use of virtualization, the system calls of guest operating systems can reach around 2300 cycles.

3. Impacted I/O calls—I/O virtualization enables virtualization of I/O—i.e. one physical network card can be virtually made available as virtual network interface controllers (NICs), thereby supporting multiple operating systems. The CPU virtualization can be extended if multiple sockets are available on machines. However, I/O virtualization is not as easy as improving the

performance aspects of CPUs. For instance, I/O bandwidth cannot be improved, as it is dependent on the bus layouts of motherboards.

4. Impacted memory—in general, physical machines do not directly expose memory units to applications executed on machines. Rather, they attempt to map the underlying memory units to secondary memory addresses. When this approach is used, memory violations do not hamper the hardware functionality of real machines.

   In virtual environments, there are multiple hierarchies of mapping units. Here, the programs' memory addresses are mapped to the virtual physical memory addresses of the guest OS; later, the virtual physical memory addresses are mapped to the real memory addresses. Thus, a virtual OS may have to maintain a shadow page table that maps the memory addresses. Typically, this paging concept leads to a substantial overhead that requires around 300–400 more cycles than normal physical machines.

3.7.4 Paravirtualization

In paravirtualization, guest operating systems are modified such that privileged instructions are directly driven to the hypervisor. It is an enhancement of virtualization technology. However, the challenge is that normal operating systems cannot be utilized as guest operating systems.

One of the most popular tools that offers paravirtualization is VMware's vSphere product, which consists of virtualized machines using ESXi paravirtualization setups and containers connected by high-speed networking connections, vCenter servers, vSphere clients to access the machines, storage units, and, so forth.

3.7.5 Hardware-assisted virtualization

In modern machines, hardware-level assistance has been available since 2015, which enables the efficient operation of full virtualization. Before this, users who preferred to adopt virtual environments had to enable the virtualization option at the basic input/output system (BIOS) level. In modern machines, these environments are enabled by default because most frameworks, including deep learning applications, are developed with the assistance of virtualization concepts.

Hardware-level virtualization [10] provides certain features that keep guest operating systems functioning in ring zero itself. To quickly identify the privileged instructions, Virtual Machine Extensions (VMX) `root` mode and `non-root` mode are implemented in modern processors. The VMX `root` mode is more similar to traditional computing systems which have four rings, and hypervisors operate in the VMX `root`. In addition, there is also a second mode of operation known as the `non-root` mode, which includes a control structure called the VM control structure. This control structure keeps track of the privileged instructions that attempt to access the machine. Hence, guest OSs are loaded in the `non-root` mode of operation.

3.8 Containers and Dockers

The majority of deep learning applications are implemented as containers or Dockers. It is therefore important to understand the key functionalities of these technologies in detail. This section explains the nuts and bolts of Dockers and containers.

Containers are software packages with self-contained information that can be executed in any environment. Containers use kernel features such as `cgroups` and `namespaces` to develop software packages and processes for handling isolated applications.

Containers may be related to images. Images are typically a bunch of files stacked in the form of layers that can be hosted on a local machine or on cloud repositories such as Jfrog. Images continue to be a recipe for containers. In fact, containers can be modified based on images. However, the images are typically immutable and are written only once.

Containers are more lightweight components than the traditional virtual machines hosted on bare metal. Obviously, containers can support large scalable environments, as VMs can easily be ported to multiple machines at run time. In addition, they require limited storage space compared to bare-metal VMs. For instance, a bare-metal VM could have a storage size of gigabytes whereas the containers would be in the range of megabytes.

3.8.1 Docker instances

Dockers are specialized container instances that utilize container technology to multiplex multiple computing instances in hardware. Dockers are often termed lightweight VM instances and are widely applied for deep learning applications [18]. These VM instances are comparatively more lightweight than any bare-metal hypervisor implementation.

Docker instances are built on machines such that the hypervisors are found above the operating system layers. This means that the user has to boot an operating system before loading the Docker instances. These VM instances are extensions of the OS—i.e. most of the kernel portions remain common among all instances. Accordingly, a Linux-based machine can only support Linux-based Docker machines; a Windows-based machine can only operate Windows-based Docker machines. Thus, cross-compatibility is not possible for Docker machines.

Dockers are created using two basic building blocks of kernels:
1. `cgroups`—which limit the utility
2. `namespaces`—which limit the views

In the modern era, deep learning applications are built based on Docker instances. The major reasons for utilizing Docker instances are as follows:
1. Agile launch—for implementations based on Dockers, only a very short time is needed between program development and launch operations. Dockers are considered to be potential candidates for DevOps. Typically, in traditional software development markets, the development team implements many

lines of code to implement some deep learning logic; later, the team has to pack the code into a specific format and distribute it with the relevant documentation to the operational team. Then, the operational team has to experiment with or test the code before it can be offered to public clients or customers. In fact, the operational team might encounter several challenges due to the following factors:

(a) The code might not work properly as expected in the operational team's working environment. For instance, the relevant package with suitable versions may be missing from the operational team's environment. Most probably, the operational team will install the code with newer software dependency versions which would have not been tested by the developers.

(b) The expertise of the operational team members might be different from that of the application developers' team, which delays the time to market.

2. Easy integration—Dockers provide an easy integration tool, because Dockers have so much subsidiary software. For instance, the Docker swarm has the ability to orchestrate Dockers among multiple machines with minimal management effort.

3. Programmability—Docker-based implementations support the microservice implementation approach, which promotes programmability support in various languages. Developers can be hired from a Nodejs background, a Golang background, or a Python background to launch distributed learning services. In this way, many programmers can be involved in developing a large set of deep learning applications.

4. Reduced storage—the storage space required for a Docker instance is minimal compared to that required for bare-metal hypervisor implementations. A deep learning algorithm, therefore, could be implemented using Docker instances. For instance, a Docker machine generally has a storage space of 200 to 500 MB, while a bare-metal machine can easily reach more than 1 GB of storage space.

5. Wide utility—Docker-based implementations have become much more popular in the modern era because deep learning applications can be written and hosted on computing machines while specifying all the prerequisites in the files. Notably, configuration files such as the DockerFile contained in Docker instances are utilized to write the step-by-step procedures required to host Docker machines.

For instance, NVIDIA has developed a set of NVIDIA GPU containers (NGCs) to support the development of deep learning applications. Users can write Dockerfiles that contain commands which fetch NVIDIA GPU images in order to execute deep learning models. A simple Dockerfile that creates an NGC container suitable for the development of deep learning applications is given below:

```
FROM nvcr.io/nvidia/TensorFlow:19.03
RUN apt-get update
RUN apt-get install -y octave
```

Here, the keyword 'FROM' represents the image from which the installation of the octave package is initialized.

3.8.2 Docker building blocks

As discussed earlier, the two building blocks used to create Dockers are cgroups and namespaces. The most basic functionalities of cgroups and namespaces are described in the following subsections:

```
namespaces
```

A namespace is a building block that is used to frame Docker instances or containers. The namespaces are responsible for limiting the views of computing resources while sharing them with multiple owners. Limiting the views of directories, file systems, networks, I/O, and so forth, creates isolation between multiple Docker instances. To provide such views, Linux kernels have specific functions which are available to system-level programming.

The namespaces offered to Docker containers are classified into broad categories, as follows:

1. Process identifier (PID) namespace—process identifiers are specific numbers that distinguish computer processes. Starting from the init process, which has a PID of zero, all other processes in a computing machine are spawned with newer process numbers. When a new machine is framed in a Docker container, the users or applications hosted on such a container should also have unique views starting from the init process identity. Since processes are spawned by the parent host machine, the child processes are given to Docker containers with new PID numbers. Thus, this approach enables OS-level virtualization, which is a concept used to provide an extended OS to machines.
2. cgroup namespace—the cgroup namespace is crucial in Docker containers in order to provide a unique view of directories or file system structures. As we all know, the Linux file system has a specific directory structure that has /var, /root, /home, /etc, and so forth. These file structures should also be reflected in the Docker container machines that are hosted on any computing machines.

3. Network namespace—the network namespace attempts to provide a new view to Docker containers. The host machine has network identifiers based on NIC cards. These network identifiers typically originate from the physical NIC card information. Depending on the number of available NIC cards, there are a few identifiers such as, eth0, eth1, and so forth. The `iptools` command provides the Internet Protocol (IP) address information of the host machine.

Since Docker containers are utilized by multiple owners, guest operating machines should get a new view of the underlying physical NIC cards. For instance, the Docker container machine should get unique IP addresses and eth tools with which to perform network-related communications. The namespace component of Linux kernels provides these features to limit the views of Docker containers while operating them on top of host machines.

4. Mount namespace—the ability to mount different devices or media drives on physical machines must be granted to Docker containers. The mount namespace building block of the kernel is responsible for offering such new views of different mounting options. In addition, several other namespace features provide a limited view to container machines, compared to that available to the host machine.

```
cgroups
```

cgroups are considered to be one of the crucial building blocks of Docker containers and are used to limit the utilization of services. This feature describes how much resource is provided by host machines to perform Docker computation.

In general, deep learning applications might require more GPU computation or memory instances when they run in Docker containers. The number of CPUs and the amount of memory made available to Docker containers is determined by the cgroup feature of Linux kernels.

The key objectives of cgroups in Docker containers are as follows:

1. to limit the resources provided to deep learning Docker containers by the host machine;
2. to audit the utilization of Docker container resources; and,
3. to isolate resources in different guest Docker containers from the host machine.

There are several cgroup components in Docker containers, such as memory cgroup, cpu cgroup, block i/o cgroup, cpuset cgroup, devices cgroup, freezer cgroup, and so forth. The important activities performed by these cgroup components that support the Docker containers utilized in deep learning applications are given below:

1. Memory cgroup—The memory cgroup is responsible for isolating the memory behavior of a group of tasks from the rest of the system. It creates a

cgroup with a limited amount of memory. It separates the memory-hungry applications from other applications. For instance, a deep learning application often requires a greater volume of data or databases. The database-enabled deep learning applications hosted on containers may be provided with larger memory spaces.

The memory cgroup enables Docker containers to provide appropriate accounting features—i.e. it offers methods that specify how many memory pages are utilized by a specific group of running processes. This information is offered in file pages or in anonymous pages, such as heaps, stacks, and so forth [25].

The memory cgroup provides opportunities to control the memory utilization of Docker containers by limiting their utilization on host machines. Typically, the control measures are implemented using two approaches, as listed below:

(a) Soft limit—in the soft-limit approach, the memory allocated to a Docker machine is not strictly honored. If the memory requirement of a Docker machine increases, then based on the availability of surplus host memory, additional memory is allotted to the Docker machine. This is especially important if the host machine has limited work while the Docker machine wants to execute a few computationally intensive deep learning tasks.

(b) Hard limit—in the hard-limit approach, memory is not allotted to a group of Docker containers if the amount of memory increases beyond any specified limit.

In fact, if they exceed the predefined hard limit, the kernels of host machines could trigger an out-of-memory (OOM) killer process to kill any running Docker processes based on the badness score of the Linux machine. To avoid unnecessary issues, it is advisable to run only one application in a container.

There is a customized solution for overriding the hard limits of Dockers which lead to the OOM killer processes. The customized solution uses the series of steps discussed below:

Step 1: all Docker processes are signaled to stop the ongoing processes. This is achieved using the 'freeze' option of Docker containers;

Step 2: notifications are submitted to the user space so that the users can be more vigilant in caring for their resource-hungry applications;

Step 3: the user can kill specific processes rather than letting the operating system of the host machine decide on its own;

Step 4: otherwise, the users are permitted to increase the hard limit of resources specified in the cgroups;

Step 5: finally, once the intended processes are killed, the unfreeze option is enabled to keep the Docker container running without conflicts.

2. Block I/O cgroup—this cgroup feature enables block I/O storage options for Docker containers. It provides limited and scoped storage units without impacting the performance of large numbers of Dockers and the underlying host machines.

3. CPUSet cgroup—if a machine has several CPUs, the ability to assign programming instructions to these CPUs must be optimized with respect to performance. For instance, a parallel program wanting CPUs sparsely spread across the larger parallel machine, could consume a large execution time due to the delay in sending packets across the wired CPUs. In fact, the performance of an application can be dramatically improved by combining CPU sets together for a parallel program. This is quite beneficial for several deep-learning-based applications.

4. Devices cgroup—It is sometimes necessary to control Docker machine access to rare devices, such as printers, USB flash drives, and so forth. The devices cgroup is responsible for limiting the access from multiple Docker containers to devices. For instance, a deep learning container may need access to attached NAS devices, while a normal container might have to be prevented from having such access.

5. Freezer cgroup—the freezer cgroup allows Dockers to perform some maintenance functions. It enables Docker machines to stop all processes or a group of processes before some actions are performed.

All these components and subcomponents of cgroups and namespaces are considered to be building blocks of Docker containers that perform specialized isolated applications, including deep learning applications.

3.8.3 Docker storage characteristics

Dockers are specific containers that are unique compared to traditional containers. The most crucial feature that characterizes Docker machines is the inclusion of a union file system. Containers are stored using a union file system approach. The union file system ensures that the contents of multiple Docker containers are unified, which improves the usage of the storage space in Docker machines. A few researchers have studied the performance of Docker storage systems [20].

If a deep learning application implemented using TensorFlow library version 2.0 is hosted in a Docker machine for the second time, the lower layers of the library are not downloaded. In addition, the storage space from the previous Docker machines is utilized. Thus, the Docker approach consumes less storage and less network bandwidth while executing applications on Docker machines.

Accordingly, several Docker machines used to execute deep learning applications are hosted on public repositories. For instance, most of the TensorFlow-based deep learning applications are hosted using Docker containers on cloud resources.

3.8.4 Docker working model

Docker is implemented using a client-server architecture that has three major components. A pictorial representation of a Docker-enabled cluster machine is shown in figure 3.4.

The functionalities of these three software components are listed below:

1. Docker client—The Docker client transfers user requests to host machines. The client requests are processed in Docker machines to execute Docker machines or host Docker images. A few popular commands such as, Docker run, Docker build, Docker ps, and so forth, are issued from the Docker clients by users.
2. Docker daemon—The requests from users are submitted to Docker daemons that run on host machines. The daemons are initiated immediately when the boot process is started in the host machines. The role of the Docker daemons is to continually watch the requests from clients and enable images or containers based on the requests. They ensure that the images are utilized to load union-file-system-based containers on host machines. If any of the required images are not found in the local machine, the daemon is responsible for communicating with the external Docker registries in order to loading the images into the host machines.
3. Docker registries—The Docker registries hold a large number of images that function as recipes for creating Docker containers. There are two types of Docker registry:
   (a) Public registries—public registries are common registries hosted by several third-party providers. These registries often contain the most popularly available deep learning and similar images that could be customized for our needs.
   (b) Private registries—in most cases, the public registries cannot satisfy the needs of a specific organization. Organizations that have several customers generally use templates or images designed to work with a particular intention or task. Such images are often hosted on these private registries.

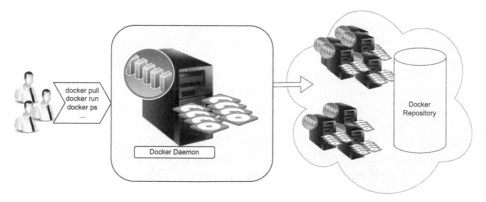

Figure 3.4. Docker architecture used to host deep learning applications.

The Docker daemon initially searches for images on the local machine. If they are not found in the local machine, it tries to search for them in the private registries. Subsequently, it searches for suitable images from the public registries before the images are loaded into containers.

3.8.5 Docker tools

Although several deep learning implementations utilize Docker-based installations, the necessity for tools is multifaceted:

1. Tools are necessary to provide ease in handling Docker-related applications.
2. Tools are important to pinpoint the performance problems of lightweight machines. Obviously, it is very difficult for normal users to quickly identify the underlying performance problems of deep learning applications that are executed on Docker machines.
3. Tools are required in order to work with Docker machines, instead of working with the basic components of Linux kernels such as `cgroups` and `namespaces`.

A few Docker tools that are very popular in providing support to deep learning application developers or business enthusiasts and their crucial visions are described below:

1. Docker Desktop—Docker Desktop [2] is a tool that produces a bundled package that contains all the Docker components, such as Docker-engine, cli, credential helper, and so forth. Accordingly, the users do not need to search for the individual bare components of Docker installations while hosting deep learning applications on Docker-based host machines.
2. Docker Compose—this tool [1] is beneficial for defining instances specific to certain applications, including deep learning applications. For instance, a deep learning application might require specialized dependency versions of languages and packages in order to execute without failure on machines. The purpose of the Docker Compose tool is to create such images using configurations specified in YAML files. Accordingly, the Docker Compose tool provides opportunities to build and run multicontainer Docker applications.
3. Docker Swarm—this tool [3] has features that coordinate Docker instances hosted on multiple machines. It is a tool to manage Docker containers hosted on clusters and is similar to orchestration tools such as Kubernetes. This tool has features such as scaling, multihost orchestration, service discovery, load balancing, and so forth.

3.9 Cloud execution models

In the modern world, deep learning applications are mainly hosted on clouds. VM-based cloud execution models are often converted to serverless execution models and Kubernetes-based deep learning container engines. This section describes the crucial developments of cloud implementation styles related to deep learning inference.

3.9.1 Serverless cloud execution model

The serverless cloud execution model is utilized in a few deep learning architectures [9]. In fact, a serverless function is a programmatic function that invokes servers to execute operations. In the serverless framework, the servers are not initially available for execution. However, based on requests initiated by the serverless functions, cloud infrastructures enable servers in cold-start or warm-start modes to host deep learning algorithms for further execution. Serverless functions may be executed in parallel containers hosted by third-party cloud infrastructures. In general, this is also called function-as-a-service.

The most important features of serverless functions in the deep learning domain offer several advantages. These advantages are as follows:

1. Any deep learning algorithms, when developed, can have a limited lifetime in the market. This is because the functions are implemented using fine-grained code logic developed by multilingual programming experts.
2. Enhanced scalability—as the functions are often fine-grained, they can be hosted by lightweight VM containers. Accordingly, the scalability feature of the intelligence or associated frameworks is increased. For instance, an online training program hosted using serverless platforms scaled to 40 000 users in six months without a single dedicated cloud server.
3. Costs—obviously, as a result of the concept of no running application servers, the serverless-based cloud execution model reduces the costs involved in the development of algorithms or logic. Deep-learning-based applications that infrequently use sensor nodes to process intelligence from sensor data can typically profit from serverless cloud technology.

3.9.2 Kubernetes solutions

Managing lightweight containers that execute deep learning algorithms is a considerable task for several application developers [17]. Docker containers have developed a Docker swarm tool to perform the managerial tasks. Like the Docker swarm tool, the Kubernetes platform was developed by cloud experts to manage containers, especially hanging containers.

Kubernetes is considered to be an orchestration tool that brings together a group of running containers or services. In addition, it is responsible for discovering services hosted on containers belonging to clusters. For instance, a training model hosted by a container could be tracked by the Kubernetes platform before performing tests on real-time data. As we may imagine, there could be tens of thousands of different flavors of training model which could be hosted on a Kubernetes cluster using containers. These services are captured in a timely fashion using the orchestration tool.

A Kubernetes cluster consists of master and slave nodes. The master node is responsible for managing slave nodes and their associated application containers, such as deep learning models hosted by containers. It is called the brain of the cluster. It contains an API server that offers representational state transfer (REST) services that support scheduling and replication tasks. The main objective of the Kubernetes cluster is to provide automated scheduling of application containers across the available nodes in a cluster. The slave nodes are also named minion nodes. These nodes host the application containers. They have two major components, as given below:

1. Kubelet—this component talks to the API server to submit the status of the current workload so that the master node can orchestrate the flow.
2. Kube-proxy—this component is responsible for directing user messages to PODs, which represent a group of containers with a single IP address.

Minikube is a minimal version of the Kubernetes orchestration tool that can be established on a single machine.

3.9.3 DL-as-a-service

In general, clouds provide service-oriented implementation support. Deep learning as a service (DL-as-a-service) is way of implementing the corresponding tasks [22]. Typically, DL-as-a-service is offered using software or hardware-cum-software approaches.

DL-as-a-service is implemented using four different approaches. The gists of these approaches and their crucial features are described below:

1. Environments—deep learning services are offered as environmental variables. By enabling these environmental variables, users can offload certain deep learning tasks to the connected cloud services. For instance, AWS environmental variables can be set to connect learning-based computational tasks with EC2 instances of AWS.
2. Plugins—some services are developed as plugins for browsers or attached software frameworks. Deep learning tasks are offloaded to cloud environments due to the performance of deep learning plugins.
3. Libraries—the majority of deep learning tasks are implemented as libraries using APIs connected to cloud infrastructures. These libraries offer functions that can be added to deep learning tasks to offload selected activities to clouds.

3.10 Programming deep learning tasks—libraries

TensorFlow [5], Pytorch [4], and similar ecosystems have been developed to help their users to program deep learning tasks so that they can be executed by computing machines, including cloud environments. TensorFlow has been widely utilized by deep learning enthusiasts. It enables a workflow model to perform deep learning tasks using the well-known Python programming language.

3.10.1 Features of TensorFlow

The important features of the TensorFlow platform that facilitate the coding of Python-based deep learning tasks are as follows:

1. Ease of operation—the TensorFlow platform delivers easy integration with several other platforms, such as Google run time collaboration services or

locally connected clusters. Users have to select appropriate compute resources using the platform in order to execute deep learning services in the cloud.

2. Ease of representation—in addition, TensorFlow focuses on making it easy to represent data. For instance, Tensors are utilized to represent text, image, or audio data. Tensors are multidimensional arrays that are mainly represented as NumPy arrays, mostly static in nature. Tensors are often represented by strongly typed array representations that are immutable during the execution period. Hence, altering tensors is not possible. However, newer tensors can be created during the execution of deep learning tasks.

3. Debugging feature—interpreters for TensorFlow have been developed, which use Jupyter notebooks. The Jupyter notebooks allow users to easily develop the code and debug errors that appear due to inefficient coding, etc. An application developer working on deep learning tasks and using more than 20 Python files could find it difficult to trace mistakes or errors using a traditional approach. However, using the TensorFlow platform, they are able to debug them in a short span of time.

4. Visualization—the platform provides a visual representation of tensors and variables to programmers. In this way, associated graphs and data can be visualized to some extent using TensorFlow.

3.10.2 TensorFlow components

Deep learning inferences made using TensorFlow libraries are carried out using specific components. If we examine the internal architecture of TensorFlow-based deep learning inference engines, the following crucial components can be identified:

1. Compute hardware—TensorFlow-based programs are executed on different computing hardware units, such as CPUs, GPUs, TPUs, Android, and so forth.

2. TensorFlow core—the abstraction of the hardware computing units happens at the kernel level, which is implemented in the TensorFlow core components. The core is developed using C++ APIs with Linux or OS kernels at the system-level programming stages.

3. Python components—Python-level interpreters are developed on top of the TensorFlow core component to create task graphs and to perform eager execution. These components, which use several Python packages, are often considered core functionalities of the TensorFlow libraries.

4. Custom components—the TensorFlow platform delivers several functions, such as tf.shape, tf.layers, and so forth. These components are developed using the Python components to deliver customization setups.

5. High-level APIs—in addition, there are a few high-level tools and APIs, such as TensorFlow Estimator, which combine all the available lower-layer implementations to deliver deep learning tasks using simple commands or functions.

3.11 Sensor-enabled data collection for DLs

A few sectors of deep learning applications involve the use of sensor nodes to apply intelligence. The data collection mechanisms for these sensor-enabled applications are particularly important for any deep learning enthusiasts [24]. This is because the data sources and the preprocessing stages are crucial aspects of deep learning applications.

3.11.1 Required mechanisms

A few mechanisms that we need to consider while processing sensor data for deep learning applications are as follows:

1. Multihop mechanism—sensor nodes often communicate via wireless media. Since they are often battery-operated, nodes may have difficulties in submitting data to deep-learning-powered inference engines or establishing proper communications. These nodes could use multihop methods to submit the data to the destination node through intermediate nodes.
2. Energy-efficient operations—energy efficiency is considered to be one of the most crucial objectives, not only for battery-operated embedded devices but also for power-sourced cloud-based machines. In fact, a poor approach to handling applications can lead to substantial electricity costs and carbon emissions.
3. In-network processing—in some cases, it is better to handle the routing or packet processing performed by communication systems at network nodes rather than submitting packets to the cloud or intended computational systems. In this way, the network latency and the processing capabilities of applications can be significantly improved.

Obviously, all deep learning applications that receive data from sensor nodes must ensure sufficient quality of service, fault tolerance, required lifetime to process data, programmability, and provision to attract data from wide density locations.

3.11.2 Sensors to DL services—data connectivity

IoT-enabled devices, such as cameras, temperature sensors, or humidity sensors can submit data to deep learning services in various ways. The approach used to submit the data depends on the network topology used for the connected nodes.

In general, a few network topologies have been used to connect IoT-enabled sensor nodes, as described below:

1. IoT local area network (LAN)—in the IoT LAN, sensors are connected each other using any topology such as star, bus, mesh, and so forth. These sensor nodes have unique local addresses that identify them. Notably, the computing machine that collects the sensor data must reside within the LAN to process sensor applications.
2. IoT wide-area network (WAN)—here, a deep learning computing engine can reside at any distant location. Multiple LANs that have unique addresses

typically reach other LANs through routers attached to the networks. Each LAN belonging to one organization is attached to a router that submits the data to the connected WAN nodes.

3. IoT direct connectivity—in some cases, sensor nodes may need to directly connect to Internet-powered nodes or cloud services that host deep learning algorithms. To do so, tunnels are created between sensor nodes and anchor points that are Global Positioning System (GPS) enabled before the data reach the intended deep-learning-based cloud services.

3.11.3 Application-layer protocols

The method by which data is distributed among networked nodes for processing by deep learning algorithms greatly influences the performance of IoT-enabled deep learning applications. In general, sensor nodes communicate with cloud services using either a publish/subscribe model or a request/response model.

A few protocols, such as Message Queue Telemetry Transport (MQTT), Secure Message Queue Telemetry Transport (SMQTT), Constrained Application Protocol (CoAP), Advanced Message Queuing Protocol (AMQP), Extensible Messaging and Presence Protocol (XMPP), Data Distribution Service (DDS), and so forth, assist sensor nodes to deliver messages. The most important gists of these protocols and data delivery patterns are described in the following subsections.

3.11.3.1 MQTT

MQTT stands for Message Queue Telemetry Transport. It is quite popularly utilized to transfer messages, typically short ones, in order to enable energy-efficient communications to take place between sensor nodes or battery-operated nodes. In general, this protocol is applied for machine-to-machine (M2M) communications, in which sensors submit data to another machine.

The uniqueness of this protocol is that it follows a publish/subscribe model for sending messages within nodes. In the publish/subscribe communications model, devices need not be actively listening for the receipt of acknowledgments or required messages. Figure 3.5 illustrates how sensor nodes can submit sensor data to subscribers via MQTT brokers.

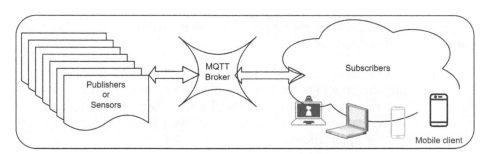

Figure 3.5. The publish/subscribe architecture of MQTT-based sensor applications for DL intelligence.

The mechanism which, in contrast to the Hypertext Transfer Protocol (HTTP), does not involve actively listening to messages, is based on the underlying MQTT architecture, which consists of three major components, namely, publishers, brokers, and subscribers. The important features of these components that are relevant to the process of submitting data to services are as follows:

1. Publishers—sensor nodes can periodically sense a few measurable properties and submit the data to brokers rather than waiting for reply messages. Accordingly, the energy consumption of the sensor nodes is dramatically reduced. The sensor nodes that publish such information to brokers are called publishers.
2. Brokers—the most important responsibility of the broker is to collect messages from sensors and transport them to known subscribers based on their demands. The subscribers are not active all the time. They can become active whenever they want the information from the sensor nodes. For instance, a deep learning engine may need sensor data only when it needs to process algorithms. Additionally, these brokers provide a secure way of authenticating publishers or subscribers. Depending on the availability of brokers, they are classified into two broad categories:
    (a) Private broker—private brokers permit only known subscribers or publishers to send or receive messages. Hence, no anonymous sensor nodes can directly utilize the deep learning services. In contrary, no deep learning services are permitted to collect sensor data from unauthorized sensor nodes.
    (b) Public broker—public brokers, as the name suggests, permit any subscriber or publisher to send or receive messages. Some popular available MQTT brokers are EclipseMQTT broker, HiveMQ, Mosquitto, and so forth.

Brokers may have to have certain characteristics before users can choose them. The most popularly recognized broker characteristics and their features are listed below:
    (a) Quality of service (QoS) assistance—brokers must provide sufficient QoS support for connected devices. In fact, wireless communications are prone to failures, including communication disruptions. By default, brokers should have the ability to enable QoS support.
    (b) Open source—normally, open source-based development offers better opportunities for future enhancements. Accordingly, the academic world could extensively innovate to extend broker functionality. For instance, the authentication schemes could be improved in open source-enabled brokers. However, the challenge would be to ensure that the broker had long-term support.
    (c) Performance—performance is one of the key characteristics for brokers or associated implementations. The performance metrics include:

    i. Latency—the message delivery time is a crucial performance metric for MQTT-based protocols.

     ii. Throughput—the throughput describes the number of messages that are processed by brokers within a specified time frame.

    iii. Scalability—scalability is a performance metric that describes the number of resources that can be handled by brokers while increasing the numbers of incoming/outgoing messages.

    iv. Availability—the availability of brokers describes the operation of the nodes even if external forces are applied or processing capabilities fail. This feature has to be consistent to process MQTT messages from various machines or sensor nodes.

(d) Interoperability—brokers must ensure that they are interoperable with various hosted services or subscriber features. For instance, messages from brokers may have to support deep learning engines that are written using languages such as Nodejs, Golang, C++, etc. Additionally, brokers may have to easily integrate with other brokers, including private brokers, if needed.

(e) Security—even if brokers are implemented as private or public brokers, the authentication and authorization mechanisms used by brokers, including key encryption mechanisms, must be carefully managed. For instance, token-enabled authentication may be employed with brokers to ensure a higher security level when connecting devices or services to brokers. Also, it is important to have mechanisms that protect brokers from various known denial of service attacks. In this way, deep learning applications can easily be integrated with brokers.

3. Subscribers—subscribers are entities that require data or messages to develop knowledge or perform actions. For instance, examples of subscribers include deep learning algorithms hosted in cloud services, which require sensor data to process applications.

The MQTT protocol [13] defines specific methods that are used to connect or disconnect nodes. These methods are given below:

1. Connect method—this helps to connect sensors with the server which executes deep learning algorithms.
2. Disconnect method—this helps to disconnect sensors from the deep learning services.
3. Subscribe method—this method enables deep learning services to subscribe to sensor data provided by brokers.
4. Unsubscribe method—this method is utilized to unsubscribe from sensor data provided by brokers.
5. Publish method—this method helps sensors to submit or publish sensor data to brokers so that the data can be fetched by subscribing deep learning applications.

Consider a situation in which water quality sensors are utilized in the water distribution sites of a smart city. The water quality sensors are battery-operated.

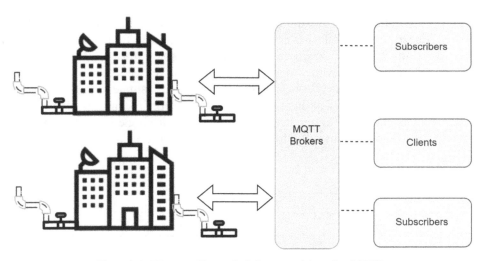

Figure 3.6. Water quality analysis in smart cities using MQTT.

Also, let us assume that the smart city official wants to update the water quality data for the distribution channels. In such cases, appropriate deep learning algorithms may be applied to predict the maintenance required by the channels. Accordingly, the official wishes to view progressive charts hosted by cloud services (figure 3.6).

In this use case, the water quality sensors installed in the various distribution channels do not respond to data based on the request from the deep learning services. In fact, according to the MQTT protocol, there is no communication between the sensor nodes and the services. Rather, the sensors, whenever they are ready to communicate the water quality information, can submit the data to the public brokers. The deep learning services, when invoked by the smart city official, connect to the brokers using the Transmission Control Protocol (TCP) and fetch the sensor data used to predicting the maintenance and relevant actions, if any.

The messaging between sensors and brokers (or publishers and brokers) is formulated using topics. The topics are a way of addressing messages between actors. They are represented using a UTF-8 string format that has hierarchies to represent the data in a structured manner.

Depending on the messages that are collected, MQTT topics are classified into two approaches:

1. Exact topic—the exact topic is a string of information that relates to an exact location. In this use case, it would be sensor information collected from a specific water distribution channel. For instance, if the water quality is monitored in the water distribution channel of a house, the specific topic for a bathroom would be represented as follows:

```
Topic—house/bath-room/waterquality
```

2. Wildcard topic—data from many sensors is accommodated or processed in a wildcard topic. It consists of a string of information that relates to multiple locations. Wildcard `topics` are further classified into two types:

(a) Single-level wildcard topic—in a single-level wildcard topic, data from many sensors is collected and processed at a single hierarchical level of the system. For instance, if water quality information from several rooms of a house needs to be studied, a single-level wildcard topic could be utilized. This is represented using a '+' symbol, as shown below:

```
Topic—house/+/waterquality
```

In the above example, the `topics` representing the sensor data from several rooms, such as house/bath-room/waterquality or house/kitchen/waterquality, are considered for the analysis.

(b) Multilevel wildcard—in the multilevel wildcard approach, the `topics` encompass several levels of the hierarchy. For instance, sensor data from the entire house (consisting of multiple rooms) could be processed using this approach, as follows:

```
Topic—Eg. house/#
```

It can be observed that the multilevel wildcard `topics` are represented using the '#' symbol.

In fact, `topics` in the MQTT protocol can be named using any names the user chooses, without any specific restrictions. However, a topic starting with the '$' symbol is restricted. These are often utilized to represent status messages, such as:

```
SYS/broker/clients/connected
SYS/broker/clients/disconnected
SYS/broker/clients/total
SYS/broker/messages/sent
SYS/broker/uptime
```

3.11.3.2 CoAP

CoAP is a Constrained Application Protocol designed exclusively for IoT-based applications. It targets constrained devices that do not have sufficient power to process instructions. The CoAP protocol is utilized for web transfers that can be applied for M2M communications in various domains, such as smart building, building automation, and smart manufacturing applications where intelligence can be implemented using deep learning algorithms.

CoAP [6] uses a request–response model for web transfers between nodes. Even though CoAP utilizes the request–response model to transfer sensor data, it appears to be an efficient protocol for power-constrained devices.

The major reasons that CoAP is capable of handling the request–response model for web transfers between nodes while achieving reduced energy consumption are as follows:

1. CoAP utilizes the User Datagram Protocol (UDP) to send messages, rather than employing the expensive TCP protocols. In general, when TCP is used as the transport layer of communication nodes, they have to perform a three-way handshake before sending packets between the designated nodes. However, TCP-based transport layers use sophisticated methods to ensure reliable packet delivery due to the continuous connections.
2. CoAP functions in the session layer or the bottom thin portion of the application layer. In general, reducing the number of higher layers is an asset when focusing on the energy consumption of applications.

To compensate for the principles of avoiding higher layers and enabling only UDP, CoAP proposes the following ideas in order to efficiently improve communication exchanges:

1. HTTP—CoAP easily integrates with HTTP so that the power-efficient nodes can communicate with traditional web-related applications. CoAP merges with HTTP-enabled browsers to provide the normal request–response architecture of Internet communications. In this context, it can use a few REST-based messages rather than submitting more detailed information that follows Simple Object Access Protocol (SOAP)-like protocols.
2. Session sublayers—CoAP incorporates two layers, namely, the req/res layer and the reliable messaging layer.
    (a) req/res layer—this layer is responsible for establishing connections and providing communication support between connected nodes.
    (b) Reliable messaging layer—this layer provides reliability support for connections, as communications are handled using the UDP protocol —i.e. a connectionless protocol. To achieve this, a few messages have been developed for CoAP communications.

The list of CoAP messages supported by the CoAP protocol and their common interests are described below:

1. Confirmable message—here, an acknowledgment is received for every sent messages between power-constrained machines/nodes. Using a similar approach to that used for HTTP, CoAP also uses GET, PUSH, DELETE, and UPDATE web verbs while exchanging messages.
2. Non-confirmable message—here, only messages are sent between the nodes. Notably, no ACK messages are involved in communications.

3. Piggyback message—in this message type, in addition to the ACK message, the data is also sent to the client as a response. However, there are issues with parsing the data and ACK messages. To do this, processes require some sophisticated machinery, which limits the utilization.
4. Separate message—here, the ACK message and the appropriate data messages are sent separately by the server to the client.

3.11.3.3 XMPP

XMPP [8] is an acronym for the Extensible Messaging and Presence Protocol. This protocol was initially named Jabber because it was developed by the Jabber community in 1999. The Jabber community formed the XMPP Foundation to look into the future aspects and development phases of XMPP-related applications.

The unique feature of this protocol is that it provides for instant messaging. It is based on an open standard that uses Extensible Markup Language (XML)-based communications between communicating nodes. XMPP can use either a publish-subscribe or request–response model for communications. Its design is standardized by the Internet Engineering Task Force's (IETF's) Request for Comments (RFC) 6120 and RFC 6121 standards.

According to the XMPP messaging pattern, XML tags are utilized for communication. The XMPP protocol functions below the application layer of the TCP/Internet Protocol (IP) standards. Communications between nodes are not centralized—i.e. there is no need for centralized servers similar to brokers in MQTT or the AMQP.

Messages are transferred based on the requirement and willingness to communicate between nodes. For instance, any client can connect to XMPP servers using the following commands:

```
<stream:stream
from='client-a@name-server.com'
to='name-server.com'
version='1.0'
xmlns='jabber:client'
>
```

As can be observed, stream tags are utilized to connect to XMPP servers; from and to indications are provided to describe how the communications should be directed between communicating nodes.

Client 'A' can be connected to an XMPP server using the following code snippet:

```
<stream:stream
from='client-b@name-server.com'
```

```
to='name-server.com'
version='1.0'
xmlns='jabber:client'
>
```

It can be seen that client 'B' connects to the XMPP server using `from` and `to` tags.
Client 'A' sends a near-real-time message to Client 'B' as follows:

```
<message to='client-b@name-server.com'>
<body>Enjoy the day! </body>
</message>
```

Messages are sent using XMPP `message` tags. In the above example, messages are sent to the specified client address along with the message payloads.
Client 'B' receives the instant message from Client 'A' as follows:

```
<message from='client-a@name-server.com'>
<body>Enjoy the day! </body>
</message>
```

The connection to the XMPP server is terminated using the `stream` tag of XMPP. For instance, Client 'A' terminates the stream as follows:

```
</stream:stream>
```

XMPP-based devices often communicate with other higher-layer protocol devices, such as gateways, in order to connect to HTTP-based Internet-enabled devices.
The major drawbacks of XMPP protocols are as follows:
1. The XMPP protocol does not offer any QoS support while communicating with other nodes.
2. XMPP has no support for end-to-end security (or encryption methods).
3. Obviously, due to these limitations, the XMPP protocol has not been very successful in some application domains.

3.11.3.4 AMQP

AMQP allows nodes to exchange messages using a publish/subscribe model. It was originally developed in 2003 as an open-standard application protocol.

Although AMQP follows a publish/subscribe model, it attempts to deliver messages using `routes` between nodes. It ensures that point-to-point

3-33

communications take place between the intended nodes by providing specialized queues in the broker architecture of the AMQP system.

The major differences between AMQP and MQTT are as follows:

1. MQTT does not have methods to provide messages to designated subscribers. It is open, so that any approved subscriber can collect messages. By contrast, AMQP employs routing mechanisms to route message queues to known subscribers.

2. The broker architecture of MQTT makes it simple to hold and pass messages to any subscriber. In fact, there are over 47 000 exposed MQTT brokers that serve subscribers. If the publisher became an attacker, the sensor could send open messages to brokers which have registered subscribers. Accordingly, this system can cause huge security problems. AMQP attempts to overcome these cybersecurity issues.

3.11.3.5 DDS

DDS is a data-centric messaging protocol [11]. Most of the previously mentioned protocols are not data-centric, although they offer better instant messaging communications.

Consider the scenario of fixing an appointment date at a preferable location for a group of colleagues. Typically, the messaging approaches based on previous protocols try to deliver messages back and forth between the connected nodes. This gives the intended recipients the burden of figuring out which messages should be reliably considered for the final decision. For instance, a calendar application will generate a huge number of messages between colleagues when fixing a location or time for a joint appointment.

With the implementation of data-centric data distribution protocols, the sensor nodes can deliver messages with the architectural changes between sender and receiver. In fact, the DDS protocol is designed such that intermediate brokers are avoided. Hence, the protocol is normally termed as brokerless protocols.

3.11.4 Lower-layer protocols

The design of the lower layers of communication systems used to develop deep learning algorithms is crucial, as performance depends on the underlying communication protocols. Several deep-learning-based applications need IoT-enabled devices to collect sensor data. However, these sensor nodes do not have communication protocols that handle deep learning tasks efficiently.

In the previous subsection, we learned about the service-level protocols that are utilized to exchange messages between nodes in a deep learning ecosystem. This subsection describes the most commonly available lower-layer protocols that are utilized to send data between the communication nodes that perform deep learning tasks.

3.11.4.1 The IEEE 802.15.4 standard

The IEEE 802.15.4 standard is mainly utilized for connecting personal area networks (PANs). Sensor nodes are often connected to nearby servers or microprocessor-based powerful computational nodes in order to send or process sensor data.

The IEEE 802.15.4 standard focuses on low-cost, low-speed, communications between PAN-connected nodes. The basic framework specifies a 10 m communications range with a transfer rate of 250 kbit/s, which is meant for short-range communications. The standard was defined by IEEE 802.15 task group 4/4b and first published in 2003; it was revised in 2006. The design of 802.15.4 takes account of the spectrum allocation rules of the US, Canada, Europe, and Japan.

The datalink layer includes two other sublayers, namely:

1. The service-specific convergence sublayer (SSCS)—the SSCS is responsible for offering assured data transmission between nodes;
2. Logical link control—this layer aims to provide a robust multiplexing mechanism for access to radio links. It typically uses the carrier-sense multiple access with collision avoidance scheme.

IEEE 802.15.4 has two different communication versions:

1. Low-speed version—this approach uses the binary phase-shift keying (BPSK) modulation technique—i.e. input symbols are phase shifted to two levels based on the input bits.
2. High-speed version—in this approach, 16 symbols are utilized to represent four input bits at a time. Each block of four input bits corresponds to a phase symbol. This modulation approach is called offset quadrature phase-shift keying or offset QPSK. Typically, the power level used by these systems ranges from 0.5 mW to 1 mW. The associated antenna transmissions fall into the line-of-sight (LOS) category. The transmission range of IEEE 802.15.4 devices generally reaches from 10 m to 30 m or 40 m.

IEEE 802.15.4 networks are composed of several types of device that are able to access connected nodes:

1. Full-functionality devices—these nodes are able to include all protocol layers. They are capable of processing deep learning tasks and transferring messages to connected cloud services. A few examples of fully functional devices are PAN coordinators, routers, and nodes.
2. Reduced-functionality devices—these devices are not capable of processing all the relevant information. The main reasons for this are the unavailability of high-end processors, memory space, or battery support. Obviously, these devices route their processing requests to connected fully functional devices in the network.

3.11.4.2 Zigbee protocol

Earlier, we discussed the IEEE 802.15.4 standard. It provides a physical and link-layer technology optimized for low-bitrate, low-duty-cycle applications. In general, sensor and control applications need a mesh networking cluster and a standard syntax for application-layer messages.

The Zigbee protocol, as applied for deep learning tasks [19], aims to deliver the following most important features on top of IEEE 802.15.4 radio links:

1. It aims to improve encryption-based communications between nodes. To this end, it recommends 128-bit Advanced Encryption Standard (AES) encryption support.
2. It only allows authenticated nodes to join the network and to engage in communication with deep learning engines.
3. It adopts sophisticated routing processes using ad hoc on-demand distance vector routing protocols.
4. It enables the formation of clusters (via mesh networks).

The recent Zigbee 3.0 protocol enables mesh networks and routing support to carry messages from IoT-enabled devices to deep learning engines with the highest security.

A Zigbee architecture includes an application layer, an application support sublayer, a Zigbee network layer, and IEEE 802.15.4 lower layers. The most important features of these layers, including the application support sublayer, are listed below:

1. They are responsible for serving as an interface between the higher and lower layers of the Zigbee stack.
2. They are responsible for forwarding the network layer packets to the appropriate application objects through the endpoints using endpoint identifiers (IDs).
3. They create a local binding table containing the information about the remote nodes and endpoints that are registered to perform communications.
4. They map a 64-bit IEEE address to a 16-bit ZigBee network node address.
5. They manage the security keys and message acknowledgments.

Zigbee protocols are efficiently applied in smart-home-related deep learning applications. For instance, washing machines and fridges communicate with shopping malls over the Internet. If a user wants to study the working patterns of fridges or washing machines in houses over a period of years, deep learning models need to be integrated with these Zigbee-enabled devices for effective communications.

3.11.4.3 WirelessHART

WirelessHART is a communication protocol designed by the Highway Addressable Remote Transducer (HART) Communication Foundation. Sensors, typically analog sensors used in industry, can be connected to analytic hosted machines using the HART protocol. This protocol is widely applied in industrial IoT systems [16]. The protocol has the ability to configure devices and fetch sensor data using 4 or 20 mA AC signals.

This protocol can create mesh connectivity between a set of remotely connected nodes. The major objective of wirelessHART devices is to enable quick installation without high data-rate communications.

This protocol uses a time-slot channel-access mechanism that includes frequency-hopping spread-spectrum techniques to prevent the connected nodes of a network from jamming each other.

To increase the reliability of the connected nodes, the WirelessHART protocol expects at least three neighboring nodes to process packets and routing configurations.

The devices used to create WirelessHART-enabled communication networks are categorized into three types:

1. WirelessHART devices—these are sensor nodes that can remotely connect to gateways or handheld communication devices. WirelessHART devices are often power-line powered or battery powered.
2. WirelessHART Adapters—these are devices that are used to create connections between wired and wireless HARTs. Typically, these devices are located near accessible locations. These devices can either be battery-powered or line-powered and have sufficient computing capabilities to relay packets from different wirelessHART nodes. These wireless adapters are also used to connect new HART devices to existing WirelessHART infrastructure.
3. WirelessHART gateways and handhelds—these devices are responsible for performing network management functions, routing calculations, and security-related tasks. In addition, WirelessHART gateways can allow at least 20 percent of their connections to be direct connections to WirelessHART devices.

The most common applications of WirelessHART protocols are to increase the process control of industrial applications. The data produced by these WirelessHART devices can be directly submitted to cloud-hosted deep learning engines to automatically assess the performance of industrial motors or appliances.

3.11.4.4 6LoWPAN

The IP version 6 (IPv6) over low-power PAN (6LoWPAN) protocol is very useful in various analytic applications, as sensor nodes utilizing this protocol can directly communicate using Internet-based devices. The major key functionalities of this protocol are reflected in the associated name, as follows:

1. IPv6—6LoWPAN works with IPv6-based sensor nodes. Obviously, the security of the networked applications is improved, as devices communicate using enhanced security features compared to those of IPv4 packets. Additionally, more sensor nodes can be connected and processed using IPv6 due to the use of 128-bit addressing patterns in the 6LoWPAN protocol.
2. Low power—this protocol uses IEEE 802.15.4-based lower layers in its networking protocol stack. As a result of this feature, several benefits of IEEE 802.15.4 directly apply to the connected nodes.
3. PAN—this protocol is utilized for PANs. Due to this feature, the communication range is restricted to less than 10 m. However, in LoS communications, 6LoWPAN can reach around 40 m.

3.11.4.5 RFID

Radio Frequency Identification (RFID) is a connectivity protocol that is utilized in shopping malls, wallets, ID cards, books, and so forth, in which identification information is digitally encoded in RFID tags. Applications such as those that forecast personal access to malls or accessibility to books collect information from RFID tags to perform their analysis. RFID performs one-way communication to submit data to connected systems or services hosted in cloud environments.

Typically, these RFID tags consist of integrated circuits with printed circuit board (PCB) antennas. The tags can generally be divided into two types:
1. Passive tags—passive tags are RFID devices that have to be powered by an RFID reader. This happens using the induction principle.
2. Active tags—active RFID tags use their own power supply to send data to readers.

3.11.4.6 WiFi

WiFi, a short name for Wireless Fidelity, is a widely utilized technology. The term 'fidelity' represents the compatibility between wireless equipment produced by different manufacturers. It attempts to provide in-building broadband coverage which is based on the IEEE 802.11 family of standards. This group of standards has several subdivisions, such as 802.11a/b/c/g.

Recently, with the development of WiFi version 6, deep learning applications using the ESP microcontrollers or the Raspberry Pi have become possible.

The major differences between WiFi v5 and v6 are listed in table 3.1.

3.11.4.7 LoRaWAN

Long-range WAN (LoRaWAN) is a low-power WAN protocol which uses a long-range technology. It is a low-power technology that supports wide-area communication ranging from 500 m to 10 km in rural areas. This communication technology was developed by Cycleao of Grenoble, France, and it was acquired by Semtech of the LoRa Alliance. It utilizes deep learning to select channels [14].

Table 3.1. Differences between WiFi v5 and v6.

	WiFi 5	WiFi 6
Speed	3.6 Gbps	9.6 Gbps
Connection to the Internet	Each device connects to the Internet one at a time.	Each device connects to the Internet at all times
Users/Devices	Single user—multiple input, multiple output	Multiple user—MIMO
	(SU-MIMO)	MU-MIMO
Signals	No beamforming	Beamforming is used
Battery utilization	No special features (little sleep time)	Allows target wake time

LoRaWAN achieves long ranges by reducing the bandwidth of communications. It is not comparable to WIFI or similar technologies. In fact, this technology only fits a few applications (in particular, those that require long range and limited bandwidth). This technology uses different frequencies for different regions, such as (i) 868 MHz in Europe, (ii) 915 MHz in North America, and (iii) 433 MHz in Asia.

3.11.4.8 Bluetooth

Bluetooth was initially developed by Dr Jaap Haartsen and Sven Mattison at Ericsson in 1994. The protocol was released in 1999 by a consortium of companies including Ericsson, Nokia, and Intel. It initially started with Bluetooth 1.0 and has now been upgraded to 4.0. It offers a low data rate in the range of 1 Mbps over a distance of 50 m. The protocol endeavors to replace cables to connect devices such as cell phones, laptops, headsets, and so forth. It offers a 2.4 Mbps data rate via a low-energy extension (Bluetooth/LE).

3.12 Edge-level deep learning systems

The use of edge intelligence has been a trending topic in recent years because of specific deep learning applications, including mobile devices, which require edge nodes. For instance, applications such as word processing, text conversion, speech processing, healthcare monitoring, and so forth, have been effectively implemented using high-end edge nodes consisting of microcontrollers.

The most commonly utilized microcontrollers that support machine-learning algorithms are the ESP32, the Jetson Nano, the Coral Dev Board, and so forth. In this section, we will describe the specifications of the ESP32 and the corresponding programming features of this microcontroller.

3.12.1 About the ESP32

The ESP32 microcontroller is widely utilized for machine-learning-related applications. The important features of the ESP32 are described below:

1. The ESP32 is a system-on-a-chip (SoC) processor developed by Espressif (ESP), a Shanghai-based Chinese company.
2. It is a popular microcontroller for IoT applications with 32-bit processing stages.
3. It consists of two Xtensa 32-bit CPU cores (dual core).
4. It follows the Harvard architecture—i.e. separate storage and signal pathways for instructions and data are available in the microcontroller.
5. The typical clock frequencies of the ESP32 are 120 MHz to 240 MHz.
6. Its operating voltage is 3.3V and its average current consumption is 80 mA;
7. It supports two eight-bit digital to analog converters and 18 12-bit analog to digital converters. As a result, both analog sensors and digital sensors are able to submit data to deep learning services hosted on local or cloud services.
8. It has integrated WiFi and Bluetooth support.

9. It can support over 26 general-purpose I/Os and 2.4 GHz WiFi based on the IEEE 802.11b/g/n standards.
10. Its antennas are based on PCB antennas.

In fact, the ESP32 has a series of microcontrollers—the NodeMCU, the ESP32-Devkit, the ESP32-WROOM, and the ESP32-WROOM-E. The ESP32 has broad support for interfacing with data or symbols, for instance: universal asynchronous receiver–transmitters (UARTs) for serial communications, Secure Digital (SD) cards for flashing code, Inter-Integrated Circuit (I2C) serial synchronous communication support, and so forth.

3.12.2 Programming ESP boards

Sending sensor data to cloud environments for further analysis requires proper programming logic. Such logic may be written using an appropriate integrated development environment (IDE). In the edge analytics domain, in particular, for the programming of ESP boards, there are two available IDEs, as follows:

1. The Arduino IDE—the Arduino IDE is a framework that supports sensor-related tiny ML applications that can be modeled and processed using its rich inherent libraries. For instance, connections to sensors and flashing code to microcontrollers are fairly straightforward in the Arduino IDE, compared to the ESP-IoT Development Framework (ESP-IDF).
2. ESP-IDF—by contrast, the ESP-IDF was designed exclusively for ESP-related boards. The compilation of code and the implementation of logic are carried out using a sequence of steps. These steps are listed below:
   (a) Setting up the build—initially, the build environment is developed using scripts such as install.sh and export.sh, which are provided by the framework.
   (b) Project creation—the relevant project folder and configuration settings are set using the default Python scripts provided by the framework, as shown below:

       idf.py create-project –path <folder><project-name>

   (c) Board selection and configuration—next, the corresponding ESP board in which the logic needs to be flashed is selected. When the board is selected, a bare minimal configuration setting is uploaded to the board through the connected interface. Additionally, several other configuration settings can be suggested before the final build operation is carried out for the logic. The entire sequence of these processes can be implemented in the ESP-IDF as follows:

```
idf.py set-target;
idf.py menuconfig
idf.py build
```

In short, several computing architectures are utilized to implement deep learning algorithms. This chapter provided a brief description of the available compute nodes, including the IoT-enabled devices and data collection mechanisms, used to perform deep learning tasks.

References

[1] Docker compose, May 2022 Page Version ID: 1088786364

[2] Docker desktop, May 2022 Page Version ID: 1088786364

[3] Docker swarm, May 2022 Page Version ID: 1088786364

[4] PyTorch, May 2022 Page Version ID: 1088786364

[5] Tensorflow, May 2022 Page Version ID: 1088786364

[6] Amsüss C, Mattsson J P and Selander G 2022 Constrained Application Protocol (CoAP): echo, request-tag, and token processing *RFC* **9175** 1–27

[7] Benedict S 2020 Serverless blockchain-enabled architecture for IoT societal applications *IEEE Trans. Comput. Soc. Syst.* **7** 1146–58

[8] Cam-Winget N, Appala S, Pope S and Saint-Andre P 2019 Using extensible messaging and presence protocol (XMPP) for security information exchange *RFC* **8600** 1–28

[9] Chahal D, Ramesh M, Ojha R and Singhal R 2022 High performance serverless architecture for deep learning workflows *2021 IEEE/ACM 21st International Symposium on Cluster, Cloud and Internet Computing (CCGrid)* vol 13151 ed L Lefèvre, S Patterson, Y C Lee, H Shen, S Ilager, M Goudarzi, A N Toosi and R Buyya (Piscataway, NJ: IEEE) pp 790–6

[10] Chen W, Lu H, Shen L, Wang Z, Xiao N and Chen D 2008 A Novel Hardware Assisted Full Virtualization Technique *2008 The 9th International Conference for Young Computer Scientists* (Los Alamitos, CA: IEEE Computer Society Press) pp 1292–7

[11] Fang S, Huang L and Li Z 2020 DDS-based protocol-compatible communication platform for mining power system *IET Commun.* **14** 158–64

[12] Foster I T and Karonis N T 1998 A grid-enabled MPI: message passing in heterogeneous distributed computing systems *SC '98: Proceedings of the 1998 ACM/IEEE Conference on Supercomputing* (Los Alamitos, CA: IEEE Computer Society Press) p 46

[13] Hunkeler U, Truong H L and Stanford-Clark A 2008 MQTT-S — A publish/subscribe protocol for Wireless Sensor Networks *Proc. of the Third Int. Conf. on COMmunication System softWAre and MiddlewaRE (COMSWARE 2008), January 5–10, 2008, Bangalore, India* ed S Choi, J Kurose and K Ramamritham (Piscataway, NJ: IEEE) pp 791–8

[14] Ilahi I, Usama M, Farooq M O, Janjua M U and Qadir J 2020 Loradrl: Deep reinforcement learning based adaptive PHY layer transmission parameters selection for LoRaWAN *2020 IEEE 45th Conference on Local Computer Networks (LCN)* H P Tan, L Khoukhi and S Oteafy (Piscataway, NJ: IEEE) pp 457–60

[15] Itsubo T, Koibuchi M, Amano H and Matsutani H 2021 An FPGA-based optimizer design for distributed deep learning with multiple GPUs *IEICE Trans. Inf. Syst.* **104** 2057–67

[16] Kim A N, Hekland F, Petersen S and Doyle P 2008 When HART goes wireless: understanding and implementing the WirelessHART standard *2008 IEEE International Conference on Emerging Technologies and Factory Automation* (Piscataway, NJ: IEEE) pp 899–907

[17] Liu Z, Chen C, Li J, Cheng Y, Kou Y and Zhang D 2022 KubFBS: A fine-grained and balance-aware scheduling system for deep learning tasks based on Kubernetes *Concurr. Comput. Pract. Exp.* **34** 11

[18] Mao Y, Yan W, Song Y, Zeng Y, Chen M, Cheng L and Liu Q 2020 Differentiate Quality of Experience Scheduling for Deep Learning Applications with Docker Containers in the Cloud *CoRR* abs/2010.127 28

[19] Sun Y, Wang X and Zhang X 2019 Deep learning-based device-free localization using zigbee *Communications, Signal Processing, and Systems—Proc. of the 8th Int. Conf. on Communications, Signal Processing, and Systems, CSPS 2019, Urumqi, China, 20–22 July 2019* (Lecture Notes in Electrical Engineering) ed Q Liang, W Wang, X Liu, Z Na, M Jia and B Zhang (Berlin: Springer) pp 2046–49

[20] Tarasov V, Rupprecht L, Skourtis D, Li W, Rangaswami R and Zhao M 2019 Evaluating docker storage performance: from workloads to graph drivers *Clust. Comput.* **22** 1159–72

[21] Wang Y and Wei G 2019 Benchmarking TPU, GPU, and CPU platforms for deep learning *CoRR* abs/1907.107 01

[22] Wu Y, Liu L, Pu C, Cao W, Sahin S, Wei W and Zhang Q 2022 A comparative measurement study of deep learning as a service framework *IEEE Trans. Serv. Comput.* **15** 551–66

[23] Ye Z, Sun P, Gao W, Zhang T, Wang X, Yan S and Luo Y 2022 Astraea: A fair deep learning scheduler for multi-tenant GPU clusters *IEEE Trans. Parallel Distrib. Syst.* **33** 2781–93

[24] Zhang P and Zhang J 2022 Deep learning analysis based on multi-sensor fusion data for hemiplegia rehabilitation training system for stoke patients *Robotica* **40** 780–97

[25] Zhuang Z, Tran C, Weng J, Ramachandra H and Sridharan B 2017 Taming memory related performance pitfalls in Linux cgroups *2017 Int. Conf. on Computing, Networking and Communications, ICNC 2017, Silicon Valley, CA, USA, January 26–29, 2017* (Los Alamitos, CAIEEE Computer Society Press) pp 531–5

[26] Flynn M 2011 Flynn's taxonomy *Encyclopedia of Parallel Computing* ed D Padua (Boston, MA: Springer)

Part II

Deep learning techniques

Chapter 4

CNN techniques

Convolutional neural networks (CNNs) [4], form a subclass of neural network models that is widely applied in computer vision-related applications. It suits applications that include image processing, classification, segmentation, identification, and other image-related data manipulation. This chapter describes the important features of CNNs and explains the concept while showcasing code snippets of social-good applications.

4.1 CNNs—introduction

Recognizing friends, family members, vehicles on roads, clothes, and so forth, is an instant and involuntary act of human brains. Brains generally organize tens of thousands of computations, depending on the images received from our retina. CNNs mimic the human brain's ability to quickly categorize objects in images or videos. Neuroscientists and AI researchers, therefore, study the conceptual basis of the processes involved in the mapping of objects in images.

4.1.1 Analogy with human brains/eyes

The human brain (see figure 4.1) captures the features of objects in images through the retinas of our eyes and submits the core information to the ventral visual stream when we view the objects. The ventral visual stream is a hierarchical processing unit of our brain. It processes the features of objects and enables us to identify objects instantaneously. In particular, the human brain quickly recognizes lines and curves due to the active involvement of visual cortex cells. Invariances in the images are flattened, sorted, and categorized in several stages when we identify the objects in images.

As mentioned above, the working of a CNN resembles that of a human brain. Delving into the working of the brain, specifically, its operation while identifying objects in complex images, should assist deep learning scientists to develop performance-efficient algorithms. For instance, we want to understand the principle behind the brain's processing of visual information in terms of lines, edges, and curves.

Parts of the Human Brain

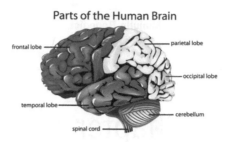

Figure 4.1. The human brain. This human brain image (https://commons.wikimedia.org/wiki/File:Human%2BBrain.png) has been obtained by the author(s) from the Wikimedia website where it was made available under the CC BY-SA 4.0 licence (https://creativecommons.org/licenses/by-sa/4.0/legalcode). It is included within this chapter on that basis. It is attributed to ErMED14.

These may represent complex structures used for identification purposes that could potentially induce neuroscientists or deep learning enthusiasts to reexamine the findings of deep learning algorithms such as CNNs.

4.1.2 Characteristics of the human brain

In short, the functioning of the human brain has the following characteristics, which remain the basis for several deep learning algorithms:

1. Dynamic: human brains are dynamic in nature—i.e. they change depending on the environmental conditions and the input fed to the system.
2. Unique structure: brains develop a unique structure for each person, due to genetic variation. The brain structure insists on an agile learning process in specific subjects rather than mastering a variety of diverse subjects. Accordingly, the learning performance varies depending on the complexity of the structure.
3. Adaptiveness: brains attempt to adapt to findings when exposed to newer learnings and the knowledge gained from any past experiences. Typically, a feedback mechanism drives the brain functions to learn newer notions and attain insights from the available data or information.
4. Collaborative inference: brains learn or increase their perceptual findings based on collaboration between minds. The movements and activities of the people around a person directly influence the functionality of the human brain, more specifically, its learning processes. For instance, inputs are tuned by the appraisal, punishment, judgment, and so forth provided by society. These evolve as new findings in human brains.
5. Workable memory: the memories contained in the brain can be tuned or modified by persistent training and reward mechanisms. There is no rigid rule about the capacity of the brain; equally, there is no promise that all information will be registered in the human brain.

In fact, CNN models follow the wider principles of the abovementioned human brain—i.e. such models follow a specific structure using layered approaches; the findings obtained from the layers vary depending on the chosen parameters; the inclusion of weights in CNN models promotes collaborative learning among perceptrons; and the learning inferences are subject to change, depending on the applied filters and activation functions. More detailed information about the CNN model and its functionalities is provided in section 4.2.

4.1.3 CNN principles—in a nutshell

CNN deals with multidimensional data and studies the input data, preferably images, using multiple layers of neurons. The output of one layer of neurons is fed as the input to the subsequent layers of neurons. In principle, the neurons are created in an artificial manner that mimics their biological description. They use activation and collective decisions about the weighted information of the input signals in order to extract the relevant features from multidimensional data. In CNNs, each layer is responsible for extracting appropriate features to benefit the process of learning from the data.

A diagrammatic representation of a single perceptron used in the CNN model is shown in figure 4.2.

4.1.4 Comparison between CNNs and ML

Although ML and CNNs utilize algorithms to predict or classify their input data within some prescribed error ranges, they exhibit fundamental differences in their learning processes. For instance, a comparison between ML and CNNs can be described in the following ways:

1. Feature engineering—ML algorithms require a robust manual feature engineering process to understand data. Feature engineering includes the filtering and extraction of information from the available data. The process of manual feature engineering might be prone to creating error conditions and tedious jobs for the developers or data scientists.

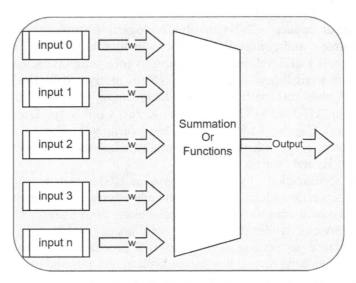

Figure 4.2. Single perceptron.

2. Data reduction—to reduce the burden of manually representing data, such as labeling data, ML learning approaches avoid including all available data. As a result, the accuracy of the model is challenged by real-world scenarios. By contrast, the CNN approach scales well with the input data, even extending to multidimensional big data solutions.

3. Small versus large data—the learning process choices available for ML algorithms are a good fit for small data. This is because the cleansing of the input data invariably takes a long time, although perceptions formulated from such data are more intuitive in nature.

4.1.5 Advantages of CNNs

CNNs have become a widespread deep learning model used for classifying images in several sectors, including financial markets. The popularity of deep learning has, in fact, been driven by the effectiveness of CNNs—note that artificial neural networks emerged decades ago. Tens of thousands of research works based on convolutional networks have appeared in recent years [3]. Platforms such as TensorFlow, R, and Python have influenced the surge of novel CNN applications in recent years. The major reasons that CNNs are advantageous are multifold:

1. Diverse applications—several applications relating to the analysis of images, such as classifying fruits, vegetables, faces, nameplates, vehicles, 3D images, and so forth, can easily be crafted using CNN models.

2. Automated feature engineering—irrespective of several other existing ML algorithms, CNN promotes automated feature engineering [10] from the input datasets. Automation could certainly benefit from greater ease and portability in learning setups.

3. Mathematical intuition—CNNs fundamentally apply mathematics to accurately represent the hierarchical layers of data. This improves the accuracy of the learning processes.

4. Biological impact—CNNs involve biological features, such as multilayer perceptrons, and connectivity factors which enthuse many interdisciplinary researchers and developers in addition to core computer scientists.

5. Platform availability—the use of CNNs is motivated by the availability of several platforms with sufficient documentary support, such as Neural Designer, H2O.ai, MXNet, Theano, Keras, ConvNetjs, Deep learning kit, Microsoft Cognitive toolkit, and DeepLearning4J. These computing platforms have been implemented in several well-known languages, such as C++, Python, R, and Nodejs.

6. Image segmentation—the advancements in CNNs can be applied to image segmentation through the use of U-Net architectures. U-Net architectures include more layers of convolution to segment objects from images. These segmented images are quickly identified from the input images while they are being tracked. For instance, segmenting skin lesions is a prominent example of the use of U-Nets. Similarly, several biomedical applications are candidates for the use of CNN-based U-Net architectures or similar segmentation-related architectures [6].

4.2 CNNs—nuts and bolts

4.2.1 Object recognition—the computer's perspective

Human eyes can recognize objects from images or scenery pretty easily and in no time. However, computers interpret the same images quite differently. Typically, cameras capture pictures and separate them into three different colors, namely red, blue, and green. The intensities of these image colors are converted to matrices such that the rows and columns represent the pixel values of the images. Three matrices are used to represent the three color channels, in which the rows and columns correspond to pixel values. Obviously, for black and white images, it is sufficient to represent images using a single channel or matrix.

4.2.2 Neurons and CNN connections

In neural networks, information capture relies on neurons or perceptrons with specific weights obtained from the inferred pixel regions. If all neurons are connected to each other, as is the case for a fully connected neural network, the amount of computation required is tremendously high.

CNNs, by contrast, reduce the number of connected neurons to a specific region, as depicted in figure 4.3. CNNs follow the same principle for the capture of visual information as that used by the visual cortex of the brain—i.e. only a small portion

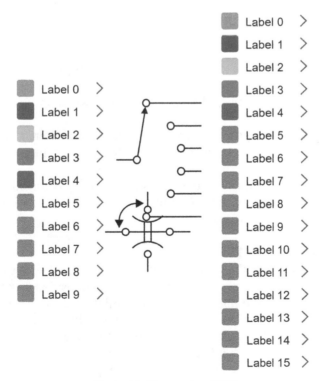

Figure 4.3. Neurons in a CNN.

of visual information is sent to a specific visual cortex portion of the brain. It has been described in the literature that our neurons send sensitive information about horizontal edges, vertical edges, and diagonal edges to appropriate reception fields in the visual cortex of the brain.

Avoiding fully connected neurons for image processing has several advantages:

1. Minimal neurons—the computational complexity is drastically reduced in CNNs with a little variation in their estimation quality, due to the inclusion of a minimal number of neurons to compute the hidden layers. It is crucial for image-processing applications to have larger numbers of input pixels— i.e. for the rows and columns of the channels to be present in large numbers.

2. Increased learning parameters—dividing the input layer into groups enables the training model to increase the number of parameters for each subsequent hidden layer. By doing so, a specific operation can be carried out such that the pixels from each group can receive input from the other groups—i.e. the knowledge is widely transferred by a minimal number of connecting neurons.

4.2.3 CNN building blocks

The building blocks used in CNNs to implement region-specific neural connections are: (i) convolution layers (CLs), (ii) activation layers (ALs), (iii) pooling layers (PLs), and (iv) fully connected layers (FCLs). The crucial activities of these layers [7] are discussed in the following subsections.

Convolution layers

The input images converted to matrices are used as the input to the CLs. The main objective of these layers is to identify the features of interest in images using appropriate filters. To do this, the CLs perform two steps: (i) mapping and (ii) averaging.

1. Mapping—if the digits zero to nine need to be filtered from an image consisting of an $x \times y$ matrix, the cells of the matrix values are multiplied by the input matrix of the images;

2. Averaging—the obtained values are subsequently averaged with the input number of cells/pixels. The outputs of the convolution layers can have positive or negative values.

Activation layers

The output matrices of the CLs are the inputs of the ALs. Here, the matrices are transformed into other matrices using activation functions (AFs) while increasing the learning inferences of the higher-order polynomials—i.e. a transformation from one form of the input data to another form of the input data. Typically, this transformation happens between linear and nonlinear functions.

Avoiding ALs in CNN's can lead to a poor learning model, as such learning systems cannot deal with the complex features of input data (which are present in several real-world training examples).

The AFs of ALs are also called transfer functions in the neural network domain. Such functions are responsible for transforming the summed weighted input from a region of collective nodes of the input layers.

Fundamentally, AFs are classified into linear and nonlinear functions. Linear functions transform the input data using a linear equation/model, and nonlinear functions transform the input data using a nonlinear equation/model. Linear functions can remain easy while challenging the quality of the pattern learning performed using complex input matrices.

Several types of AF were implemented in the past in order to address different problems, depending on the input data (see figure 4.4):

- Sigmoid function—the sigmoid function is a nonlinear AF category in which the curve has an 'S' shape. It is also called the logistic activation function. As the name indicates, this activation function fits problems for which the probability of the input needs to be predicted—i.e. the sigmoid function predicts values from zero to one.
- Tanh function—the tanh activation function is a nonlinear AF category in which the logistic curve of the function ranges from negative to positive infinity values. In general, the tanh function is better than the sigmoid function due to its range of predictability.
- Softmax function—the softmax function, based on physics and statistical domains, expresses probabilities for real numbers. It creates probable real numbers such that the sum of the attained vector is one. It is also called multiclass logistic regression. This activation function can be applied to a special class of classifier problems in which the input classes are mutually exclusive.
- Softsign function—the softsign function is a variant of the softmax function that deals with a quadratic polynomial. This function transfers the input values into a range between -1 and 1. It is similar to the tanh function in that it is zero centered. However, it is different from the tanh function in terms of

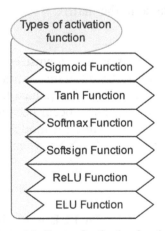

Figure 4.4. Types of activation function.

its convergence—i.e. the tanh function converges exponentially, whereas the softsign function converges in a polynomial form.

- Rectified linear unit (ReLU) function—the ReLU function is the most widely applied activation function in image classification and prediction problems. It is considered to deliver better performance than the performances of the most commonly available activation functions such as the sigmoid or tanh functions. ReLU applies gradient descent methods to transform the input data into a near-optimal linear function. It outputs zero for negative input values and non-negative values, otherwise. As a result of this phenomenon, it fits well with multilayer inputs by solving the vanishing gradient problem. Due to the use of a threshold approach, the ReLU function is computationally inexpensive compared to many other activation functions.
- Exponential Linear Unit (ELU) Function—the ELU function aims to improve the computation time in neural networks such as CNNs. ELUs eliminate the gradient descent problem of activation functions by providing an identity for non-negative values. This function provides a smooth transition of its output values until it reaches infinity for positive input values.

4.2.4 Pooling layers

The PLs of CNNs receive their inputs from the outputs of the activation layers. The main objective of the PLs is to reduce the matrix size. Accordingly, it becomes easier for the next layer of the CNN to classify images rapidly. This reduction mechanism is also known as downsampling the feature maps of CNNs. Downsampling is achieved by windowing the convoluted images into smaller matrix sizes using the two approaches described below.

Max pooling
Windowed matrices, also called strides, are collectively represented in one cell after the max pooling process is completed. For instance, 8×8 matrices, when windowed to a 2×2 matrix, can result in two cells of 4×4 matrices. Each of these cells can include the maximum cell value in the matrix.

Average pooling
By contrast, the average pooling approach downsizes the convolved matrix. Here, the windows are averaged to form the resultant matrix.

The main objective of PLs in CNNs is to reduce the possible overfitting issues associated with prediction problems. These occur because, by default, the formation of downsized matrices introduces noise into the modeling system. Thus, the learning rate increases for the deeper layers of CNNs when input images are fed to the models.

4.2.5 Fully connected layers

The last part of a CNN is its FCL. An FCL is the basis of a traditional neural network. The input nodes of traditional neural networks are connected to each other while they formulate weights and calculate values. The output of the PL is typically represented as a 2D matrix. This matrix must be converted to a 1D array or vector before the fully connected layers can be applied. To convert the multidimensional matrix into a 1D matrix, the FCL adopts a flattening method. The flattening method reads the cell values of the 2D or 3D matrices and sequentially inputs them into a specific array.

The FCL is also responsible for comparing the results obtained from the final array of the predefined cell values of the images. Depending on the obtained summed value of the relevant cell values of the FCL output, the input value is classified as a specific character, number, or element.

4.3 Social-good applications—a CNN perspective

We can apply CNNs for various social improvement applications. Social issues are typically caused by the misguided activities of a few people or a group/community. These issues occur knowingly or unknowingly due to the gradual impact on specific subjects. Social problems need to be handled with care, as many diverse conflicts are possible. For instance, social issues such as air pollution can be caused by industrialists. Obviously, air pollution can lead to health concerns or climate change issues [5].

There is a dire need to tackle societal problems or issues in order to add goodness to markets. This section focuses on the applications of CNNs in dealing with social problems. The social problems discussed are based on the Sustainable Development Goals (SDG) [1].

The list of SDG goals that are considered as possible uses for CNNs is given below:

1. Climate change—SDG goal 13 (at present) relates to the interest in reducing climate change. For instance, it is known that climate change is dramatically increasing. This causes a rise in sea levels and other harmful effects. Deep-learning-based solutions can reduce these impacts by proactively controlling the forecasted dangers.
2. Good health—SDG goal 3 focuses on improving people's health conditions. It promotes collaborative efforts to address health concerns by applying novel methods or techniques. For instance, IoT-enabled intelligent solutions based on deep learning can be solutions that target this SDG goal.
3. Clean energy—SDG goal 7 aims to improve energy transformation or utilize renewable energy sources. In fact, several energy sources emit polluted air or water into the environment. These energy sources have multiplied by orders of magnitude and drastically harm sustainable living. Techniques involving deep learning mechanisms could help to reduce the associated failures.
4. Waste Management—SDG goal 6 attempts to manage waste disposal procedures. The main target is to improve water distribution and sanitation processes using novel technologies. However, the approach to handling wastes, including water, interests various deep learning architects who are interested in framing solutions.

4.4 CNN use case—climate change problem

Handling climate-change-related issues using the CNN approach leads to highly targeted solutions. It is a known fact that most of the detrimental climate changes happen due to humans rather than nature itself, especially due to the increase of industrial revolutions—i.e. the utilization of fossil fuels such as coal, gas, and so forth, has increased natural greenhouse gases, such as CO_2 and methane. As a result, the temperature of the Earth will drastically increase. It is expected that the temperature will increase by at least 0.2 degrees Celsius in the 2050s.

Climate change is a complex phenomenon that involves several factors that impact the temperature. It depends on the atmosphere, land, snow conditions, water levels, air pollution levels, sunlight levels, the solar system, and so forth. All these ingredients must be influenced in a natural way to control the rise in Earth's temperatures.

4.4.1 Reasons for climate change

Some of the most notable reasons for climate change are as follows:

1. Increased energy industry—several energy sources, mostly fossil fuels, contribute to the increase in climate change. Fossil fuels drastically increase the global temperature, which prevents animals or living beings from achieving their normal growth. Fossil fuels release CO_2 in addition to from the normal emissions from natural sources. The excessive amount of CO_2 emissions increases the heat present on the Earth's surface. Accordingly, several issues such as glacial warming, sea-level rises, and so forth happen in our daily lives.

2. Deforestation—cutting down trees and removing forests as a whole creates more CO_2, as carbon is released into the atmosphere. A large loss of trees could drastically increase the carbon emissions from one region, which creates holes in the ozone layer.

3. Transportation wastes—another important cause of climate change include the gas emissions from transportation systems. In fact, a large number of these contributions are due to air transportation—i.e. airplanes fly at high altitudes, emitting gases that are harmful to the environment. Additionally, wastes from public road transportation vehicles that are not protected by air filters are also considered to be sources of climate change.

4. Livestock farming—additionally, in recent years, tens of thousands of livestock farms have been constructed to feed the human population with sufficient meat. In general, animals release methane and nitrous oxide through their wastes. A large volume of animal farming in a region is prone to emitting tons of CO_2 into the environment. Subsequently, global warming increases.

Apart from various human contributions, nature finds its way to worsen the climatic situation through natural disasters. For instance, volcanic eruptions and forest fires contribute to global warming. In addition, tsunamis, solar flares entering our atmosphere, an increase in the Sun's radiation, and a few other natural sources can keep the global temperature increasing relatively quickly over a long period.

4.4.2 Ways to reduce climate change

There have been efforts to reduce the global warming situation in several ways: organizing awareness conferences, producing technological solutions, adopting chained growth policies across countries, and so forth. In recent years, AI-assisted solutions have been a new way of quickly detecting or predicting climate change situations across regions or countries of the globe. In this way, various precautionary methods or penalties can be offered to defaulters. The next section discusses a way in which a CNN has been used to address the issues related to climate change conditions by leveraging climatic conditions—i.e. predicting forest fire occurrences [9].

4.4.3 Forest fire prediction

The prediction of forest fire, a social-good application, can be achieved using several learning algorithms. These learning algorithms are explained and compared below:
1. CNNs—the basics of CNNs and their layering/learning concepts were explained in the previous portion of this chapter.
2. Single-perceptron NNs—single-perceptron NNs consist of a single neuron that learns from the data set.
3. Extra-tree classifier—the extra-tree classifier is an ensemble-based prediction algorithm that uses trees to learn classifications. The decision trees are constructed during the training phase; the evaluations are carried out during the testing phase of the program.
4. K-neighbor classifier—the K-neighbor classifier is a non-parametric supervised learning algorithm that requires a training data set to construct nearest neighbors based on the input parameters. The algorithm is more suitable for studying nonlinear decision boundaries (if any) than linear regression methods.
5. Support vector classifier—support vector classifiers fall into the category of supervised learning in which the data points are distinguished by hyperplanes. The hyperplanes are placed such that there are few overlaps between two distinct sets of data points.
6. Logistic regression—a learning mechanism in which the parameters are estimated such that minimal errors are obtained. This algorithm is often utilized when the outcome is categorical.

4.4.4 TensorFlow-based CNN code snippets

If the CNN model is applied to learning processes, several steps are undertaken, as depicted in figure 4.5.

These steps for predicting forest fires in any region are carried out using the TensorFlow machine learning library.

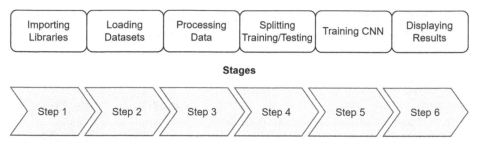

Figure 4.5. Steps utilized for predicting forest fires.

Step 1: Importing libraries:

In TensorFlow-based implementations, it is important to load the required libraries, as shown below:

```
import tensorflow as tf
from tensorflow import keras
from tensorflow.keras import layers
from keras.models import Sequential
from keras.layers import Dense
```

Here, the TensorFlow and Keras packages are imported at the implementation stage, as these packages support the modeling and testing phases for datasets. CNN models can be implemented in sequential mode using an appropriate number of hidden layers. Accordingly, the relevant packages, such as `Sequential` and `Dense`, need to be invoked by the program.

Step 2: Loading the data set:

To predict fire scenarios in forests, a minimal set of data that illustrates the fire spill in certain forests is considered. The data may be available in CSV format, JSON format, or any other known format. The data needs to be loaded in the form of a data frame consisting of certain rows and columns, in which the rows represent a few instances of such occurrences and the columns represent the variables that influence the learning processes.

```
df = pd.read_csv('/path/to/csv/forestfires.csv')
```

Step 3: Processing data:

The data cannot be directly applied to CNN models due to several prerequisites of the learning algorithms. Therefore, it has to be preprocessed. A few notable preprocessing stages for CNN algorithms, which are specific to this societal problem, include (a) removing NULL data, (b) converting data types into numeric formats, and (c) normalizing data. Typically, NULL data needs to be removed to improve the performance of learning algorithms; converting data into numeric formats makes it easier for algorithms to perform mathematical computations. Accordingly, the data sets need to be formatted in most cases; normalizing the data used by algorithms improves the accuracy of learning inferences, especially for CNNs.

The, pandas library is typically utilized to process or fine-tune the data as per the requirements of learning algorithms such as CNN.

The required packages for this step are listed below:

```
from tensorflow.keras.layers.experimental.preprocessing
import Normalization import pandas as pd
```

Step 4: Splitting data for training versus testing
Once the data are ready for the learning algorithm, the data can be split into training and testing datasets. The datasets are chosen such that 40 percent of the data from the input data set is allocated to the test data set and the rest of the data are allocated to the training data set. Code snippets that are utilized to split a data set into training and testing datasets are given below:

```
testing = df.sample(frac=0.4, random_state=111)
training = df.drop(testing.index)
```

Step 5: Training a CNN
Once the training data set is available, the CNN algorithm is utilized to train and complete the model for predicting fire in forests (if any). To do so, the following submodules are organized while training the CNN model:

1. First, it is necessary to select an appropriate batch size. Choosing an apt batch size improves the learning accuracy over a certain number of iterations. If the batch size is larger than the normal training size, the algorithm takes a little time to complete. However, the prediction accuracy is very poor. On contrary, if the batch size is reduced to an optimal level, the accuracy can be improved at each subsequent iteration.

    A code snippet utilized to sample the training data set to get a batch size of 32 is given below:

```
training_batch = training.batch(32)
```

2. It is now necessary to define the learning model. For the fire prediction problem, dense layers are defined based on the batch size (32) including all

relevant variables; the activation function and the dropout components of the layers are then added before receiving the final model output. A code snippet for this stage of the prediction problem is given below:

```
model_def = layers.Dense(32, activation="relu")('features')
model_def = layers.Dropout(0.5)(model_def)
model_out = layers.Dense(1, activation="sigmoid")(model_def)
```

3. The model is then compiled using the required compilation knobs, such as the filter knob, the optimization knob, and the metric knob. In this program, adam, binary entropy, and the accuracy metric were chosen to compile the model, as shown below:

```
model.compile("adam", "binary_crossentropy", metrics=
["accuracy"])
```

4. Finally, the training of the model is carried out using a GPU, a CPU, or another computational device using the model.fit command, as given below:

```
history = model.fit(training, epochs=1000, batch_-
size=32, steps_per_epoch=10)
```

The number of epochs selected for the training phase defines the prediction accuracy improvement while predicting fires in forests.

Step 6: displaying results

Once the training and validation stages are complete, it is necessary to observe the prediction accuracy achieved by the model. Hence, this step is mandatory in various learning techniques. The displayed results can be shown on screen to reveal the raw result data or viewed in a visual form using graphs and tables. Example code that displays the prediction accuracy of the learning algorithm for the fire prediction problem is shown below:

```
import matplotlib.pyplot as plt

plt.plot(history.history["loss"])
plt.plot(history.history["val_loss"])
plt.title("Model loss value")
```

```
plt.ylabel("Loss Values")
plt.xlabel("Number of Epochs")
plt.show()
```

The results are typically plotted using the `matplotlib` Python package. A graphical representation of the loss function for the learning model can be plotted and displayed on screen.

4.4.5 TensorFlow-based single-perceptron code snippets

Implementing a single-perceptron neural network to predict fire in forests is broadly similar to the CNN prediction approach. In fact, the steps such as importing libraries, loading datasets, processing data, spitting training/testing datasets, and displaying results remain the same. However, the code has slight variations in following these steps. For instance, the layering of a deep learning framework is reduced to only one layer—i.e. one input layer that receives the output data.

```
model_def = layers.Dense(32, activation="relu")('features')
model_out = layers.Dense(1, activation="sigmoid")(model_def)
```

4.4.6 Scikit-learn-based extra-tree classifier

In general, if the extra-tree classifier algorithm is required, the TensorFlow library is not a very popular solution. It can be implemented using Python packages made available in the past. For instance, the `scikit-learn` tool based on Python can be utilized to develop this learning algorithm. The following code snippet shows how the model could be designed and the associated packages executed using the `Scikit-learn` Python library.

```
from sklearn.ensemble import ExtraTreesClassifier
model = ExtraTreesClassifier()
model.fit(ETC-Features,ETC-Labels)
```

4.4.7 Scikit-learn-based K-neighbors classifier

We can easily apply the K-neighbors classifier algorithm using the `Scikit-learn` Python packages. Using a similar approach to that used for the extra-tree classifier, the implementation can be written in two to three lines of code to model forest fire predictions. The implementation can be interpreted using `Jupyter Notebook`, which provides better visibility for developers. It imports the `KNeighborsClassifier` package from `sklean.neighbors` to model the forest fire prediction data set.

The following code snippets illustrate the simplicity of implementing the algorithm for the prediction problems:

```
from sklearn.neighbors import KNeighborsClassifier
model = KNeighborsClassifier(neighbors=n).fit(KN-Features,
KN-Labels)
```

4.4.8 `Scikit-learn`-based support vector machine

The implementation of a support vector machine (SVM) can also achieved using the `Scikit-learn` package. In fact, several other packages and programming languages support SVM implementations. For instance, SVMs can be implemented using the R language, C/C++, Python, and so forth. A few parallel implementations of SVMs can be found in the literature. However, to deliver a solution similar to those discussed so far, the following snippet exemplifies the implementation of an SVM using the `Scikit-learn` package:

```
from sklearn.svm import SVC
model = SVC().fit(SVM-Features,SVM-Labels)
```

4.4.9 `Scikit-learn`-based logistic regression

Logistic regression is a categorical learning algorithm that is implemented using the `Scikit-learn` Python packages. The flow and the steps involved in an implementation intended to learn the forest fire data set remain the same. A code snippet that reveals the most important changes in the modeling processes is given below:

```
from sklearn.linear_model import LogisticRegression
model = LogisticRegression().fit(LR-Features,LR-Labels)
```

4.4.10 Flood prediction

Floods are considered to be societal problems that fall under the category of climate change. They are considered a natural disasters in which lives could be saved if proper awareness were available. Floods occur due to heavy rainfalls, storms, or melting snows. They can also be caused by tsunamis in coastal regions. Humans need to get early warnings of floods well in advance in order to protect themselves from major losses. The learning algorithms utilized to predict floods based on a data set remain the same as those already shown for the forest fire prediction use case.

Additionally, for this example, we discuss a few more supervised learning algorithms. The list of learning algorithms added to the previously discussed learning algorithms is explained in the following paragraphs:

1. Stochastic gradient descent (SGD) classifier—the SGD classifier is a simple learning approach that learns specific objective functions based on loss functions that occur during the learning process. The learning process obeys parameters that influence the input training data. The learning process iteratively captures suggestions for improvement using an optimized way of handling the learning parameters. It is frequently applied for classification purposes, although it can be applied for regression problems.

2. Linear regression—linear regression is considered to be a naive learning approach among the available statistical methods. It tries to find the linear variation in prediction problems given a set of dependent variables and the independent variable of the data set. The dependent and independent variables are picked from the data set such that a linear equation can be derived from them.

3. Bayesian regression—the Bayesian regression approach is based on a linear regression technique in which the dependent variable predicts some linear mathematical combinations with the independent variables of the data set. It works in the context of Bayesian inference, which applies Bayes' theorem to predict occurrences. In other words, this approach does the following:

    (a) follows mechanisms to observe the likelihood of the data,
    (b) finds the data distribution and associated parameters, and
    (c) applies Bayes' theorem to find the posterior distribution of the data.

4. Ridge regression (RR)—RR is a variant of the linear regression approach. It reduces the overfitting problems of regressions which often happen for several training datasets. In general, an overfitting problem is considered to be a problem in which the training data fits the developed mathematical model properly without any exposure to varying real datasets. Accordingly, the prediction results obtained using validation or test sets are poor. RR attempts to handle these situations.

5. Least absolute shrinkage and selection operator (lasso) regression—lasso regression is also considered to be a variant of the traditional linear regression method. Here, during the learning phase, a penalty is included depending on the importance of the coefficients. This learning algorithm is also designed to solve the overfitting problems in a similar way to the previously discussed RR model. The major difference between least absolute regression compared to RR is the utilization of the absolute value of the coefficients in least absolute regression instead of the least squares of the coefficients in RR. Least absolute regression uses a variable selection mechanism in addition to solving the overfitting problem of trained models.

6. Elastic net regression—elastic net regression is considered to be an extended learning algorithm of lasso regression. It is designed to overcome the challenges of least absolute regression and RR. Elastic regression shrinks coefficients and sets some coefficients to zero—i.e. it is a combination of

both **RR** and least absolute regression. ER is therefore considered to be a more effective regression approach, compared to the previous regression approaches.

7. LARS lasso regression—in the field of statistics, LARS stands for the least angle regression model. It mainly focuses on applying linear regressions to high-dimensional data. For instance, if the number of independent variables in the prediction problem is high, this learning algorithm can be utilized. In LARS lasso regression, the features of both the `Lars` and `lasso` algorithms are merged so that the advantages of both learning algorithms are obtained by any single execution.

8. Online one-class SVM—the idea of the online one-class SVM algorithm is to detect novelties in datasets. In fact, datasets might have some features that are not exposed after many iterations of some implementations. These rare events need to be captured for better classification or regression. This algorithm attempts to learn such rare events.

9. Random forest (RF) regression—the random forest regression algorithm is an ensemble-based bagging technique that creates models during the training phase. It constructs multiple decision RF trees; it bags data to appropriate trees while building the training model. RF is considered to reduce the overfitting problem during the training phase. It picks up a few samples from the training data set and starts to create RF trees so that RF can average the RF trees' results. It is an attractive algorithm that maintains its prediction accuracy, even if a sequence of data is missing while it creates the training model from the training data set.

10. Multilayer perceptron (MLP)—the MLP approach to learning features from datasets is to apply a feedforward artificial neural network approach. It is based on neurons that learn the features of the data. This particular algorithm uses fully connected neurons which keep more data correlations and are compute intensive in nature.

4.4.11 `Scikit-learn`-based stochastic gradient descent

For flood prediction or forest fire prediction problems, an SGD classifier can be applied to suggest whether a forest fire is likely to occur or a flood is imminent. Most of the steps used in predicting the forest fire problem remain the same—i.e. importing libraries, loading datasets, processing data, splitting the training versus the test data, and displaying the prediction results. However, the modeling component differs for the implementation, as follows, based on the `Scikit-learn` package:

```
from sklearn.linear_model import SGDClassifier
model = SGDClassifier(loss="hinge",penalty="xx",max_iter=10)
```

As discussed, SGD can incorporate penalty components over iterations to learn the model for a data set.

4.4.12 `Scikit-learn`-based linear regression

The Python-based `Scikit-learn` package offers implementations for linear regression models which can be used after the required stages of the learning processes. It is based on the `linear_model` package of the sklearn packages. The methods used for prediction algorithms are often very simple. The code snippets used to model the linear regression algorithm are given below:

```
from sklearn import linear_model
model = linear_model.LinearRegression()
```

4.4.13 `Scikit-learn`-based Bayesian regression

As discussed earlier, Bayesian regression is a variant of linear regression that applies Bayes' theorem to data to calculate the likelihood of data. For social-good problems, these algorithms can be implemented using the `Scikit-learn` package, as shown in the following code:

```
from sklearn import linear_model
model = linear_model.BayesianRidge()
```

Notably, the Bayesian implementation is part of the `linear_model` package of sklearn.

4.4.14 `Scikit-learn`-based ridge regression

RR, which is a variant of linear regression, can be carried out using the `Scikit-learn` package. The package offers a parameter named `alpha` that controls the regularization strength of the linear regression model. The implementation of the model becomes a normal linear regression implementation if the parameter `alpha` becomes zero. Code snippets that can be used to implement RR for social-good applications are given below:

```
from sklearn import linear_model
model = linear_model.Ridge(alpha=0.1)
```

4.4.15 `Scikit-learn`-based lasso regression

Most of the learning algorithm implementations of lasso regression can be developed using different programming languages such as R, Python, C/C++, and so forth. The following code snippet exemplifies the implementation of this model using the `Scikit-learn` package. The parameter `alpha` is responsible for controlling the regularization strength of the model, which is similar to the approach used for RR. This implementation can change from the lasso model to the normal linear regression model if the `alpha` parameter is set to zero. `from sklearn import linear_model` `model = linear_model.Lasso(alpha=0.1)`

4.4.16 `Scikit-learn`-based elastic net regression

Using a similar approach to that used for the previously discussed lasso-based regression and ridge-based regression methods, elastic net regression can be implemented using the `Scikit-learn` package. In fact, the package delivers a very simple approach to handling these different learning algorithms. For instance, the implementation of the modeling step only varies in the method that is followed for the learning process. The crucial parameter, named `alpha`, remains the same, along with its purpose. The code snippets for the elastic net regression model are given below:

```
from sklearn import linear_model
model = linear_model.ElasticNet(alpha=0.1)
```

4.4.17 `Scikit-learn`-based LARS lasso regression

The LARS lasso regression technique is implemented using `Scikit-learn` package such that the `alpha` parameter is utilized without a normalization factor. The algorithm imports the same `linear_model` package from the `Scikit-learn` package. Code snippets that demonstrate the modeling step for social-good applications are given below:

```
from sklearn import linear_model
model = linear_model.LassoLars(alpha=0.1, normalize=False)
```

4.4.18 `Scikit-learn`-based online one-class SVM regression

The implementation of the online one-class SVM regression using the `Scikit-learn` package is based on the `linear_model` package. Although the name one-class SVM suggests the necessity of including an implementation of the SVM package of the library, this is not really the case. In fact, the online one-class SVM regression utilizes the method from the normal linear regression implementation of the package. For instance, see below for the implementation of the modeling step:

```
from sklearn import linear_model
model = linear_model.SGDOneClassSVM()
```

4.4.19 `Scikit-learn`-based random forest regression

RF regression, being representative of an ensemble-learning approach, is implemented as a separate package in the `Scikit-learn` package. The modeling step of the learning algorithm is imported from `RandomForestClassifier` as shown below:

```
from sklearn.ensemble import RandomForestClassifier
model = RandomForestClassifier(n_estimators=n)
```

The parameter `n_estimators` of the algorithm defines the number of decision trees that are utilized for learning the variances of datasets.

4.4.20 `Scikit-learn`-based multilayer perceptron

The MLP, as discussed earlier, is an implementation based on neurons. The `Scikit-learn` package offers support for such neuron-based implementations, which can be used to predict the features of training/testing data. As MLP is an extension of the neural network package, the appropriate package needs to be imported in order to model the data set, as shown below:

```
from sklearn.neural_network import MLPClassifier
model = MLPClassifier()
```

4.5 CNN challenges

CNNs are widely applied in various applications, with a particular emphasis on image processing applications. However, there are a few notable challenges that the algorithm suffers from, which apply to all generic applications. The list of challenges is shown below [2] and the countermeasures are discussed in the following sections:
- Insufficient data
- Low speedup
- Hidden layers
- Missing coordinates
- Inaccurate datasets
- Black-box approach
- Positional challenges
- Overfitting/underfitting problems

4.5.1 Insufficient data

CNNs require a large volume of data to effectively pretrain the model. If the data volume is small, CNNs can converge faster than expected, but they cannot produce reasonably accurate results with real-world examples or datasets. Evaluating the amount of data required can typically be assessed using an accuracy metric for the algorithm. For instance, increasing the training data to the point that the accuracy metric of the testing data is slightly lower than the accuracy of the training data is an acceptable approach for CNNs.

In general, CNNs require at least thousands of data points for basic execution and millions of labeled data points for better learning accuracy. If the amount of data used is lower than usual, there is a high chance that the accuracy of the test data set will converge much faster than in the training phase of the algorithm.

4.5.2 Low speed

Most existing CNN implementations experience a poor speedup, even if they are combined with better computational resources. This is because most CNNs have many processing requirements that represent neurons. The computations involved in the `max pooling` processes of the layering processes of CNNs can persist for hours to months. The algorithm is computationally very expensive, with the result that power-constrained IoT devices and minimal GPU devices are unable to complete its execution.

4.5.3 Hidden layers

The hidden layers, which are located within the input and output layers of CNNs, require large amounts of computation and communication. In addition, these layers have weights that determine the learning rates. In addition to the existing issues, the batch size of the algorithm also causes impacts that slow down the users when compared to other traditional machine learning algorithms.

4.5.4 Missing coordinates

For image-based applications, CNNs consider images to be clusters of pixels. Like the human eye, CNNs do not have coordinate frames. This limits the ability of the algorithm to search for the correct coordinates while detecting objects. The coordinates are often oriented to other directions when they are articulated by the hidden layers of CNNs.

4.5.5 Inaccurate datasets

Data plays a major role in arriving at a robust learning model. CNNs struggle to achieve an accurate representation of the independent variables when the data are inaccurate [8]. The sample data utilized to train a CNN should represent the real-world scenario of the problem.

In addition, CNN's sample data from the given data set to apply activation functions and weights through hidden layers. If the sampling process leads to a biased mode of learning, the resulting model does not provide more accurate results for the training/validation datasets.

It can also be the case that the training data is of poor quality—i.e. the data is not reasonably acceptable for the problem domains. This is makes it difficult for CNNs to produce more accurate predictions, as the learning process is a challenging one.

Some datasets have inappropriate features which may be hard to cluster or group. In such cases, there is a need for a large number of hidden layers which increase the computation performed by the algorithm.

4.5.6 Black-box approach

The major challenge of CNNs is the hidden logic used to obtain the intended output. This means that although the algorithm produces better prediction accuracy, the network fails to produce an explainable result at the end of its execution. In fact, it is a challenging task for researchers or practitioners to unbox the algorithm and learn its internal logic in order to reproduce the same behaviors.

In recent years, there have been efforts to override the concept of the black-box approach to CNNs. However, a few researchers and practitioners still prefer the black-box approach, as the results are highly accurate in the majority of cases even though the users have no idea how the results were generated.

4.5.7 Overfitting/underfitting problems

CNNs can easily have issues related to overfitting and underfitting problems. Overfitting [11] is a scenario in which the model quickly fits the training data—i.e. the model has learned almost all data provided to it as a training data set. The major drawback of having the overfitting problem in the learning model is that it results in poor prediction accuracy for test datasets. Some known methods used to solve the overfitting problem of CNNs are:
1. Increase the amount of training data that is input to the model.
2. Avoid the possible noise found in the training datasets.

In contrast to the overfitting problem, the underfitting problem is related to a failure to train a model using the training data. The major reasons for the occurrence of underfitting problems are:
1. the model is not complex enough to handle the large number of hyperparameters;
2. there is too much training data for the model to learn from it;
3. the computations involved in the modeling process are too few, leading to training processes with a limited learning model, etc.

References

[1] United Nations 2022 *The Sustainable Development Goals Report 2022* (Geneva: United Nations)
[2] Alzubaidi L, Zhang J, Humaidi A J, Al-Dujaili A Q, Duan Y, Al-Shamma O, Santamaría J, Fadhel M A, Al-Amidie M and Farhan L 2021 Review of deep learning: concepts, CNN architectures, challenges, applications, future directions *J. Big Data* **8** 53
[3] Aslam N, Ramay W Y, Xia K and Sarwar N 2020 Convolutional neural network based classification of app reviews *IEEE Access* **8** 185619–28
[4] Fong R 2020 Understanding convolutional neural networks *PhD Thesis* University of Oxford

[5] Gerges F, Boufadel M C, Bou-Zeid E, Nassif H and Wang J T L 2022 A novel deep learning approach to the statistical downscaling of temperatures for monitoring climate change *ICMLSC 2022: 2022 The 6th International Conference on Machine Learning and Soft Computing* (New York: ACM) pp 1–7

[6] Jiang Y, Liu W, Wu C and Yao H 2021 Multi-scale and multi-branch convolutional neural network for retinal image segmentation *Symmetry* **13** 365

[7] Shen H, Chen S and Wang R 2021 A study on the uncertainty of convolutional layers in deep neural networks *Int. J. Mach. Learn. Cybern.* **12** 1853–65

[8] Son H, Jang Y, Kim S-E, Kim D and Park J-W 2021 Deep learning-based anomaly detection to classify inaccurate data and damaged condition of a cable-stayed bridge *IEEE Access* **9** 124549–59

[9] Wang S, Zhao J, Ta N, Zhao X, Xiao M-X and Wei H-C 2021 A real-time deep learning forest fire monitoring algorithm based on an improved pruned + KD model *J. Real Time Image Process.* **18** 2319–29

[10] Xiao G, Li J, Chen Y and Li K 2020 MalFCS: an effective malware classification framework with automated feature extraction based on deep convolutional neural networks *J. Parallel Distrib. Comput.* **141** 49–58

[11] Xiao M, Wu Y, Zuo G, Fan S, Yu H, Shaikh Z A and Wen Z 2021 Addressing overfitting problem in deep learning-based solutions for next generation data-driven networks *Wirel. Commun. Mob. Comput.* **2021** 8493795

Chapter 5

Object detection techniques and algorithms

Object detection is a computer vision technique in which algorithms are utilized to identify objects in images and/or videos. Typically, predefined categories of object have to be detected in the given natural images. The human eye can detect the images in no time. In computer vision systems, however, computing devices have to implement specific algorithms, such as recurrent convolutional neural networks (R-CNNs), You Only Look Once (YOLO), and so forth, to mimic the natural scenario and to detect objects. This chapter explains different object detection algorithms and illustrates the concepts using suitable examples.

5.1 Computer vision—taxonomy

Computer vision problems enable computers to derive information from images that shows how the human eye observes objects in images captured from real-world situations. These tasks typically involve procedures such as capturing, processing, analyzing, and understanding the objects in images.

Computer vision problems are often classified into several subdomains, as discussed below:

1. Object classification—this is a method of classifying objects in a given image [14, 15]. Object classification is utilized to classify a specific type of object using the predefined labels of several objects. If two objects of the same type appear in an image, object classification is not a viable solution. In such cases, it is preferable to detect objects using bounding boxes or similar techniques.
2. Object detection—object detection is an approach that detects or tracks all available objects using specific object detection models. For instance, objects such as tables, chairs, human beings, animals, and so forth, can be detected using object detection techniques. Even if an image has more than one similar object, this technique can detect them to a specific

percentage accuracy [1]. Typically, bounding boxes that have a rectangular shape are added to the output image or video to represent the detected objects.

3. Object segmentation—this is a process in which computing machines are trained to detect objects and segment them by scanning the pixels of images. By segmenting objects from an image, it is also possible to alter the detected pixels so that different colors may be added to them. In addition, it is possible to manipulate objects with some other objects after performing the object segmentation process. For instance, the application of a deep-learning-based object segmentation method to the monitoring of a fruit growth process is explained in [5].

4. Object localization—this is a technique for identifying objects in given images. The difference between object localization and object detection is that the former only detects a single object and the latter detects multiple objects in the same image.

Figure 5.1 depicts the list of problems related to computer vision.

The taxonomy of computer vision tasks is depicted in figure 5.2. As can be observed, object recognition tasks are divided into image classification and object localization problems. These problems can develop into detecting objects or segmenting objects in images.

In this chapter, we focus on the techniques involved in object detection-related tasks.

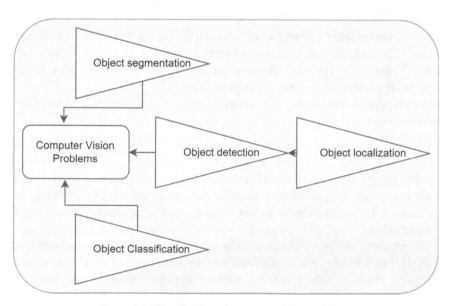

Figure 5.1. Classification of computer vision problems.

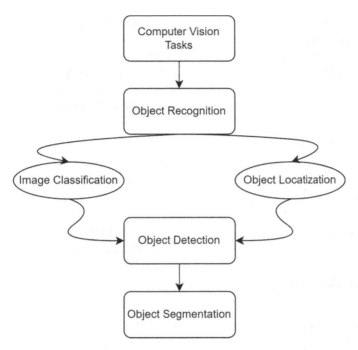

Figure 5.2. Taxonomy of computer vision tasks.

5.2 Object detection—objectives

In general, object detection is widely applied in various research works and industrial establishments. The techniques adopted to detect objects in images or video data have increased the utility of object detection.

Object detection algorithms are designed by considering certain objectives. The most frequently considered objectives of performing object detection in images/videos in the computer vision domain are listed in the following sections.

5.2.1 Locating targets

Object detection algorithms play a major role in detecting object instances from a list of object categories in a given image or video frames. It is a known phenomenon that machines cannot learn newer things or infer from images if objects are not precisely detected in the given images.

The main objective of developing object detection algorithms is to identify objects by creating bounding boxes in images. The creation of bounding boxes can be carried out in various ways, as discussed in a future part of this chapter.

5.2.2 Semantic representations

As machines cannot identify objects on their own, computer vision tasks aim to guide machines while they identify objects. For instance, the objects from images or videos need to be captured so that they can be represented in the form of text or language. In this way, the data can be processed and changed back from text into semantic object representations.

Obviously, the process of transforming objects into semantic texts and vice-versa has to be carefully designed to fulfill the objectives of deep-learning-based object detection algorithms. In the modern world, various approaches to automating the process of creating labels and dictating the appropriate semantics have been discussed.

5.2.3 Robust algorithms

One main task of an object detection algorithm is to choose an apt deep-learning-based algorithm from several existing algorithms. In general, an object detection algorithm used for a computer vision problem might turn out to be a vitiated approach for certain object detection tasks. Obviously, there is a need to select robust object detection algorithms based on some predefined metrics or approaches. Efforts have been made in the past to compare different learning algorithms [13].

5.3 Object detection—challenges

In most cases, object detection algorithms can be revised if probable challenges are identified. This section explains a few notable challenges that object detection algorithms encounter while parsing objects in images or video frames. These challenges are described below.

Angle orientation

Images that are captured from different angles drive object detection algorithms into complex situations. They appear differently, inviting false predictions or causing detection complexities. The use of traditional bounding-box approaches cannot be a candidate solution for targeting such angular variations. An application developer focusing on object detection has to think carefully about variations in the angles of objects observed in images.

Poor training dataset

Algorithms trained with poor data sets cause challenges for object detection algorithms. For instance, a deep learning algorithm utilized in exam proctoring software with certain styles of input quiz format as the training dataset could not detect the real exams. This is because the features utilized for the training data of an object detection algorithm might not comprehend the testing data or the real-world situations in which the images selected for tests are to be detected.

Occlusion

Occlusion is a situation in which images are not completely utilized for detecting objects [7]. These images are often cropped or show removed borders. Occlusion is a common problem for several object detection algorithms, as the training and testing processes vary in effective detection procedures. In occlusion-related images, objects are partially covered in such a way that they are not identified by the object detection algorithms. This is also a major challenge for face-detection algorithms, as discussed in the later chapters of this book.

Luminous variations

Objects captured with a certain intensity of light are captured and learned by object detection algorithms to produce specific training models. These trained models are not suitable for detecting objects, as the features identified in the training data can be different from those in the test data or video frames. Obviously, the object detection algorithms fail to understand the objects, as these objects are captured in specialized contexts under varying light conditions.

Numerous classes

Object detection algorithms encounter a huge performance problem when the number of classes used to categorize objects increases. In fact, distinguishing objects, especially in supervised learning contexts, is quite successful with two or less than ten classes. However, increasing the number of classes invites a large execution time. In addition, several implementations of deep-learning-based object detection algorithms expect to place different classes in separate folders. Subsequently, when these algorithms are executed using largely separated folder structures, they can cause performance concerns—i.e. the object detection algorithms are not fit for real-time applications in such cases.

5.4 Object detection—major steps or processes

The detection of objects in images or video frames is carried out in stages. The stages are common to several notable object detection algorithms.

5.4.1 Step 1—requirement identification

Initially, identifying object detection algorithms that are specific to the problem domain is crucial for object detection tasks. The identification of an object detection algorithm is based on the applicable algorithms, as follows:
- Real-time detection
- Non-real-time detection

Real-time object detection

The detection of objects in images or video frames can be processed in real time. This approach is beneficial for several applications that require an instantaneous report for the objects. For instance, if a blind person is willing to detect obstacles using object detection gadgets, the obstacles have to be processed in real time.

Not all object detection algorithms can function in real time. However, algorithms such as YOLOv3, YOLOv4, StreamYOLO, IncrementalYOLO, and so forth, are utilized to detect objects in real time.

Non-real-time object detection

If object detection algorithms are not restricted by time limits, they are termed non-real-time object detection algorithms. The processes involved in non-real-time object detection approaches are more similar to other object detection algorithms. However, the variation is due to the non-inclusion of a time for tasks to be completed. Algorithms in this category attempt to improve the accuracy of object detection rather than finding the bounding boxes of objects within a limited time frame.

5.4.2 Step 2—image processing

Most object detection problems need to be processed before they can be applied to appropriate object detection algorithms. For instance, detecting speeding vehicles in a smart city assumes that city officials will identify the vehicles only after applying the appropriate image processing methods. Typically, drones are utilized to capture videos or images from aerial locations of cities to detect speeding vehicles, especially when the drivers of those vehicles have committed crimes or accidents.

Input images needs to be obtained by processing video or captured images. The most stages commonly applied before images are processed to detect objects are as follows:

1. Collecting images: object detection algorithms, which require images in real time or non-real time, are fed with appropriate images collected in various forms, as listed below:
   (a) Images from data sets—several data sets are openly available for researchers to improve the performance of deep learning algorithms. These image data sets are categorized or labeled in most cases. For instance, one can find image data sets that represent flowers, fruits, and other household objects and directly provide them to the algorithms.
   (b) Images from websites—in some cases, suitable image collections may not be found in data repositories. For instance, there are no sarcasm-related data sets for images at the time of writing this book. In such situations, object detection algorithms may have to collect relevant images from web servers hosted in multiple locations. The collection of such images is carried out using web crawling techniques and other search engine support.
   (c) Image augmentation—in some cases, it is useful to perform image augmentation techniques to increase the number of images available for input to training algorithms. Image augmentation methods such as flipping, intensity variations, noise additions, and so forth have been widely discussed in the literature. Image augmentation methods are applicable if there are a few available image data sets.
   (d) Image generation—in rare cases, it is also possible to generate images in the absence of any input images using GANs or high-end deep learning algorithms. These methods provide near-accurate learning processes and could be a probable practice in some object detection situations.

In general, collecting images from cameras is implemented using OpenCV-enabled packages. For instance, OpenCV has methods to collect frames from video. A code snippet utilized to capture frames from videos is given below:

```
import cv2
frames = cv2.VideoCapture('video_file')
success,image = frames.read()
```

The cv2 package's methods, namely videoCapture() and read(), are widely applied in several object detection-related applications.

2. Normalizing images: in most cases, normalizing images improves the quality of object detection algorithms. The normalization of images attempts to modify image data such that the mean of the dataset becomes zero and the standard deviation becomes one. The main reasons for normalizing images before applying images for detecting objects using object detection algorithms are as follows:

  (a) Range fixation—by normalizing data, the range of data is standardized. Typically, this value is fixed to lie between zero and one. In this way, the algorithms are able to process the data using tensors or matrices with better accuracy.

  (b) Learning speed—as associated hardware units can be fine tuned to process values ranging from zero to one, the training model is able to learn the objects in images more quickly than if it has to handle large variations in the image data. In addition, the data distribution pattern and the other associated parameters could easily be charted using normalized data sets.

3. Preprocessing images: images can be preprocessed using several available methods in TensorFlow or PyTorch implementations. For instance, images can be preprocessed in several fashions:

  (a) Resizing: input images obtained from data sets or web sources can have varying sizes. These variations can alter the accuracy of the results of deep-learning-based object detection algorithms. Hence, it is important to resize images to a fixed value. For instance, TensorFlow offers three approaches to resizing images to a fixed size in contrast to any input image size, as follows:

```
import tensorflow as tf
tf.image.resize
tf.image.resize_with_pad #pads values to images
tf.image.resize_with_crop_or_pad #pads or crops images
```

  (b) Brightness: in general, brightness is a data augmentation method. Increasing the brightness of images is useful in some image processing applications. Typically, increasing the brightness of images is carried out in TensorFlow as follows:

```
import tensorflow as tf
tf.image.adjust_brightness(image data)
```

    (c) Contrast, hue, and saturation: Similarly to increasing or decreasing the brightness of images, it is possible to improve the contrast, hue, or saturation of images in various deep learning platforms, such as TensorFlow, as follows:

```
import tensorflow as tf
tf.image.adjust_contrast(image data)
tf.image.adjust_hue(image data)
tf.image.adjust_saturation(image data)
```

4. Conversion to specific data formats: apart from providing raw input images to object detection algorithms, there are a few other data formats that ease the implementation strategies of deep learning-based object detection algorithms.

    Supervised object detection algorithms commonly require labels in order to distinguish images. These algorithms sometimes mandate the use of the Common Objects in Context (COCO) data format, the YOLO data format, Visual Object Classes (VOC) data format, and so forth. The accuracy of object detection in custom test data sets is improved by the use of the algorithm-friendly data formats.

    The reasons for the use of different data formats by object detection algorithms are multifaceted:

    (a) Images represented in CSV, JSON, or similar file formats can break object detection algorithms, especially when the image size is very large.

    (b) Images that are represented hierarchically can lead to performance issues, such as memory overheads.

    (c) The objects in images need to be represented in bounding boxes for several object detection algorithms. It is easier to represent the bounding boxes using data formats such as YOLO, VOC, or COCO in a majority of use cases. For instance, applications utilizing the YOLO-based object detection algorithms apply the YOLO data format, which has a numerical matrix representation of RGB or gray-scale images.

5. Compressing images: In several object detection mechanisms, there is a critical need to improve the storage space or increase the transmission speed

of images. Compressing images, therefore, offers an significant improvement to object detection tasks. In general, Joint Photographic Experts Group (JPEG) compression techniques are applied in object detection or deep learning algorithms.

In addition, compressing images plays a vital role when images are processed by edge devices. Typically, edge devices, which are constrained nodes that are unable to perform strong computations such as object detection tasks, attempt to submit images to cloud services. If these edge devices are storage conscious, they should compress images using the JPEG format or another image-compression format before they are submitted to the connected services.

6. Storing images: Images are collected and input to deep learning algorithms for further object detection.

5.4.3 Convolutions and object detection

Matrices are fed to convolution networks to selectively learn objects from input images in order to detect objects.

5.5 Object detection methods

Detecting objects in images or videos is considered to be a crucial task for most computer vision applications, such as automated cars, traffic monitoring, and so forth.

A few notable object detection models are used to identify objects in images or video instances. These object detection models are as follows:

1. R-CNN
2. Fast R-CNN
3. Faster R-CNN
4. YOLO
5. Single-shot detector variants

In the following subsections, the functions of these object detection models, the layers involved, their advantages, and applications are analyzed.

5.5.1 R-CNN

R-CNN is a region-based convolutional neural network approach used for computer vision. It was first implemented in 2014. The objective of R-CNNs is to detect the objects in images or video frames and to provide bounding boxes for these objects after creating regions.

Compared to normal CNNs, R-CNN attempts to identify objects of the same category, including smaller objects [2]. Traditional CNNs were mostly applied to classify objects in an image followed by fully-connected layers. However, the problems faced by traditional CNNs in detecting objects can be illustrated using the example shown in figure 5.3.

Figure 5.3. Cat versus cats in images.

The first image has a single cat. It could be easily and logically classified as 'cat'. However, it makes little sense to feed the second image to the computer and ask it to classify the objects. In this case, it is important to detect all cats rather than to classify the objects. The other issue that is part of the CNN object detection problem is the utilization of all convolutional regions to identify the objects. This process can lead to computationally intensive tasks for computing nodes.

R-CNN plays a vital role in detecting objects by reducing the computation time involved in the detection processes. To do so, it undertakes the following steps:

1. Input image—images, either in the form of still pictures or video frames, are fed to the computer for object detection.
2. Selective search—in the given image or video frame, R-CNN selects nearly 2000 best possible regions of interest. This is carried out by segmenting portions of the image, applying a greedy algorithm that selects the major regions of interest, and proposing the best possible regions which contain objects.
3. Warping images—the selective regions of the images are warped to a fixed image size and used as inputs to traditional CNNs.
4. Classification—CNNs output a 4096 feature vector which is utilized to classify the object using algorithms such as support vector machine (SVM).

Figure 5.4 depicts the steps involved in applying the R-CNN algorithm. As can be observed, due to the application of the selective search mechanism and the proposal of selective regions in the input images, the computation involved in the identification of the warped regions is reduced.

5.5.2 Fast R-CNN

Fast R-CNN is an improved version of computer vision, compared to R-CNN [6]. It was implemented in 2015—i.e. very soon after the development of R-CNN. In Fast R-CNN, convolutional feature maps are generated by CNNs together with region selection algorithms such as edge boxes used to identify potential regions of input images and recommend them for analysis. As observed earlier, in R-CNN, over 2000 potential regions are identified in the input images. Feature detectors or filters

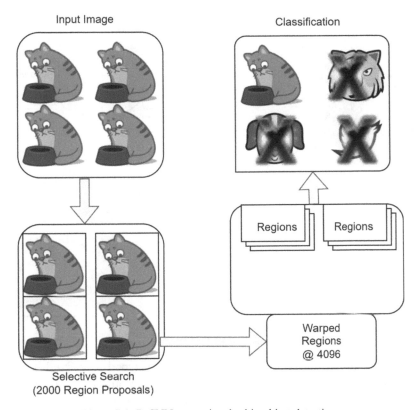

Figure 5.4. R-CNN—steps involved in object detection.

are typically utilized to detect the features present in images, such as edges, horizontal or vertical lines, curves, and so forth.

In the Fast R-CNN approach, convolutional feature maps are utilized to represent the regions of interest in the entire input images rather than splitting them into smaller regions and processing the regions one after the other. Obviously, limited computation is required by the Fast R-CNN method of detecting objects. As can be observed, the splitting of images and computing them to identify around 2000 regions, as performed in R-CNN, is avoided in this approach.

The steps involved in detecting objects in the Fast R-CNN approach are given below:

1. Input image—initially, the input image in which the available objects are to be identified is fed to the computer that executes the Fast R-CNN algorithm.
2. CNN-based feature maps—the identification of potential regions of interest in the input images is performed by CNNs—i.e. a CNN is applied to extract the feature maps from the entire image. In doing so, the analysis of over 2000 regions, which involves cropping and resizing region proposals, is not required. The CNN algorithm attempts to recognize the right proposals immediately when a few regions are identified as having features.

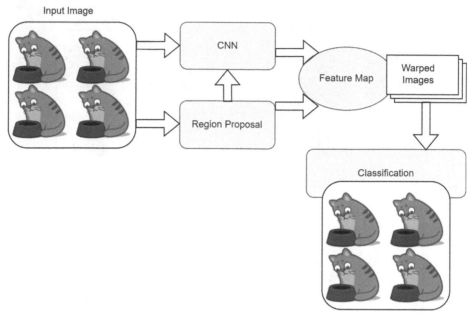

Figure 5.5. Fast R-CNN—steps involved in object detection.

3. Warping images—the identified regions are warped to a fixed image size so that further analysis of the image can be carried out. The warping of images is applied to effectively utilize the computational power of the involved hardware units, including GPUs.
4. Classification—finally, potential objects are classified and marked into bounding boxes in a similar way as for the previous R-CNN approach.

Figure 5.5 highlights the crucial steps involved in detecting objects in images.

5.5.3 Faster R-CNN

Faster R-CNN [12] utilizes a region proposal network to identify the potential regions of interest in the entire image. As a region proposal network is utilized to identify the regions, this approach to extracting crucial features from images is faster than the previous approaches.

In the faster R-CNN approach, a specialized network consisting of a convolutional neural network is utilized to identify convolutional feature maps. The faster R-CNN algorithm is similar to Fast R-CNN in two respects: (i) it utilizes an entire image for the analysis; (ii) it includes convolutional networks for image analysis.

The steps involved in the faster R-CNN method are as follows:

1. Input image—the input image is fed to the faster R-CNN algorithm. This image is fed in its entirety to the region proposal network.
2. CNN RPN—the region proposal network consists of layers of functionalities. These layers are responsible for picking up the entire image and

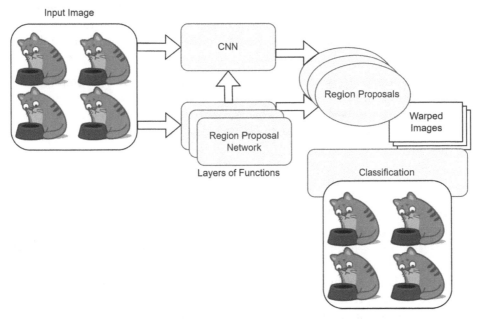

Figure 5.6. Faster R-CNN—steps involved in object detection.

attempting to identify feature maps corresponding to the images. The network highlights probabilities as scores in order to represent objects in the input image.

3. Warping—similarly to the other approaches, faster R-CNN includes a warping process to fix the size of the regions so that objects in the images can be predicted or classified.

4. Classifier—depending on the regions proposed by the CNN, classifiers are utilized to categorize the image. Faster R-CNN is also applied to regression problems in certain use cases.

Figure 5.6 specifies the steps involved in detecting objects in images. As can be observed, an entire image is submitted to a network designed using CNNs that suggests feature maps. In doing so, the faster R-CNN method is comparatively faster than the other algorithms discussed so far.

5.5.4 You Only Look Once

As compared to the previously discussed region-based object detection algorithms, such as R-CNN, fast R-CNN, and faster R-CNN, the YOLO algorithm does not use regions or CNNs to predict the regions of interest. Rather, YOLO applies CNNs to the entire image to predict the bounding boxes of probable objects and specifies the probabilities of objects in a single run of the algorithm.

The YOLO algorithm is popular due to its emerging applications in real-time use cases—i.e. it ensures higher speed and accuracy when detecting objects in images.

The YOLO object detection method is applied in several applications, such as traffic monitoring, parking predictions, language assistance [17], and so forth.

The steps involved in detecting objects using the YOLO algorithm are discussed below:

1. Input image—images, in the form of still pictures or video frames, are input to the algorithm for detecting objects.
2. Grid formation—the images are subdivided into grids of equal size with dimensions of SxS to evaluate the bounding boxes and probability scores of objects.

   If objects are identified within each grid of the image, they are marked using bounding boxes with higher probability scores. The bounding boxes represent the width, height, and class of the object and the central point of the bounding box. However, in reality, objects need not fit into the equally split dimensions of the images.
3. Intersections—each initial grid cell of the object expands such that it overlaps with the other nearby grids over iterations during the process of identifying the eligible bounding boxes. YOLO applies the intersection over the union (IOU) concept to intersect and overlap the other nearby grid cells. During this process, unnecessary bounding boxes have no appropriate objects are eliminated.
4. Bounding boxes—finally, bounding boxes with the projected width and height from the initial grid size of the cell are marked in the images. In addition, the classification of the objects at a specified percentage of accuracy is depicted on the bounding boxes.

Figure 5.7 highlights two cases of detecting objects in images. In the first case, an image consists of four objects, and in the second case, the image contains one object. While the images were split into equal grid sizes, the objects were contained within

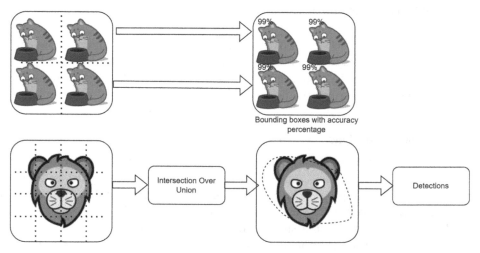

Figure 5.7. YOLO—cases for object detection.

the grid cells in the first case. In contrast, the object did not fit the grid size of a cell in the second case. Accordingly, identifying the bounding boxes, which consist of the height, width, the central point of the grid cell, and the class of the object, is much more straightforward in the first case. However, in the second case, the grid cells have to forecast the bounding boxes to fit the objects into the cells. Accordingly, the IOU concept was applied in the second example before the objects could be detected.

5.5.5 YOLO variants

The implementation of the YOLO algorithm was initiated in 2016. Subsequently, a couple more releases of the YOLO algorithm were ushered in in 2017 and 2018—v2 and v3. Later, in 2020, three more versions named YOLOv4, YOLOv5, and PP-YOLO were released.

The major enhancements of the different variants of the YOLO architecture are given below:

YOLOv2

YOLOv2 increased the number of iterations performed, compared to YOLOv1 [17]. In YOLOv2, anchor boxes were introduced to represent objects. The version was heavily utilized by researchers and academics.

YOLOv3

YOLOv3 attempted to improve the classification features of previous versions. In addition, the main focus of the algorithm was to showcase the accuracy achieved in predicting objects. To do so, the algorithm introduced the concept of writing the prediction accuracy on top of the bounding boxes. The YOLOv3 version was very actively applied by various industries and academics [11]. This is because the previous versions of YOLO engendered strong feelings regarding the necessity of such algorithms for detecting objects in images.

YOLOv4

In 2020, Alexey contributed more features to previous YOLO versions. This algorithm was designed to improve the feature abstraction processes and activation processes. The algorithm attempted to improve the accessibility of data sets while performing object detection. The algorithm tries to fit one of the anchor points automatically using evolutionary algorithms and k-means approaches. Fitting to one of the anchor points keeps the algorithm functioning and searching for the best fit for rectangles or objects in images. The algorithm is used in several applications, including traffic sign detection [4].

PP-YOLO

In 2021, the Paddle-Paddle You Only Look Once (PP-YOLO) algorithm was developed by Baidu and his coauthors. The major improvements of this algorithmic variant, when compared to the other previous algorithms, are the inclusion of a model backbone, DropBlock regularization, and Matrix non-maximum suppression (NMS). PP-YOLO is getting attention in the market [8]. However, this approach has seen a diminishing role because of the naming variant of the algorithm.

5.6 Applications

This section describes the applications of object detection algorithms in several domains. As object detection is one of the key concepts for computer vision problems, its algorithms are undoubtedly applied in several domains. Additionally, object detection algorithms are a crucial step toward the most popular deep learning techniques, which involve convolutions and computational instances.

In general, object detection algorithms are used in applications that have tasks requiring the detection of objects in images or video frames. The most commonly available applications that utilize object detection algorithms are described below.

5.6.1 Tracking

Object detection algorithms are very commonly utilized for tracking objects, vehicles [16], people, movements, and so forth. A few use cases in which object detection algorithms can be applied are listed below:

1. to identify the number of people present in a city or airport station;
2. to identify vehicles that move along smart city roads;
3. to detect lost objects, such as vessels, in smart home environments;
4. to quickly trace wild animals living in forests;
5. to examine the quality of objects in images, etc.

5.6.2 Geo-classification

The classification of terrain [9], groundwater levels, sea/land, geographical maps, and so forth are typical examples of the geo-classification category of application. These applications typically utilize GPS-connected devices and images captured from satellites. The satellite images are processed using object detection algorithms to categorize the locations in maps.

5.6.3 Healthcare solutions

Object detection algorithms have been a key method of classifying medical images, such as x-rays, magnetic resonance imaging (MRI) scans, and so forth. These algorithms have demonstrated the importance of quickly and precisely diagnosing diseases. For instance, diagnosing brain tumors in images is a challenging task for medical practitioners. This is because the tumors [10] are sometimes inactive and they are not very noticeable, even for skilled practitioners—i.e. skilled medical practitioners can miss certain important features that categorize images of brain tumors. However, deep-learning-assisted object detection algorithms can quickly identify them using previously trained models.

5.6.4 E-learning solutions

E-learning has become a popular and mandatory technique in the education sector which has received more emphasis in the post-COVID era. In fact, COVID-19 prompted industrialists, including educational institutions, to organize learning systems in an online mode. Before COVID-19, many universities and educational institutions organized lectures and exams based on direct involvement/interaction with students and teachers.

During COVID-19, the repetitive lockdowns and inaccessible institutions made people rethink the applicability of remote classes. They subsequently increased the utilization of online classes with the assistance of AI solutions. Deep learning algorithms consequently increased the tendency to apply possible algorithms, including object detection algorithms.

Object detection algorithms can be applied for educational purposes in the following ways:

1. to undertake contactless attendance in classrooms [3] or lecture halls;
2. to learn the emotional state of students, such as anger, sadness, happiness, disgust, fear, and so forth;
3. to calculate diets from foods served in the canteens of institutes;
4. to evaluate yoga postures or athletic postures;
5. to improve teaching materials that are provided as images using supportive details from Internet sources;
6. to proctor exams by examining the candidates or screen actions, etc.

5.7 Exam proctoring—YOLOv5

Exam proctoring is an application that applies image analysis, such as deep learning algorithms, to automatically invigilate exams. It is a recent application that evolved in academic institutions during the post-COVID-19 period to support the invigilation of online exams. Compared to several traditional applications in domains such as transportation and healthcare, exam proctoring is considered to be the most novel application.

5.7.1 Crucial applications

Exam proctoring applications can be useful in several situations:

1. it is useful when exams need to be organized through web transfer protocols such as HTTP;
2. it is essential when exams are remotely conducted within an organization;
3. it is beneficial when exams are proctored for a large number of students, which is the case in leading organizations such as the Technical University of Munich (TUM) (Germany), Cardiff University (UK), and so forth.

5.7.2 Requirements

The important requirements of exam proctoring applications are as follows:

1. Screen capture—the proctoring system should have the ability to capture screens with varying time frames. In general, increasing the time frames used

to detect the images could increase the file size of the output. Thus, there should be an attempt to restrict the number of sample images that need to be captured from screens.

2. Image classification—the proctoring system has to classify the captured images into exam or non-exam categories based on the classification algorithm specified in the proctoring system.

3. Anomaly detection—methods are required to detect anomalies that pinpoint exam violations, such as moving away from the exam site, reading web materials, watching exam answers on websites, and so forth.

4. Real-time analysis—one of the crucial characteristics of a proctor application is to access exam invigilation at run time rather than pinpointing anomalies in an offline mode.

5. Scalability feature—in addition, the proctoring application needs to be scalable so that it can accommodate tens of thousands of candidates and automatically invigilate them at run time.

5.8 Proctoring system—implementation stages

In general, a proctoring system consists of the following system components: (i) interface, (ii) screen recording, (iii) image categorization, (iv) object detection, (v) anomaly records, and (vi) object detection systems. Figure 5.8 explains the training and test phases of the exam proctoring system in which anomalies are tracked.

The most important functionalities of these components are described in the following sections along with the code snippets required to implement the proctoring system.

5.8.1 Interface

The proctoring system should be interfaced with popular online educational portals, such as Moodle. Typically, Moodle is utilized in various universities to assist teachers and students by sharing files, folders, contents, and so forth. In addition, it is used to organize quizzes, collect assignments by a deadline, and grade them online. The proctoring system should have the capability to integrate with such portals to

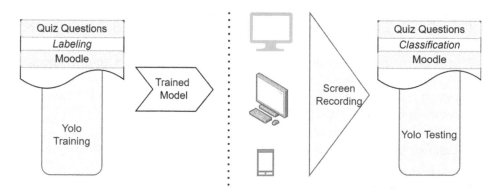

Figure 5.8. Exam proctoring system architecture.

incorporate online proctoring systems into them. The interfaces should be implemented as extensions to Moodle or similar tools.

5.8.2 Screen recording

Computer screens are periodically recorded to understand whether the students taking exams have violated the exam rules or not. Screen capture could be implemented using the OpenCV Python packages. The code snippet below exemplifies the procedure used to record screens using the `pyautogui` package of Python.

```
import pyautogui
collect_image = pyautogui.screenshot()
```

In addition, the images need to preprocessed using NumPy packages while collecting the entire information on the screen, including color images, as follows:

```
import numpy as np
collect_image  =  cv2.cvtColor(np.array(collect_image),
cv2.COLOR_RGB2BGR)
```

5.8.3 Image categorization

Image categorization requires sophisticated object detection algorithms that are capable of capturing objects in images. In the proctoring application, the system has to identify exam quiz questions in the input images.

YOLO preparation and training
The YOLO algorithm is an object detection algorithm that is widely applied in several application domains. To observe quiz objects in images, sufficient training is required using exam images.

To achieve this, a set of images representing Moodle quizzes was obtained and the images were labeled using the `labelImg` software. This software allows the exam images to be labeled with *question* and *moodle* labels by drawing bounding boxes to represent the question and Moodle pages.

These labeled images are exported in the YOLO data format, which consists of a matrix of numerical values representing the objects in images. The training and test data set folders are then prepared as inputs for the training module of the proctoring application, and models are created using the YOLOv5 algorithm.

YOLO testing and anomaly detection
By setting the initial values of YOLOv5 as follows to define the test components, object detection can be performed in the proctoring application.

```
img_size=(640, 640)
conf_thres=0.4
iou_thres=0.45
max_det=1000
anomaly=False
```

For each input test image, the entire image is parsed and converted to arrays using the NumPy package, as follows:

```
image = torch.from_numpy(image).to(device)
```

The inference step, which uses PyTorch of YOLOv5, is simple. We need to invoke one function for the image:

```
# Inference step
pred = model(im)
pred = non_max_suppression(pred, conf_thres, iou_thres,
max_det=max_det)
```

After applying a non-max-suppression component, the prediction value is found in the YOLOv5 algorithm. This prediction value contains data if objects such as 'exam' and 'moodle' are detected in the test images. However, the prediction value becomes NULL if the algorithm cannot find the specified objects.

Based on the outcomes of the prediction values, anomalous images are recorded—i.e. those related to students who have violated exam rules by viewing websites or web-related materials. The anomaly information is uploaded to cloud services or sent to the proctoring software or the relevant tutors in real time.

The proctoring application was designed at TUM (Germany) and the Indian Institute of Information Technology (Kottayam) to assist teachers during the invigilation process using the YOLOv5 object detection algorithm.

References

[1] Ahmed M, Hashmi K A, Pagani A, Liwicki M, Stricker D and Afzal M Z 2021 Survey and performance analysis of deep learning based object detection in challenging environments *Sensors* **21** 5116

[2] Chen C, Liu M-Y, Tuzel O and Xiao J 2016 R-CNN for small object detection *Computer Vision – ACCV 2016* (Lecture Notes in Computer Science vol 10115) ed S-H Lai, V Lepetit, K Nishino and Y Sato (Berlin: Springer) pp 214–30

[3] Cheng Q, Rong B, Sun B and He J 2019 Class attendance checking system based on deep learning and global optimization *ICCPR '19: Proceedings of the 2019 8th International Conference on Computing and Pattern Recognition* (New York: ACM) pp 331–6

[4] Dewi C, Chen R-C, Liu Y-T, Jiang X and Hartomo K D 2021 Yolo V4 for advanced traffic sign recognition with synthetic training data generated by various GAN *IEEE Access* **9** 97228–42

[5] Fukuda M, Okuno T and Yuki S 2021 Central object segmentation by deep learning to continuously monitor fruit growth through RGB images *Sensors* **12** 6999

[6] Girshick R B 2015 Fast R-CNN *2015 IEEE International Conference on Computer Vision (ICCV)* (Los Alamitos, CA: IEEE Computer Society Press) pp 1440–8

[7] Li F, Li X, Liu Q and Li Z 2022 Occlusion handling and multi-scale pedestrian detection based on deep learning: a review *IEEE Access* **10** 19937–57

[8] Li Y, Huang H, Chen Q, Fan Q and Quan H 2021 Research on a product quality monitoring method based on multi scale PP-YOLO *IEEE Access* **9** 80373–87

[9] Mikolka-Flöry S and Pfeifer N 2021 Horizon line detection in historical terrestrial images in mountainous terrain based on the region covariance *Remote Sens.* **13** 1705

[10] Nazir M, Shakil S and Khurshid K 2021 Role of deep learning in brain tumor detection and classification (2015 to 2020): a review *Comput. Med. Imaging Graph.* **91** 101940

[11] Pandiyan P, Thangaraj R, Subramanian M, Rahul R, Nishanth M and Palanisamy I 2022 Real-time monitoring of social distancing with person marking and tracking system using YOLO V3 model *Int. J. Sens. Netw.* **38** 154–65

[12] Ren S, He K, Girshick R B and Sun J 2015 Faster R-CNN: towards real-time object detection with region proposal networks *Advances in Neural Information Processing Systems 28: Annual Conference on Neural Information Processing Systems 2015, December 7–12, 2015, Montreal* C Cortes, N D Lawrence, D D Lee, M Sugiyama and R Garnett (Red Hook, NY: Curran Associates, Inc.) pp 91–9

[13] Sindhwani N, Verma S, Bajaj T and Anand R 2021 Comparative analysis of intelligent driving and safety assistance systems using YOLO and SSD model of deep learning *Int. J. Inf. Syst. Model. Des.* **12** 131–46

[14] Socher R, Huval B, Bath B P, Manning C D and Ng A Y 2012 Convolutional-recursive deep learning for 3D object classification *Advances in Neural Information Processing Systems 25: 26th Annual Conference on Neural Information Processing Systems 2012. Proceedings of a meeting held December 3–6, 2012, Lake Tahoe, NV* P L Bartlett, F C N Pereira, C J C Burges, L Bottou and K Q Weinberger (Red Hook, NY: Curran Associates, Inc) pp 665–73

[15] Wang D, Wang J-G and Xu K 2021 Deep learning for object detection, classification and tracking in industry applications *Sensors* **21** 7349

[16] Wang K and Liu M 2022 2022 YOLOv3-mt: A YOLOv3 using multi-target tracking for vehicle visual detection *Appl. Intell.* **52** 2070–91

[17] Zhang J, Huang M, Jin X and Li X 2017 A real-time Chinese traffic sign detection algorithm based on modified YOLOv2 *Algorithms* **10** 127

Chapter 6

Sentiment analysis—algorithms and frameworks

Sentiment analysis (SA) is a natural language processing technique that gauges sentiments expressed in the text, audio, or video of an individual or group. It analyzes input data to gauge positive, negative, or neutral responses to subjects. In addition, it offers knowledge and opinions to people who formulate guidelines or feedback. This chapter explains the principles behind applying SA to social-good applications, especially for recommendation systems that improve the economic status of humans.

6.1 Sentiment analysis—an introduction

Imagine a situation in which a politician wants to attract a large number of followers in a region or a country. The politician could use social media sites such as LinkedIn, Twitter, Facebook, or similar sites to issue a statement. In countries such as India, where there are a large number of sensitive communities, certain statements could immediately cause trouble, leading to the downfall of a party. In such scenarios, the likes, dislikes, and comments of the followers have to be keenly observed using tools or techniques such as SA applications. Obviously, corrective measures may be taken by the tools in an automated fashion to improve the situation.

6.1.1 History—sentiment analysis

The emergence of SA with the inclusion of deep learning and the other modern sophisticated methods/techniques evolved since the 2000s. However, analyzing the opinions of the public had been practiced for several decades. For instance, in earlier years, hand-crafted templates and survey portals were utilized to collect the opinion on products or services of an industry.

Applying SA using modern methods evolved based on the talk by Prof. Lillian Lee of Cornell University. Subsequently, the opinion mining concept was practiced by several researchers and developers by applying suitable algorithms and techniques [14].

6.1.2 Trends and objectives

The field of SA has exponentially grown since the inception of the idea market. The number of related articles grew from 96 in 1990 to 7773 in 2020. Although this domain has started to decline since 2019, its use as a research topic has increased in diverse fields, including the Internet of things (IoT) and applications for social good. Figure 6.1 highlights the number of relevant papers published in Scopus-indexed journals over the last few years. These publications had the keywords 'Sentiment Analysis' in the article title. In addition to scholarly works, which have reached over 80 000 articles to date (as of July 2021), the number of patents related to SA has exceeded 2000 across the globe.

Finding customer insights in opinions about products or services has understandably attracted a large number of implementations in the past. Almost all of the companies who developed products or services wished to incorporate this technology into their web services or their e-commerce web sites. In fact, their older approach to getting feedback/opinions from valuable customers through surveys was an arduous task.

The major reasons that companies shifted their processes toward this newer approach are as follows:

1. The traditional survey method led to cost inefficiency, as the work was often outsourced to third-party companies.
2. The survey mechanism used to collect opinions had limited options for incorporating the required intelligence into the feedback processes.
3. The problem caused by the negligence of a wider group of customers, especially those from different countries/regions, increased.
4. The survey mechanism required sufficient manpower to understand the tone of the customer opinions.
5. The personnel engaged to review the opinions were required to have sufficient expertise in the traditional approach to handling opinions.

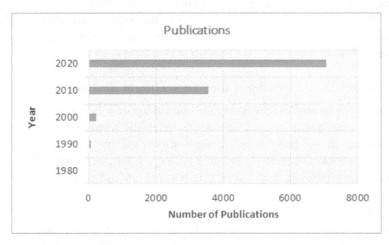

Figure 6.1. Publications related to SA.

The major tasks or objectives of SA are listed below:

- to classify the tones of texts into positive, negative, or neutral based on the input received from social media sites or comments obtained from feedback sites
- to identify the features that influence the tones of texts, voice, or video
- to distinguish opinions after extracting features from the input data

6.2 Levels and approaches

This section describes the levels and approaches/techniques used to perform SA in a system. In addition, the SA methods are discussed in detail.

6.2.1 Levels of sentiment analysis

SA techniques are performed at several levels of data mining. In the context of text mining, SA is adopted at the following levels:

1. Document level—in *document-level* SA, an entire document in the .pdf, .tex, or .doc format or so forth, is fed into the system to perform opinion mining. As the size of the document is typically large, fine-grained analysis [12] of the entire document provides near-accurate solutions—i.e. the SA might not be accurate.
2. Sentence level—in *sentence-level* SA, sentences are evaluated to distinguish opinions such as positive, negative, or neutral tones [23]. E-commerce applications, in general, utilize sentences rather than documents to analyze comments or review opinions hosted on web sites. The exponential growth of e-commerce applications has triggered a requirement for sentence-level SA.
3. Aspect level—in *aspect-level* SA, certain phrases in sentences are analyzed [15] for possible opinions or tones. This level of SA offers more fine-grained categorization of the aspects or sentiments expressed in texts or videos. The aspects involved in the analysis of sentiments from documents can be classified into two categories, depending on their use: (i) explicit and (ii) implicit. In explicit aspect-level SA, the aspects are specified before the analysis, whereas in implicit aspect-level SA, the aspects are derived based on certain techniques.

6.2.2 Approaches to and techniques used for sentiment analysis

SA techniques can be carried out using two broad approaches, namely, lexicon-based and learning-model-based approaches. SA is generally applied to analyze the sentiments contained in public or user reviews submitted on web sites. For instance, analyzing the reviews of recently launched movies, product sentiments, fashion designs, and so forth, has attained attraction among researchers and production-level markets.

6.2.2.1 Lexicon-based SA
In lexicon-based SA, the content and polarity of the texts of reviews are analyzed using the relevant vocabulary. To do so, sentences from reviews need to be tokenized

and analyzed to discover their polarity. The tokens consist of words or bags of words in the form of dictionaries used to perform lexical analysis.

Lexicon-based SA is performed using SA tools such as SentiWordNet, Linguistic Inquiry and Word Count (LIWC), Multi-Perspective Question Answering (MPQA) subjectivity lexicon, and so forth. Lexicon-based SA attempts to identify the emotions of texts and words in sentences.

SentiWordNet was formulated from a dictionary database for opinion mining processes. It attempts analysis after the substantial seed words have been identified in sentences. In addition, potential positive and negative labels are captured in the sentences for opinion mining.

LIWC is a computerized text analysis tool that parses the input texts and suggests the psychological insights contained in the texts. For instance, the usage of words such as 'I', 'we', and so forth is studied in the words of documents. Additionally, the positive emotions, negative emotions, and emotional tones of sentences are captured using LIWC.

The MPQA subjectivity lexicon comprises an array of annotation databases, such as news corpora, opinion corpora, and so forth, that are manually annotated for further use by SA algorithms.

Most of the abovementioned lexicon-based SA methods involve the manual labeling of words to identify emotions or polarities. In the field of modern lexicon-based SA approaches, semi-supervised training models, supervised training models, and unsupervised learning models have been developed. The authors of [21] studied the application of lexicons to Twitter-based SA problems.

6.2.3 Processing stages

In general, the processing of sentiments in texts or images undergoes certain stages. The important features of these stages and their functionalities are discussed in the following subsections.

6.2.3.1 Learning-model-based SA
SA and classification problems require appropriate learning models such as logistic models or classifier models [6] in order to automatically learn the emotions and polarities of texts without manual intervention.

Typically, model-based SA parses sentences, words, and contexts to extract appropriate features. These features are learned from a set of training data sets and the derived inferences are validated using the validation data set. If the validation data set does not yield the expected results, the training inferences are fine tuned to the expectations. Later, depending on the refined learning models, SA of the texts is performed with more accuracy.

The learning models most commonly applied for SA include:

1. Naive classifier—a naive Bayes classifier functions using Bayes' theorem of probability. During the learning phase of the algorithm, the likelihoods of words in sentences and the emotions expressed in sentences are studied. Using the probability study, future instances of words or the polarity of words can be predicted.

2. SVM—support vector machine is a machine learning model which identifies the hyperplanes between data points represented in the form of words. These hyperplanes distinguish the tones of words in sentences using lines. The algorithm places the separation line in such a way that the distance between data points is high [6].

3. Logistic regression—in general, the logistic regression algorithm is well suited to binary classification problems. In SA problems, this algorithm is quite beneficial, as most of the data points are sparse in nature—i.e. the words occur infrequently. Obviously, binary classification problems such as identifying the positive or negative tones of words can significantly benefit from using this algorithm.

4. Deep learning—recent years have seen remarkable growth in the evolution of learning models [8, 16]. For instance, the application of deep learning models, such as the convolutional neural networks studied in chapter 4, provides more accuracy and reduces complexity.

6.3 Sentiment analysis—processes

SA, which is derived from natural language processing (NLP), involves a few stages of processing before it identifies the tones or polarity of sentences in documents, texts, or videos. Often, such processing is divided into three stages:

- Preprocessing
- Learning
- Classifying

The preprocessing of texts obtained from pdf files, web links, or web pages involve the following steps (see figure 6.2):

1. Tokenization—tokenization attempts to split words from the input sentences, sentences from paragraphs, paragraphs from files, and so forth. Tokenized words, sentences, or paragraphs, are stored in a vector of arrays used to infer the uses of words from the contexts of documents.

2. Lowercase conversion—collecting words without capital letters is beneficial for pursuing word processing in raw texts. In fact, analysis of the tones of words utilized in sentences or paragraphs does not expect capital letters to be used—i.e. representing words with capital letters leads to more computational complexity but does not offer any advantages. Moreover, identification of the tones of words can be utilized to rephrase sentences or words if they are written in lower case.

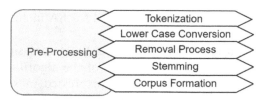

Figure 6.2. Steps used in preprocessing texts.

3. Removal process—punctuation marks are also removed while preprocessing texts for SA, because they do not add any value to the analysis process. In short, it is expected that the words in raw texts should be reduced to keep the computational complexity of the SA process at a minimal level. The removal process is quite important for several classification-related SA problems, such as identifying the positive and negative sentiments of texts. However, it is not advisable to remove the punctuation from raw text if sentiments need to be transformed to another language.

   It is also a good practice to remove other language symbols, such as, %, $, #, and so forth, from raw texts.
4. Stemming—stemming is the process of identifying the base word of the identified words of texts. Base words can be obtained by reducing the suffixes of words. For instance, words such as *write*, *writes*, and *writing* can be written as *write* instead of *writing*. In doing so, the dimensions of the words are reduced for further SA processing—i.e. the computational complexity is reduced.
5. Corpus formation—corpus formation is the process of identifying the combinations of words in texts. The corpus enables the creation of n-grams from words, which can be applied in the creation of newer sentences. A 1-gram is called a unigram, and a 2-gram is known as a bigram. As an example, 'South India' is a bigram representation of text. The formation of n-grams from a corpus enables probabilistic studies of framing newer corpora in NLP applications to take place.

The learning and classification stages of the SA processes are detailed in the following section, which discusses the recommendation systems that use SA.

6.4 Recommendation system—sentiment analysis

Recommendation systems apply SA to filter information from a large volume of data found in web sites or documents. The most common applications of recommendation systems include (a) housing recommendations, (b) hotel recommendations, (c) tourism recommendations [7], (d) movie recommendations, (e) online course recommendations, (f) product recommendations, and so forth.

A brief outline of these recommendation systems is found below:
1. Housing recommendations—understanding the sentiments or emotions of residents expressed on social media sites, such as Facebook, LinkedIn, Google+, and so forth, can be utilized to recommend the best housing options for residents. In fact, the Malaysian government has planned to grant public housing to citizens after emotions were studied on social sites.
2. Hotel recommendations—observing the reviews written by the guests of popular hotels plays a key role for travelers intending to book hotels in major cities. It has been the practice of travelers to not only view the facilities of the hotels, such as the availability of air conditioners or heaters, but also to monitor the reviews of previous travelers. If travelers find unfavorable

reviews of a hotel, they need not opt for it even if the facilities are appealing. A manual study of each and every hotel in a city could become an arduous task and a time-consuming activity. SA-enabled recommendation systems can rapidly ease this process.

3. Tourism recommendations—planning tourism locations during summer or winter vacations, depending on budget and personalized requirements, has shifted the focus of modern tourists. The traditional approach to planning tourism has been seen as counterproductive to travelers' productivity. E-tourism recommendation systems have been developed for different platforms, such as mobile, web, and desktops. These recommendation systems are engaged in delivering functions such as guiding, planning, budget control mechanisms, report preparation, feedback analysis, and so forth. The tourism recommendation system is a knowledge management system.

4. Movie recommendations—a movie recommendation system combined with semantic intelligence has been widely applied in movie markets. It is a sort of collaborative effort between the various viewers of a movie. A person viewing a movie for the first time shares their opinion about the movie in the form of a recommended review. The collective reviews from various viewers are used by the SA system to produce efficient recommendations [13]. Additionally, the personal behaviors of viewers can be analyzed to support future movie recommendations. In recent years, SA scores have been combined with hybrid recommendations, such as collaborative filtering and content-filtering-based recommendations.

5. Online course recommendations—past student experiences with the growing number of online courses are captured, analyzed, and recommended by online course recommendation systems [17]. The traditional approach to selecting online courses includes rule-based methods, association methods, collaborative methods, and so forth. The inclusion of SA into the collaborative filtering mechanism personalizes the selection of courses. For instance, the collaborative filtering approach enables the selection of an online course based on the similarity found with similar-caliber students in the system. However, sentiments can provide more personification to the online recommendation system, which encourages the student to complete the course with interest.

6. Product recommendations—purchasing mobile phones or similar products that fit an anticipated budget is a difficult exercise for many people. Several factors associated with products need to be optimized to satisfy both the budget and the expected benefits [11].

Figure 6.3 showcases a list of the available recommendation systems found in the market.

The scraping of web information is considered the be one of the basic steps in creating the abovementioned recommendations. The web scraping method is a process of collecting information from the web that contains relevant information used to create recommendations. For instance, collecting reviews about a product or an online course from web pages is termed web scraping. The reviews or pieces of

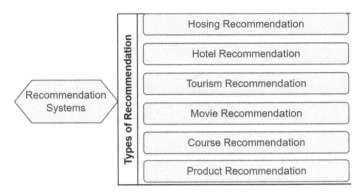

Figure 6.3. Recommendation systems.

information are often represented in different formats, such as comma-separated values (CSVs), JavaScript Object Notation (JSON), or .txt file formats after the data are collected in specified data structures.

Web scraping techniques require parsers that fetch the appropriate information from web pages. These parsers can lead to overheads. The authors of [24] studied the performance impact of different web parsers during the web crawling processes in recent years. Similarly, Rohmeth *et al* [20] compared the performance efficiencies of different web scraping techniques for web pages.

Applying intelligence while scraping information from web pages in an automated fashion has attracted various researchers and web application developers. For instance, the authors of Rizwan *et al* [18] studied the application of bots to automatically feed data to web servers and investigate the crimes that happened in web sites. The authors of [22] applied intelligent supervised machine learning algorithms to web page processing methods.

In the context of recommendation systems that apply SA, the techniques are classified into (i) collaborative filtering, (ii) content-based, (iii) knowledge-based, (iv) demographic, (v) context-based, (vi) review-based, (vii) hybrid, and (viii) decision-tree approaches, as shown in figure 6.4.

Apart from recommendation systems, text classification based on sentiments or other text processing methods is carried out as follows:

1. News text analysis—the contents of news and news headlines are analyzed by these algorithms [10]. In general, this information needs to be handled in real time by commodity devices, including heterogeneous devices. The users of such tools prefer to obtain news headline information that is recommended using their own interests.
2. Topic categorization—sentiment-based semantic information retrieval from texts is one of the most popular use cases of text analysis [19]. For instance, students may be interested in collecting information on a particular topic rather than utilization metrics.
3. Quiz analysis—text processing can apply SA mechanisms to create quiz questions in a constructive manner or to process quiz answers using test classification methods.

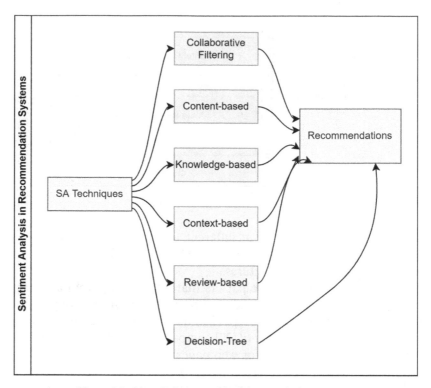

Figure 6.4. SA techniques used in recommendation systems.

6.5 Movie recommendation—a case study

As a case study, this section explains movie recommendations. Based on the earlier discussion, the reviews need to be fetched from selected web pages.

Fetching reviews from web pages requires the appropriate Python packages, as given below:

```
import requests
from bs4 import BeautifulSoup
import re
```

The *requests* package of Python submits Hypertext Transfer Protocol (HTTP) requests to web sites. The response to this request provides all the details of the web page, enabling further processing of review contents. For instance, the code below shows the procedure used to collect contents from the web site domain.com. In addition, user credentials can be included in the protected links to collect the information. Methods such as get are responsible for fetching the responses from web pages for HTTP requests. However, the contents are available in the .text method of the Uniform Resource Locator (URL).

```
htmlUrl = requests.get("https://domain.com/", auth=('username',
'pwd'))
 print(htmlUrl.text)
```

The *BeautifulSoup* Python library is responsible for parsing HTTP responses. It creates a perfect soup from the specified web sites. It is also possible to prettify the contents using the HTML tags provided in the web pages.

```
soup = BeautifulSoup(htmlUrl.text,'lxml')
```

Here, *soup* prepares contents from the web page based on *lxml* parsing information. The output of *soup* enables us to prettify the contents or find particular texts in the input web page. Similarly, it is possible to find all the information following an HTML tag such as <div>, <p >, <a >, or so forth, using the classes of the web page.

```
soup.prettify()
 soup.find_all('div', class_ = 'movieReviews')
 soup.find(text="movie")
```

soup can be utilized to iteratively surf web contents, as reviews typically occur one after the other for different movies.

The movie reviews can be exported in several formats, including CSV format, so that SA can be applied to the reviews after sufficient preprocessing of the data, such as tokenization, stemming, n-gram provisioning, and so forth.

There is a popular movie recommendation data set named the Internet Movie Database (IMDB) data set, which can be accessed using the TensorFlow/Keras packages. This can be realized using packages, as follows:

```
import tensorflow
from tensorflow.keras.datasets import imdb
```

The *imdb* data set from Keras consists of 25 000 movie reviews that are preprocessed from movie links. The data consists of a vector of integers referring to movie reviews fetched from the appropriate movie review pages.

This data set can be used to evaluate the performances of several SA models that learn the associated reviews. The most commonly utilized learning algorithms for

SA are (a) CNNs, (b) recurrent neural networks (RNNs), (c) long short-term memory (LSTM) models, and (d) hybrid (LSTM and convolutional) models.

6.5.1 Convolutional neural networks—sentiments

The CNN algorithm analyzes the sentiments of movies after processing review information from web sites. Preprocessing movie reviews is quite important in order to improve the accuracy of SA performed using the movie reviews. The most commonly applicable preprocessing steps are as follows:

1. padding additional information,
2. splitting data into training/testing phases,
3. labeling data, and so forth.

The preprocessed movie reviews are subjected to convolutions performed using the CNN algorithm. CNN establishes windows of information to absorb features or filters.

The CNN algorithm embeds words according to the number of reviews provided. The embedding provides an almost equal representation of real-valued numbers for different words in similar contexts. The embedding of words in SA is represented in Python as follows:

```
model.add(Embedding(words, dimensions, length=reviews))
```

Later, spatial dropout is performed to easily exploit the dropout functionality of adjacent feature maps. This functionality is more similar to the traditional dropout features. To do so, the following function of the Python package can be applied:

```
model.add(SpatialDropout1D(dropout))
```

Later, the Conv1D function is utilized to convolve the data set using the CNN algorithm. The CNN algorithm typically involves a rectified linear unit (RELU) activation function. The main purpose of applying the RELU activation function in the algorithm is to reduce activation by all neurons. The code used is as follows:

```
model.add(Conv1D(iterations, kernel, activation='relu'))
```

A max pooling operation is then performed on the data. In general, the max pooling operation attempts to reduce the size of the data so that the computations are effectively improved. Since the 1D max pooling technique is utilized, one-dimensional data are utilized with a specific window size. For instance, if the window size is three, 1D max pooling selects the maximum of the three matrix cells, as shown in figure 6.5.

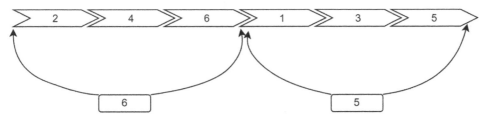

Figure 6.5. 1D max pooling.

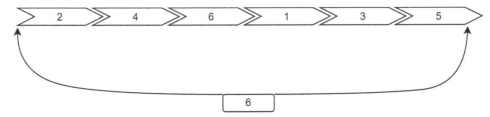

Figure 6.6. Global 1D max pooling.

In the SA of movie reviews, global max pooling is applied. The major difference between 1D max pooling and global 1D max pooling is due to the application of window size. In the latter case, the entire window size is applied (see figure 6.6).

A code snippet that provides global max pooling in the movie SA is as follows:

```
model.add(GlobalMaxPooling1D())
```

Next, dense layering and activation functions are utilized in the CNN algorithm to perform SA using movie reviews, as follows:

```
model.add(Dense(layers, activation='relu'))
model.add(Dense(1, activation='sigmoid'))
```

6.5.2 Recurrent neural networks—sentiments

An RNN is a division of a neural network. In an RNN, neurons are recursively connected to establish learning models for time-dependent sequences. Using this approach, a sequence of data inputs is processed in a similar way to the processing of memory layouts that takes place in the human brain.

Figure 6.7 shows an RNN architecture and explains the series of time steps that corresponds to the historical input data sets. Here, the weight associated with the previous state's input and the weight associated with the previous state's output are multiplied. Later, appropriate functions are utilized to acquire the new state. This means that the history of sentiments at time step t is loaded into the RNN

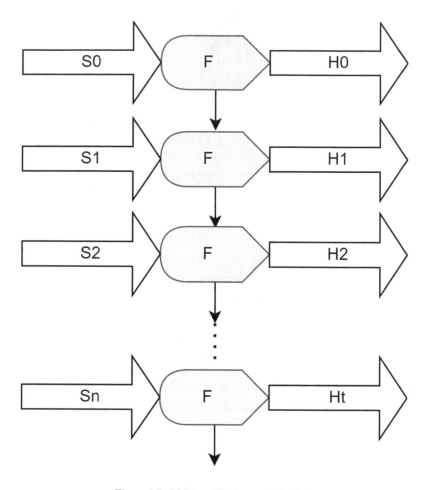

Figure 6.7. RNN architecture used for SA.

architecture with appropriate weights in order to find the output sentiment values or vocabularies. Figure 6.7 illustrates the folded functions used to retain the memory structure in RNNs. Notably, RNNs utilize the same function, F, to construct the memory or to relate the historical information.

In fact, RNN can offer better results if more time-series information is included. However, this approach leads to a vanishing gradient problem in the learning process. Hence, RNN restricts the number of time steps or time series used to process the historical sentiment information.

6.5.3 Long short-term memory—sentiments

RNN encounters issues such as gradient vanishing problems, challenging its application to long sequences of sentiments/vocabularies. In RNNs, gradients with longer sequences offer no significance. Accordingly, the learning processes deteriorates in the RNN approach.

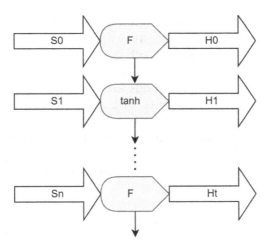

Figure 6.8. LSTM architecture.

For instance, sentences such as '*school students play volley ...*' clearly suggest that the next word is '*ball*'. However, if words have long-term dependencies, such as '*Germans play football. In October, they celebrate ...,*' the previous information about Germans could become stronger and predict '*Octoberfest.*' Obviously, in some scenarios, the older contexts are required to correctly predict information.

LSTM, in contrast to RNNs, attempts to provide long short-term memories. The LSTM approach is a good fit for a large array of time-series-based problems, including SA problems—i.e. the LSTM approach remembers the earlier history of information in order to predict/evaluate future words in a sequence of words.

LSTM is similar to RNN in terms of its repetitive nature in the functions used in the architecture. However, the major difference between them lies in the interacting layers of the architecture. The functions of LSTM are represented as states which can be controlled by multipoint gate structures. As a result, LSTM offers a reasonably good learning process during the modeling stage (figure 6.8).

6.6 Metrics

SA relates to traditional classification problems in which the broader classes of sentiments are identified in sentences, documents, voice, or video data. The most crucial metrics that apply to SA-based problems are as follows:

1. Precision—in the majority of SA problems, especially on social sites, terms such as positive, negative, neutral, and mixed sentiments are frequently identified. Keywords such as 'amazing, love, best' observed in texts or documents are some examples of positive sentiments; words such as 'not, blurry, awkward' relate to negative sentiments; a few words do not suggest whether they express positive or negative tones, and texts such as 'why is it so hard to understand?' relate to mixed sentiments. The term 'precision' also

means 'accuracy'. It defines the correctness in predicting the texts to be either positive or negative sentiments. It is a known fact that sentiments are not always predicted in accordance with the accurate sentiments. Hence, baseline predictions are made to ensure normality in predictions.

In practice, baseline predictions are obtained for SA by evaluating the positive and negative sentiments for a specified number of documents. For instance, if around 1000 documents are to be used for analyzing sentiments, 50 percent of the documents are used for training and 50 percent for testing the sentiments. If around 90 percent of the predicted positive or negative sentiments are obtained, then the baseline predictions for the specific context are declared to be 90 percent.

The mathematical representation of the precision is as follows:

```
Precision = True Positives / (True Positives + False Positives)
```

2. Recall—the recall measure of SA relates to the number of sentiments identified in the selected documents. In some text documents or videos, SA algorithms are unable to classify the sentiments as either positive or negative. This is because the sentiments are merged with complex sentence structures and word combinations in the texts. The recall measure represents the efficiency of the SA algorithm and the challenges of the texts.

The mathematical representation of the recall measure is as follows:

```
Recall = True Positives / (True Positives + False Negatives)
```

3. F score—this measure, which is also called the F1 score, is a combination of precision and recall. It is the harmonic mean of both the precision and recall represented using values from 0.0 to 1.0. SA that achieves an F score of 1.0 offers the best value in predicting sentiments from texts/documents.

The mathematical representation of the F score measure is as follows:

```
F-Score = ((Precision * Recall) *2) / (Precision + Recall)
```

6.7 Tools and frameworks

Although the theoretical aspects of SA were discussed earlier, it is important to understand the existing tools and frameworks that promote SA in various flavors.

6.7.1 The necessity for sentiment analysis tools and frameworks

The key reasons to use tools to pursue SA are listed below:

1. Tools enable us to automate or simplify the processes when certain integrations are required. For instance, if any opinion needs to be collected from different authors of books, the tools could do this in addition to performing the required SA.
2. Tools can customize operations so that they are more tailored to the needs of the user, which bare implementations can hardly offer.
3. Tools can be connected to a few other services, typically cloud services such as storage services or scaling services, to improve the performance of analysis-based implementations.

Some well-known SA tools that are found in the market (see figure 6.9) and their key functionalities are discussed in the following subsections.

6.7.2 HubSpot tool

The HubSpot tool is a service-based SA tool that collects customer feedback and can qualitatively evaluate feedback surveys. Typically, customers provide feedback including positive and negative contents. The HubSpot service-based tool applies SA algorithms to obtain the numbers of positives and negatives in order to assess the value of the product.

This tool has the ability to utilize third-party survey systems, such as NPS surveys, to provide a mass-level review mechanism. It enables the owners of the products to view the comments pictorially using a scorecard representation on a dashboard. It also offers the user a bird's eye view of all feedback with an option to zoom in on individual customer feedback.

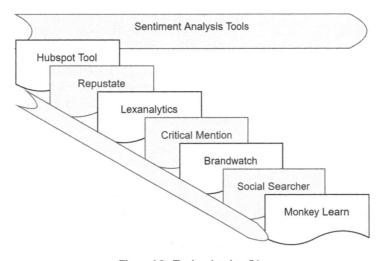

Figure 6.9. Tools related to SA.

6.7.3 Repustate sentiment analyzer

Repustate [4] is an SA tool utilized to assess feedback submitted by customers. This tool is operated by Repustate Inc. It has support for over 23 languages across the globe. The tool mainly focuses on textual analysis of customer responses. Additionally, the tool has the ability to assess the emojis used in customer feedback messages. Many of the users of Repustate find the tool convenient, as the tool helps the user to customize its API in a way that is specific to their requirements or decisions. In short, the tool offers control over utilizing SA for customer feedback purposes.

6.7.4 Lexanalytics

The Lexanalytics tool [2] is developed by the Lexanalytics company. The major focus of this tool is to provide bare text analysis that can be applied for business purposes. Its development approach is not only limited to customers for product developments but can also be used for more generic applications of SA. The tool has a focused agenda of extracting (i) intents, (ii) positive/negative opinions, (iii) named entities, and so forth.

6.7.5 Critical Mention

Critical Mention is designed to perform SA that focuses on media-related monitoring and reviewing support. The tool is developed to pursue SA in three major directions: social monitoring, media monitoring, and online news monitoring. The tool has APIs that help its users to plug in their services to get a broader viewpoint of the utility of media comments and messages. It can analyze daily news and other articles in business reviews, which seem to be useful for several enterprises. Extracting sentiments from current news and assessing current affairs or communal issues are considered to be crucial aspects of this tool.

6.7.6 Brandwatch

Brandwatch [1], a commercial product that performs SA, is mainly focused on providing insights into products. This tool lets companies connect products to their SA services. The key outcomes of this tool are services such as getting an opinion from Forrester Wave, aggregating followers, observing the latest activities of the followers, and filtering customer opinions.

6.7.7 Social Searcher

Social Searcher [5] is a tool that applies SA and text analysis performed by deep learning platforms based on keywords, hashtags, or usernames. It has a search panel similar to that provided by any search engine, such as Google, Bing, and so forth. However, the main focus of the search is to provide results based on the current trends analyzed from tens of thousands of web pages across the globe. The tool focuses on mentions, names, and trends while searching for an appropriate analysis.

6.7.8 MonkeyLearn

MonkeyLearn [3], which is very popular for collecting and assessing feedback, has enormous support for SA. To effectively utilize this tool, the user has to provide a few categorization tags and suggest some important parts of the text. Once the user has manually provided this information, the tool can simultaneously surf tens of thousands of files and provide a pictorial representation of the contents. In addition, it offers the 'Word Cloud' tool to project the major causes of certain keywords from the findings.

6.8 Sentiment analysis—sarcasm detection

SA can be applied for several applications related to financial information, customer satisfaction, media analysis, newspaper analysis, trending post analysis, and so forth. In the previous sections, a movie recommendation system was discussed. In this section, we present an application of SA used to detect sarcasm.

In general, sarcasm detection is a subdivision of NLP [9]. Sarcasm is a linguistic approach to expressing the context of a scenario oppositely. It is often used in any language to mock the activities of the actors discussed in sentences. In various texts extracted from movie reviews, Twitter comments, or customer opinions, sarcastic content is observed when people have the intention to express certain things in a positive manner which conveys a negative message about them.

6.8.1 News headline data set

In this section, a data set that contains sarcasm information from news headlines is utilized to demonstrate the important code snippets that become part of the learning process. The data set is represented in JSON file format with three attributes in each row:
1. the web address of the article;
2. news headline information, represented as a string; and,
3. a label indicating whether the string contains sarcastic information or not.

A sample record of the data set of the file named 'Sarcasm_Headlines_Dataset. json' is shown below:

```
"root":3 items
"article_link":string" :string"https://www.huffingtonpost.com
/entry/versace-black-code_us_5861fbefe4b0de3a08f600d5"
"headline":string"former versace store
clerk sues over secret black code for minority shoppers"
"is_sarcastic":int0
}
```

6.8.2 Data processing using TensorFlow

As discussed earlier, SA consists of a few stages, such as tokenization, preprocessing words, stemming, padding, and/or corpus formation, followed by data modeling. The most important code features that target these different SA stages are described below:

Tokenization

The tokenization process for sarcasm detection using TensorFlow is based on a few packages imported from TensorFlow and Keras. For instance, the Tokenizer package contains sufficient code to handle the tokenization process of the sarcasm detection task.

The code snippets used to perform tokenization in the SA code are as follows:

```
import tensorflow as tf
from tensorflow.keras.preprocessing.text import Tokenizer
```

It is also important to specify the number of embeddings when tokenizing texts from data sets; also, the out-of-vocabulary tokens required to process the tokenization need to be specified in the code snippet, as follows:

```
tokenizer = Tokenizer(num_words=vocab_size, oov_token="<OOV>")
tokenizer.fit_on_texts(X_train)
word_index = tokenizer.word_index
```

Here, tokens returns a `word_index`, which maps words to the `vocab_size`. It is important to observe that `word_index` is utilized to find the length of the word vector of the data set.

Preprocessing, stemming, padding, and corpus formation

The preprocessing stage of SA only happens after the tokenization of the data. The tokenization operations are carried out by the tokenizer.

In addition, padding is performed in the code to ensure that the data set has the required shape and size. Typically, the data set will not have a suitable computational size, which undermines the performance of the learning processes. When padding is used, additional zeros are added to the input of the learning model so that the data set has a consistent size and shape.

6.8.3 Training using neural networks

Training using neural networks or based on neural networks can be implemented using the TensorFlow library and its associated packages. The keras high-level API of the TensorFlow library can be utilized to perform sarcasm detection in the news headline data set. The `keras` API has methods that embed words, create hidden layers for learning purposes, map the learning inferences to one dense layer, and perform activations such as RELU, sigmoid, etc.

The implementation of `keras` in the form of a `Sequential` pattern enables one tensor input and one tensor output with the required activations during the learning processes.

The most significant code portions of the training model creation stage are:

- layering
- compiling
- fitting

Code snippets that can be utilized to create hidden layers and activation functions based on the input data sets used for sarcasm detection are given below:

```
model = tf.keras.Sequential([
  tf.keras.layers.Embedding(vocab_size,  embedding_dim,
input_length =max_length),
 tf.keras.layers.GlobalAveragePooling1D(),
 tf.keras.layers.Dense(24, activation='relu'),
 tf.keras.layers.Dense(1, activation='sigmoid')
 ])
```

After layering is complete, compilation is applied to determine the optimizers, loss functions, and metrics, such as accuracy units for the neural network. Code snippets that represent the compilation stage of the sarcasm detection approach are given below:

```
model.compile(loss='binary_crossentropy',optimizer='adam',
 metrics=['accuracy'])
```

Finally, a fitting process is carried out based on number of iterations needed to learn the training data set, as follows:

```
history=model.fit(training_padded,training_labels,epochs=30,
validation_data=(testing_padded, testing_labels),verbose=2)
```

6.8.4 Training using long short-term memory

Applying LSTM is typically the right choice for SA-related applications, including the sarcasm detection algorithms. The initial stages used before the learning model is applied, such as tokenization, preprocessing, stemming, and corpus formation, remain the same and are similar to the previous code snippets. However, in order to include LSTM-based learning processes, it is necessary to use different layer formation and compilation stages in LSTM models.

In particular, in LSTM, hidden layers relating to LSTM need to be fed into the model definition phase—i.e. after the embedding process and before the dense layers of the model. Code snippets which describe the LSTM model definition for the sarcasm detection problem are given below:

```
model = tf.keras.Sequential([
  tf.keras.layers.Embedding(vocab_size, embedding_dim,
  input_length = max_length),
  tf.keras.layers.Bidirectional(tf.keras.layers.LSTM(32)),
  tf.keras.layers.Dense(24, activation='relu'),
  tf.keras.layers.Dense(1, activation='sigmoid')
])
```

As previously mentioned, after model definition, the model needs to be compiled using the relevant optimizer and metric specifications before it can be fitted with sufficient iterations of the learning processes. The code snippets for these stages are as follows:

```
model.compile(loss='binary_crossentropy',optimizer='adam',
metrics=['accuracy'])
history = model.fit(training_padded, training_labels, epochs=30,
validation_data=(testing_padded, testing_labels), verbose=2)
```

References

[1] Brandwatch tool, May 2022 Page Version ID: 1088786364
[2] Lexanalytics tool, May 2022 Page Version ID: 1088786364
[3] Monkeylearn tool, May 2022 Page Version ID: 1088786364
[4] Repustate tool, May 2022 Page Version ID: 1088786364
[5] Social searcher tool, May 2022 Page Version ID: 1088786364
[6] Al-Hashedi A, Al-fuhaidi B A, Mohsen A M, Ali Y, Al-Kaf H A G, Al-Sorori W and Maqtary N 2022 Ensemble classifiers for Arabic sentiment analysis of social network (Twitter data) towards COVID-19-related conspiracy theories *Appl. Comput. Intell. Soft Comput.* **2022** 6614730
[7] An H 2022 Design of recommendation system for tourist spot using sentiment analysis based on CNN-LSTM *J. Ambient Intell. Humaniz. Comput.* **13** 1653–63
[8] Chandrasekaran G and Hemanth J 2022 Deep learning and TextBlob based sentiment analysis for coronavirus (COVID-19) using Twitter data *Int. J. Artif. Intell. Tools* **31** 2250011
[9] Chen W-Q, Lin F, Zhang X, Li G and Liu B 2022 Jointly learning sentimental clues and context incongruity for sarcasm detection *IEEE Access* **10** 48292–300

[10] Hossain A, Karimuzzaman M, Hossain M M and Rahman A 2021 Text mining and sentiment analysis of newspaper headlines *Information* **12** 414

[11] Hu S, Kumar A, Al-Turjman F, Gupta S, Seth S and Shubham 2020 Reviewer credibility and sentiment analysis based user profile modelling for online product recommendation *IEEE Access* **8** 26172–89

[12] Huang F, Yuan C-a, Bi Y, Lu J, Lu L and Wang X 2022 Multi-granular document-level sentiment topic analysis for online reviews *Appl. Intell.* **52** 7723–33

[13] Kumar S, De K and Roy P P 2020 Movie recommendation system using sentiment analysis from microblogging data *IEEE Trans. Comput. Soc. Syst.* **7** 915–23

[14] Liu B 2010 *Sentiment analysis and subjectivity Handbook of Natural Language Processing* ed N Indurkhya and F J Damerau 2nd edn (London: Chapman and Hall/CRC)) pp 627–66

[15] Liu Y, Xiao L, Huang Y-C, Xue Y, Hu X, Zhao H and Li Y 2022 Aspect-level sentiment analysis with local semantic and global syntactic features integration *Artif. Intell.* **36** 2250013

[16] Nassif A B, Darya A M and Elnagar A 2022 Empirical evaluation of shallow and deep learning classifiers for Arabic sentiment analysis *ACM Trans. Asian Low Resour. Lang. Inf. Process.* **21** 14

[17] Onan A 2021 Sentiment analysis on massive open online course evaluations: a text mining and deep learning approach *Comput. Appl. Eng. Educ.* **29** 572–89

[18] Rahman R U and Tomar D S 2020 A new web forensic framework for bot crime investigation *Digit. Investig.* **33** 300943

[19] Rodrigues A P and Chiplunkar N N 2022 A new big data approach for topic classification and sentiment analysis of twitter data *Evol. Intell.* **15** 877–87

[20] Gunawan R, Rahmatulloh A, Darmawan I and Firdaus F 2019 Comparison of Web Scraping Techniques : Regular Expression, HTML DOM and Xpath *2018 Int. Conf. on Industrial Enterprise and System Engineering (IcoIESE 2018)* **2** 283–7

[21] Shayegan M J and Molanorouzi M 2021 A lexicon weighted sentiment analysis approach on Twitter *Int. J. Web Based Communities* **17** 149–62

[22] Suchacka G and Iwanski J 2020 Identifying legitimate web users and bots with different traffic profiles–an information bottleneck approach *Knowl. Based Syst.* **197** 105875

[23] Sweidan A H, El-Bendary N and Al-Feel H 2021 Sentence-level aspect-based sentiment analysis for classifying adverse drug reactions (ADRS) using hybrid ontology-XLNet transfer learning *IEEE Access* **9** 90828–46

[24] Uzun E 2020 A novel web scraping approach using the additional information obtained from web pages *IEEE Access* **8** 61726–40

Chapter 7

Autoencoders and variational autoencoders

Autoencoding is a deep learning technique that applies data encoding methods to convert higher-dimensional data/images into lower-dimensional data/images in a compressed form. This technique has become quite popular in image-related applications in which the compression techniques and reduced representations are important. This chapter discusses the inherent modules of autoencoders and the wide variety of applications in this field of research.

7.1 Introduction—autoencoders

Autoencoders represent the input data by vector-based encodings of the dimensions of its learned attributes. Conversely, decoders attempt to reconstruct images/data based on the encodings [12].

Image compression is appreciated in applications in which images need to be transported from one location to another. Alternatively, it is considered to be the principal approach to holding data in resource-constrained storage devices. Image compression is traditionally practiced using lossy or lossless compression techniques— i.e. lossless compression techniques ensure that compressed images can be retrieved to their original state without deterioration, whereas lossy compression techniques increase the compression ratio by reducing the quality of the retrieved images.

In general, the transportation of medical images, smart city surveillance images, or industrial footage requires sufficient image compression in order to store and analyze them. For instance, computer vision tasks such as identifying the objects in images need compression methods in order to perform the learning process. In deep learning, image compression appears in the form of reducing the number of pixels, and it attempts to reduce the number of dimensions used to represent data.

In the machine learning domain, autoencoding is a technique that attempts to learn a procedure that can be used to compress data, particularly images. For instance, the compression level of data and the retrieval process used for the images/ data are learned by autoencoders when they encode images.

Autoencoders are considered to be unsupervised learning mechanisms [1] that are built using artificial neural networks. The autoencoding technique attempts to reduce the input data size or the dimensions of the data by adopting certain learning mechanisms. It is a technique that deals with lower-level representations of higher-level data using encoding options [11]. Obviously, this technique reduces the noise contained in the data. This technique is utilized in image processing applications to examine the noise contained in images and automatically denoise them by applying specific algorithmic procedures.

7.1.1 Advantages of compression

The advantages of applying compression techniques to input data (images, files, or videos) using autoencoders are multifold:

1. Reduction in file size—most real-world applications need to reduce file sizes for storage or communication purposes. For instance, an Internet of things (IoT) application may have to transfer images to fog or cloud nodes. Transferring data from sensor nodes to clouds across the network would increase the network bandwidth. This could be avoided by the use of autoencoders.

2. De-noising—learning the noise patterns contained in data improves the quality of images or applications. Applications often struggle to infer the right information from data sources when the data is transported over bandwidth-constrained networks or failing networking sites. Adopting appropriate compression techniques by removing the noise patterns improves the quality of learning techniques.

3. Reduced training—by reducing the dimensionality of images or input data using compression techniques, autoencoders are able to reduce the training time required for a given set of input files.

7.1.2 Unsupervised learning

Autoencoders perform unsupervised learning of representations from the input data. In general, unsupervised learning is considered to be a type of learning process in the machine learning (ML) domain. The unsupervised learning process does not need a labeled training dataset; the data are trained on the available information without the use of a pre-labeling processes. This method provides enough new insights into the information (figure 7.1).

The major advantages of using unsupervised learning in autoencoder techniques are given below:

1. Reduced manual work—labeling images or input data is a tedious and laborious process. In supervised learning, it is mandatory to have labels or trained solutions. Labels can also easily cause erroneous predictions if the labels are wrongly applied before the learning process takes place.

2. Flexible training samples—autoencoders are able to append or add training samples at any stage of the learning processes. As a result of their unsupervised

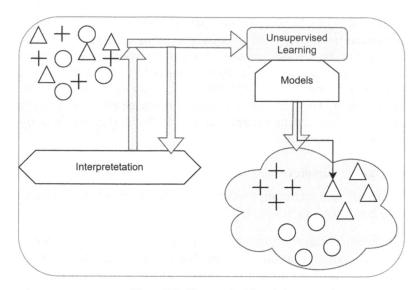

Figure 7.1. Unsupervised learning.

learning mechanism, the training module adapts to the incoming training samples, which gives more flexibility to the learning procedure.

3. Flexible data formats—due to their unsupervised learning capabilities, autoencoders can support any raw data format, such as text, video, audio, and so forth. Consequently, this technique offers higher flexibility in handling data formats.

7.1.3 Principal component analysis versus autoencoders

There is a similarity between principal component analysis (PCA) and autoencoding —i.e. they both attempt to reduce the data dimensionality. Additionally, these two techniques have the ability to learn nonlinear data features.

However, there are a few differences between them. In general, PCA spots potential components of the input images/data with acceptable variations based on features. Once these components are categorized (such that about 80–90 percent of the information can be decoded from the reduced data), the relevant principal components are conserved for encoding purposes. PCA encounters challenges in dealing with higher dimensions of the input data. It has been reported in several forums that the accuracy of autoencoders is comparatively higher than the accuracy of the results obtained using PCA implementations. Accordingly, researchers and practitioners have demonstrated more deep learning architectures using autoencoders than PCA approaches. Autoencoders, by contrast, are based on neural networks, in which layers of networks can robustly or flexibly handle the structures of the input data. In doing so, autoencoders are fundamentally able to withstand a large number of dimensions during the compression process.

The autoencoder technique is useful in deeply layered architectures, especially when algorithms such as restricted Boltzmann machines are considered. This technique has contributed much to completing the final fine-tuning or shaping processes in the final layers of deep learning architectures.

7.1.4 Autoencoders—transfer learning

Transfer learning mechanisms benefit greatly from the autoencoding approach. In general, transfer learning endeavors to fine-tune the existing findings of a problem domain related to an underlying problem [3]. The tuning of the the learning inferences formulated in a specified problem domain can be revised based on other subdomains or problem spaces.

There are two major advantages of the transfer learning concept:

1. The subdomains do not require large quantities of learning time and space. Energy-conscious subdomains, such as IoT-enabled sensor nodes, may typically have to learn from the inferences of their vicinities; and,
2. The sensitivity of information belonging to a specific target or subdomain can be preserved.

Transfer learning has turned into an important step in training deep learning applications. This is the case because incremental learning processes are feasible, given the inherent nature of the transfer learning process.

As knowledge is transferred from one domain to the other, deep learning architectures have a reduced requirement to use computation. Therefore, the energy consumption of these computing machines is reduced. Reducing the energy consumption of computing architectures such as central processing units (CPUs), graphics processing units (GPUs), or tensor processing unit (TPUs), has an indirect impact on environmental hazards. For instance, powering on a CPU/GPU machine can heat up computational nodes, increasing the need for cooling mechanisms. The most commonly used cooling mechanisms in supercomputing or computing centers, namely, air-cooling mechanisms, create CO_2 emissions. These activities damage the natural environment, leading to hazards.

7.1.5 Autoencoders versus traditional compression

Traditional compression techniques, such as Joint Photographic Experts Group (JPEG) compression, Moving Picture Experts Group (MPEG) compression, MP3, and so forth pretend to have the same kind of purpose: compression. However, there are a few notable differences which support the use of autoencoders for deep learning approaches—i.e. the compression produced by autoencoders is different from those produced by traditional compression algorithms such as MP3 or JPEG.

JPEG, MPEG, MP3, and so forth are popular lossy compression techniques for images, video, or audio files. These compression techniques focus on compressing only specific data types, such as audio, video, or images. Autoencoders, by contrast, reduce the dimensions of data or compress data with more emphasis on specified domains. For example, autoencoders trained to reduce the dimensions of plant-related images could be different from autoencoders trained for animal-related images. This means that autoencoders have more flexibility to handle the subtypes of different data formats.

7.2 Autoencoder architectures

The architecture of an autoencoder consists of three major parts. The functionalities of these parts are given below:

1. Encoder—the encoder attempts to compress an image into a smaller amount of information; in neural network terms, an encoder is a representation of the input data that reduces its data dimensions to smaller ones. For instance, an encoder can encode input data that has a size of 24 x 24 pixels to far less than 576 pixels in the intermediate layers. To do so, the encoder should be much more efficient at adopting measures to reduce the dimensions that fit the latent representational space in the code portion of the architecture.

   In general, encoders establish blocks of convolutional layers along with the required pooling layers in order to perform the transformation efficiently.

2. Code—this part of the network provides input to the decoder; this portion of the architecture is also called a bottleneck. This portion of the architecture elegantly decides which portion of the input data needs to be removed to increase the compression ratio of the system while maintaining the accuracy of the output data. The code portion of the architecture has comparatively fewer parts than the other portions.

3. Decoder—the decoder is the lossy reconstruction part of the architecture that restores the data to its normal input dimensions. The decoder is another part of the neural network that attempts to reconstruct a model with a limited data representation to a higher data representation. It uses weights and biases to reconstruct images across layers. For instance, the decoder may have to increase an image that has 256 pixels to the required 576 pixels of an input image. Obviously, a lossy compression method is used in the decoder part of the architecture.

The architecture is designed such that the input and output dimensions remain the same. However, the dimensions of the inner layers of the architecture are minimized to increase the compression levels of the input images.

7.2.1 Training phase

The training phase of autoencoders uses a code size parameter. The code size determines the number of nodes in the hidden layer of an autoencoder. This parameter is considered to be a crucial one, as it determines the level of compression in the training phase. Reducing the code size parameter can result in a higher compression rate—i.e. the conversion from higher-dimensional data to lower-dimensional data is greater.

Additionally, during the training phase of the autoencoder, the number of hidden layers defines the depth of the learning. Greater depth in an autoencoder can increase the complexity involved in solving applications; in contrast, reducing the depth of the layers in an autoencoder provides only a limited compression intensity. However, by reducing the number of layers in autoencoders, the computation time of applications can be drastically decreased.

Each hidden layer can involve several nodes used to process the compression. The process used to define weights is dependent on the number of nodes per layer.

7.2.2 Loss functions

The loss function of the autoencoder architecture defines the amount of loss that occurs in the learning processes. It consists of two major components:

1. Reconstruction loss—this is a loss that describes the estimation failures caused by the layers in the learning system. The majority of the reconstruction loss is dependent on the decoder part of the architecture and the data format used for the algorithm. For instance, if the autoencoder needs to process image-based input data, the reconstruction function may utilize the mean squared error (MSE) loss parameter, which defines the mean square error of the model. It defines the deviation of a predicted value from the original value for a given set of hyperparameters used by a model.
2. Divergence/regularizer loss—this is a loss function that defines the closeness of the predictions to reality. The regularizer loss function is a good fit if the data is converted to lie within the range from zero to one, as opposed to images or data formats.

7.3 Types of autoencoder

Autoencoders have been widely utilized in several applications in recent years. Applications such as image de-noising, image compression, inpainting, and so forth, have typically involved major modifications to the general autoencoder architecture.

Based on their functionalities and application domains, autoencoders are classified into the following types:

- Convolutional autoencoders
- Sparse autoencoders
- Deep autoencoders
- Contractive autoencoders
- De-noising autoencoders
- Undercomplete autoencoders
- Variational autoencoders

7.3.1 Convolutional autoencoders

Convolutional autoencoders apply convolutional layers to encode input images or text data. The encodings are utilized to reconstruct images using the reverse convolutional operations by the decoder part of the autoencoder.

While applying convolutional layers in the encoder or decoder components of architectures, convolutional autoencoders endeavor to improve the quality of reconstructions and can attempt to modify the shapes/sizes of the input images or data.

Convolutional autoencoders generally apply three layers in their encoders and decoders. This approach is considered a naive approach to applying the encoding and decoding processes of a generic autoencoder architecture.

7.3.2 Sparse autoencoders

Sparse autoencoders form a specialized group of autoencoders in which the number of nodes in the middle layers is not reduced, as it is for convolutional autoencoders [5]. However, the weights and loss functions of the hidden layers are defined such that the reconstruction of images is elegantly defined—i.e. only a few neurons are involved in the learning processes of the intermediate layers of the autoencoders.

In sparse autoencoders, the number of hidden layers is typically higher than in convolutional autoencoders. However, these hidden layers are fewer than those of the deep autoencoder architectures. This architecture is designed to solve the overfitting problem caused by hidden layers. This is achieved by utilizing sparsity between the encoder and decoder layers.

7.3.3 Deep autoencoders

Deep autoencoders are extended versions of convolutional autoencoders. However, these encoders use greater numbers of hidden layers to pursue a deep learning process. The greater numbers of hidden layers enable deep autoencoders to infer more information from the data. Each hidden layer can be responsible for learning specific features from the data. Consequently, it is possible to comprehensively learn the detailed information contained in the images/data.

Deep autoencoders typically have more than four hidden layers [7] to encode the data features of the input dataset and more than four hidden layers to decode the encodings. Obviously, deep autoencoders are often used to increase the accuracy of image reconstruction by compensating for the underlying computational costs or the execution time of the computation.

7.3.4 Contractive autoencoders

Contractive autoencoders do not compensate for noise—i.e. any small noise components contained in the input data are not digested by the autoencoder while learning the data. To do so, contractive autoencoders attempt to include penalty components in the encoding and decoding processes. When this approach is used, a small variation that occurs during the input representation process is flagged to the higher layers of the architecture. This is a type of regularizing technique that is used to improve the image or input data components. For instance, a poor-quality picture can be regenerated by filtering its noise and losses.

7.3.5 Denoising autoencoders

De-noising autoencoders are typically variations of generic autoencoders, such as convolutional autoencoders. These autoencoders consist of encoders and decoders that represent data in a similar way to other autoencoders. In de-noising autoencoders, the input image has noise added to overcome the over-fitting problems that occur in several other autoencoder architectures. The authors of [6] studied the use of de-noising autoencoders for surface detection problems.

By introducing noise content into the input data, de-noising autoencoders attempt to reconstruct the original image by mapping the features extracted from images. This autoencoder develops a robust mechanism for the reconstruction of input images by creating a strong encoding scheme at the encoder. The algorithm is quite often applied to improve the quality of images.

7.3.6 Undercomplete autoencoders

Undercomplete autoencoders are designed to capture maximum number of features from the input datasets. These autoencoders have considerably smaller numbers of hidden layers in both the encoding and decoding parts of the autoencoder architecture. However, the architecture attempts to capture the input features by increasing the penalties for learning the representations.

Obviously, this architecture could be a potential candidate for overfitting cases due to its approach to handling data representations. This architecture generally tries to produce the same input image at the output layers while focusing on extracting the features of input datasets.

7.3.7 Variational autoencoders

The last type of autoencoder considered is the variational autoencoder. In most of the previously described autoencoders, the attributes of the input data/images are encoded into a specific value that is registered in vectors. These vectors are utilized to reconstruct images during the reconstruction phase, i.e. the decoding process of the architecture.

In variational autoencoders, however, the latent representations of input data formulated in the encoders are not represented as evaluated values [9]. Instead, these values evolve from the outcome of probability distributions.

In this approach, the latent representations of input images are continuous, so that the decoders of the architectures can pick any random value which falls within the scope of the probability distribution to represent the output image. In this way, the architecture prevents overfitting problems and improves the various features of input images. Figure 7.2 showcases the autoencoders that have been utilized by researchers or practitioners in the past.

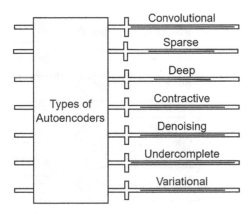

Figure 7.2. Different types of autoencoder.

A detailed description of variational autoencoders is given in a later section of this chapter.

7.4 Applications of autoencoders

There are several applications for autoencoders in social-good applications, such as water quality analysis, air pollution control analysis, forest fire predictions, face variation analysis, and so forth (see figure 7.3).

The key fields in which autoencoders have been applied in the past are described below:

7.4.1 Image reconstruction

Autoencoders are applied to reconstruct images that have missing information. In several applications, especially forensic applications, images are only partially collected, as some pieces of images are lost for various reasons. These partial images can be reconstructed using autoencoders.

The most commonly found applications are listed below:

1. In tourism, images need to be reconstructed with timelines. For instance, images without trees could be reconstructed with trees to represent previous situations.
2. Similarly, images of vanishing rivers can be modified to show sufficient water in the rivers. This is a common problem in several cities and urban areas where the water levels in rivers have diminished in the recent past. Using reconstruction approaches, people can view historical locations again in a way that agrees with their old memories.
3. Image reconstruction also paves the way to removing any unnecessary problems from input images. For instance, it is possible to remove an obstacle found in a rare image of a monograph that cannot be recreated in the normal way.

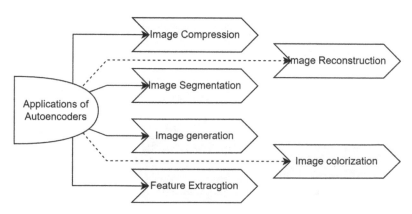

Figure 7.3. Applications of autoencoders.

Image inpainting is a technique that falls under this image reconstruction category [10]. In the image inpainting method, the lost portions of images are reconstructed by collecting features from the latent space of the images. The image inpainting approach is becoming quite popular in digital image artwork systems, as there are several fields in which reconstruction would be very useful for the users.

7.4.2 Image colorization

Image colorization is an application that improves the color spaces of images [8]. The common colors, namely, red, blue, and green (RGB) are typically mixed to form various color combinations. However, the colors can be lost by the color spaces used in some images. These lost spaces can be be recovered to reconstruct images with the maximum quality. The application of autoencoders supports such enhancements of image color quality.

In addition, old gray-colored images can be colorized with red and blue combinations to create a lively feeling using autoencoders. The layers of autoencoders extract the latent space representation of colors from images. The combination of an encoder and a decoder can colorize images with specified colors, as seen in modern pictures. Autoencoders can colorize objects in images as well. Using these applications, mountains and sky, for example, identified in images can be colorized brown and blue, respectively, by autoencoders.

7.4.3 High-resolution image generation

Many travelers and hobbyists wish to create high-resolution images from old pictures or poor camera-captured images. Autoencoders can increase image resolution after images have been learned by the encoder stage of the architecture. For instance, the authors of [4] developed a color image generation mechanism using autoencoders. In modern systems, a predefined image resolution is required.

7.4.4 Recommendation systems via feature extraction

In most cases, autoencoders are applied for image processing applications and compression improvement systems. Apart from traditional applications, these deep learning architectures can also be applied for recommendation systems that involve comments or texts. For instance, autoencoders can be applied to extract data features from web-crawled review comments so that the inherent preferences of the users or customers can be observed. Autoencoders, therefore, are candidate deep learning platforms for several recommendation systems, including movie recommendation and university recommendation systems.

7.4.5 Image compression

One of the most important applications of autoencoders is to reduce the dimensionality of input data—i.e. to perform image compression. By reducing the dimensionality of images, the hidden layers of autoencoders are able to collect the inner features of images. if the number of hidden layers is increased, the number of dimensions can considerably reduced compared to those of the input image. Thus, autoencoders are very well suited for image compression-related applications, even though they were intended for image processing and learning purposes.

7.4.6 Image segmentation

Image segmentation is also possible using autoencoders. Image segmentation is the process of segmenting objects to quickly identify them and perform some decision-related processing. For instance, in a smart transportation system, image segmentation can be applied to collect the features of roads or traffic scenes. In this way, automated cars could be realized with minimal computational effort by smaller devices.

7.5 Variational autoencoders

Variational autoencoders follow the same principle as autoencoders, i.e. the input images undergo feature extraction in order to reduce the high-dimensional images to low-dimensional ones.

7.5.1 Variational autoencoder vectors

However, the encoders of variational autoencoders use two vectors, as described below:

1. Mean vector—this vector collects the mean data from the conversion space of the encoder or decoder.
2. Standard deviation vector—this vector collects the standard deviation data values from the conversion space of the autoencoder components.

7.5.2 Variational autoencoder loss functions

Similarly to autoencoders, variational autoencoders also include reconstruction loss factors when they capture the learning losses. However, in the variational autoencoder approach, the major objective is to stay closer to the reconstructions of the original images. Hence, the loss function includes these two terms, which are used to perform the mathematical operations.

Variational autoencoders do not feed the vectors directly to the decoders. Instead, they collect the sampled values from a distribution of values. In this way, the complexity involved in the encoding processes is minimized. However, this creates a huge risk to the process of obtaining the most equivalent or expected results.

7.5.3 A pictorial way of understanding the variational autoencoder

As shown in figure 7.4, an image consisting of several objects is captured and its latent feature sets are observed by a variational encoder. For instance, an image consisting of mountains, the Sun, a river, and so forth processed by a variational encoder architecture undergoes the following:

1. initially, the image is collected and the corresponding features of the latent space are observed;

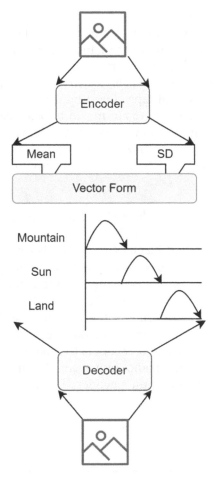

Figure 7.4. Variational autoencoder—understanding the features.

2. the feature values are represented as mean values;
3. the standard deviation vectors from the image data are also collected in another vector;
4. the image features are then represented in the form of probability distributions, as shown in figure 7.4;
5. the decoder is then allowed to choose values taken from the broad values of the probability distributions by samplers;
6. finally, the decoder reconstructs the image using the sampled values.

7.5.4 Variational autoencoder—use cases

Variational autoencoders are widely applied to automatically regenerate images or datasets. The most commonly applied applications that regenerate images or datasets using latent space exploration are described below:

7.5.4.1 Number construction

Given some sets of numbers input from handwritten documents, variational autoencoders can be used to capture the handwritten numbers and thereby create similar machine-fed handwritten numbers.

In variational autoencoders, the handwritten features of numeric number representations are observed and reproduced by robots in a similar way to human writing. Variational autoencoders are not meant to produce the exact images found in the input datasets; rather, they attempt to deliver slightly variable ones. Obviously, handwritten numbers vary in any normal situation. Hence, variational autoencoders are found to be the best fit for such situations.

7.5.4.2 Music generation

Musical notes typically have well-defined latent spaces [2]. Consider a 4/4 rhythm played on a piano. Players express specific pauses. After each pause, it is possible to play slightly varying music that blends with the earlier music.

Variational autoencoders could be applied in music generation systems that identify the latent spaces before introducing variations into the next set of musical bars. The upcoming music bar could be selected from a wider probability distribution by a sampler. Accordingly, the resulting music would have different musical notes without too much variation from the previous musical notes. A few authors have applied variational autoencoders to generate piano music by capturing the latent features from input piano sequences. Figure 7.5 describes a robotic architecture that uses variational autoencoders to generate piano music or handwritten numbers.

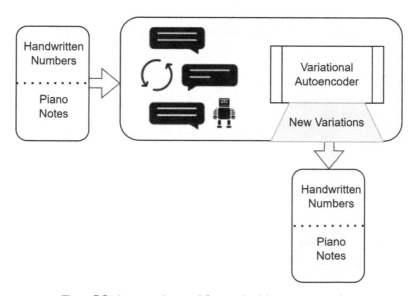

Figure 7.5. Autoencoders used for number/piano reconstruction.

The principle of learning the latent spaces and applying variational autoencoders to generate music is not limited to the piano; it can also be used to generate drum beats for different beats such as 4/4, 2/4, 7/8, and so forth.

7.6 Autoencoder implementation—code snippet explanation

The TensorFlow library can be utilized to create autoencoders. The Keras packages are most commonly utilized by this library. This section explains the bare minimum implementation of an autoencoder intended to create numbers from handwritten number datasets.

The major steps involved in implementing autoencoders using Tensorflow libraries are shown in figure 7.6. Additionally, the code snippets utilized in the implementation stages are described as follows:

7.6.1 Importing packages

To enable an autoencoder, we need to import the relevant packages for the TensorFlow libraries. A code snippet that demonstrates the process of importing software components is given below:

```
import tensorflow as tf
import keras
from keras import layers
```

7.6.2 Initialization

The next step is to initialize the variables and datasets required to enable autoencoders for computing components. The computing components can be

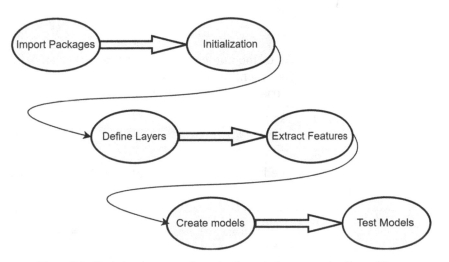

Figure 7.6. Variational autoencoders—implementation steps using TensorFlow.

GPUs or CPUs. As is understandable, GPU-based computations take less time than CPU-based computations because of the huge parallelism of GPUs—i.e. array-based matrix operations are faster when performed by GPUs. A code snippet that describes how to input images and parse the shape features is provided below:

```
dimension = 32
image = keras.Input(shape=(982,))
```

Here, 'dimension' represents the compression requirement for the input images.

7.6.3 Layer definition

The layers are now defined such that encoding and decoding processes are activated, as shown below:

```
# definition for encoder
encoder = layers.Dense(dimension, activation='relu')(input=
image)
# definition for decoder
decoder = layers.Dense(982, activation='sigmoid')(input=
encoded)
```

As can be observed, this defines the autoencoder encoder and decoder functions. Notably, the encoder layers are assigned the input images, and the decoder layer inputs are the encoded attributes. From the code snippets, it can be seen that the final outcome is compressed, as the dimensions specified are 32 for layers that need 982 dimensions.

7.6.4 Feature extraction

Once the encoders and decoders of the autoencoder are defined, the following code snippet is applied to extract the latent space attributes and perform the required functions, such as image reconstruction or generation:

```
model = keras.Model(image, decoder)
```

7.6.5 Modeling and testing

The model can now be compiled and set up for future predictions or accuracy estimations as follows:

```
model.compile(optimizer='adam', loss='binary_crossentropy')
model.fit(x_train, x_train,
```

```
epochs=100,
batch_size=32,
shuffle=True,
validation_data=(x_test, x_test))
```

Here, the model is compiled with an ADAM optimizer, and losses are calculated for different input images. The images are generally provided in two broad categories: training images and test images.

The code sequences shown above are considered to represent the bare minimum setup required to create autoencoders for any relevant applications that require images to be automatically generated from images or data by fetching the latent space attributes.

References

[1] Baldi P 2012 Autoencoders, unsupervised learning, and deep architectures *ICML Workshop on Unsupervised and Transfer Learning* vol 27 ed I Guyon, G Dror, V Lemaire, G W Taylor and D L Silver (Bellvue, WA: PMLR) pp 37–49

[2] Bretan M, Oore S, Eck D and Heck L P 2017 Learning and evaluating musical features with deep autoencoders arXiv:1706.04486

[3] Deng Z, Wang Z, Tang Z, Huang K and Zhu H 2021 A deep transfer learning method based on stacked autoencoder for cross-domain fault diagnosis *Appl. Math. Comput.* **408** 126318

[4] Gomes P R, Sabuj H H, Uddin M A, Reza M T, Faiz R I and Alam M A 2021 *A Deep Learning Approach for Reconstruction of Color Images in Different Lighting Conditions Based on Autoencoder Technique International Conference on Electronics, Information, and Communication, ICEIC 2021, Jeju, South Korea, January 31–February 3, 2021* (Piscataway, NJ: IEEE) pp 1–4

[5] Ju Y, Guo J and Liu S 2015 A deep learning method combined sparse autoencoder with SVM *2015 International Conference on Cyber-Enabled Distributed Computing and Knowledge Discovery, CyberC 2015 (Xi'an, China, September 17–19, 2015)* (Los Alamitos, CA: IEEE Computer Society Press) pp 257–60

[6] Kang G, Gao S, Yu L and Zhang D 2019 Deep architecture for high-speed railway insulator surface defect detection: denoising autoencoder with multitask learning *IEEE Trans. Instrum. Meas.* **68** 2679–90

[7] Li W, Shang Z, Gao M, Qian S, Zhang B and Zhang J 2021 A novel deep autoencoder and hyperparametric adaptive learning for imbalance intelligent fault diagnosis of rotating machinery *Eng. Appl. Artif. Intell.* **102** 104279

[8] Pradhan N, Dhaka V S, Thakur S and Bhakar S 2021 Deep learning technique for image colorization *International Conference on Data Science, Machine Learning and Artificial Intelligence* D S Jat, C Stanley, J G Quenum, N Dey and A Jain (New York, NY: ACM) pp 147–52

[9] Pu Y, Gan Z, Henao R, Yuan X, Li C, Stevens A and Carin L 2016 Variational autoencoder for deep learning of images, labels and captions ed D D Lee, M Sugiyama, U von Luxburg, I Guyon and R Garnett *Advances in Neural Information Processing Systems 29: Annual*

Conference on Neural Information Processing Systems 2016, December 5–10, 2016, Barcelona, Spain (Red Hook, NY: Curran Assoc. Inc) pp 2352–60

[10] Qin Z, Zeng Q, Zong Y and Xu F 2021 Image inpainting based on deep learning: a review *Displays* **69** 102028

[11] Raslan W and Ismail Y 2021 Deep learning autoencoder-based compression for current source model waveforms *28th International Conference on Electronics, Circuits, and Systems, ICECS 2021* (IEEE: Piscataway, NJ) pp 1–6

[12] Zhu Z, Wang X, Bai S, Yao C and Bai X 2016 Deep learning representation using autoencoder for 3D shape retrieval *Neurocomputing* **204** 41–50

Chapter 8

GANs and disentangled mechanisms

Generative Adversarial Networks (GANs) are unsupervised learning methods within the machine learning domain. In any machine learning system, data remains a crucial component of accurate modeling. The data arrives in various forms and formats, such as short characters, words, files, videos, audios, and so forth. Many machine learning algorithms perform badly if they derive models from limited data sets. GANs generate data sets for unsupervised learning algorithms. This chapter explains the concept of two different models utilized in GANs and provides suitable code snippets from real-world examples.

8.1 Introduction to GANs

In 2014, Ian Goodfellow, a PhD student from the University of Montreal, coined the concept of establishing parallel neural networks that could competently support each other in gaining knowledge. This idea revolutionized the world of machine learning, as learning made machines capable of generating data of their own.

In general, the goal of a deep learning architecture is to discover the hierarchical architectures that tend to represent the probability distribution of the data. In addition, information encountered in artificial intelligence (AI) applications, including realistic images, audio files, and even keywords and sentences contained in collections of natural language dictionary data sets [3], needs to be investigated using such architectures.

Discriminative models were used for creating newer images or data sets before GANs were used in deep learning architectures. In discriminative models, high dimensional classes of the input are mapped to class labels. Discriminative models apply piecewise linear units for the dropout process and backpropagation techniques. However, these models were not popular, as they found it difficult to approximate some complex probabilistic computations.

There was a clear need for an architecture that could propose a new generative model estimation procedure that would sidestep the difficulties mentioned above.

GANs were designed as examples of generative models. A generative model is a model that inputs a training set consisting of samples drawn from a distribution of data and learns to represent an estimate of the distribution.

8.2 Concept—generative and descriptive

Before diving into the internal details and architectures of GANs, let us introduce two basic GAN concepts that often arise in discussions—i.e. generative models and discriminative models.

8.2.1 Generative models

Generative models are the class of models that are capable of generating data sets [5]. For instance, these models can generate data sets from voice, video, data, and so forth. Notably, the data created by the models need not exist. A camera capturing facial images in an Internet of things (IoT) application can generate a few facial images without the existence of real-world faces. Thus, a generative model is the one that is capable of generating images that are not present in the data set.

Generative models involve several hidden layers of neural networks that train complex images or data sets. An important task of such models is to learn data sets and their corresponding distributions. When a generative model has successfully been trained, it can estimate the similarity between given samples and create new samples.

Let us consider an example that provides a deeper understanding of the concept. For example, let us consider that we need to create an image of an elephant that never existed on the Earth but should look relatively similar. Existing deep learning architectures cannot address this problem domain.

Using GANs, we can train a model to understand elephants' features using an existing data set of elephants. The features include the pixel values of the images, the edges of the images, brightness levels, and so forth. The generative model attempts to learn these features and derive rules or policies that enable it to create new images. In fact, this process is not a naive solution. It requires a strong foundation that can establish suitable rules or policies to create features and images.

To override the inherent complexities of the generative models, it is better to apply probabilistic theory for creating rules rather than deterministic theory. Generative models learn using the concept of maximum likelihood processes. However, the uniqueness of the generative model remains as an alternative to the likelihood approaches. Trained models are capable of generating images on their own. However, challenges exist. In GAN frameworks, discriminators are applied to compete with the generative models to improve model accuracy. A deeper study of discriminators will be addressed in the following section.

The generative models of GANs are typically implemented using TensorFlow libraries [1]. The generative models comprise layers that produce the definitions used to create dense layers, perform normalization, and specify the activation function. The models later perform a sequence of similar batches of convolutions. Code snippets that exemplify the implementation of these models are given below:

```
model = tf.keras.Sequential()
model.add(layers.Dense(7*7*256, use_bias=False, input_-
shape=(100,)))
model.add(layers.BatchNormalization())
model.add(layers.LeakyReLU())

model.add(layers.Reshape((7, 7, 256)))
assert model.output_shape == (None, 7, 7, 256)

model.add(layers.Conv2DTranspose(128, (5, 5),
strides=(1, 1), padding='same', use_bias=False))
assert model.output_shape == (None, 7, 7, 128)
model.add(layers.BatchNormalization())
model.add(layers.LeakyReLU())

model.add(layers.Conv2DTranspose(64, (5, 5),
strides=(2, 2), padding='same', use_bias=False))
assert model.output_shape == (None, 14, 14, 64)
model.add(layers.BatchNormalization())
model.add(layers.LeakyReLU())

model.add(layers.Conv2DTranspose(1, (5, 5),
strides=(2, 2), padding='same', use_bias=False, activation
= 'tanh'))
assert model.output_shape == (None, 28, 28, 1)
return model
```

8.2.2 Discriminative models

Discriminative models are the teaching modules of the generative models in GANs. As they are unsupervised learning models, GANs require mechanisms to strengthen their accuracy. Discriminative models attempt to suggest generative models so that the rephrased data sets, including images, are realistic in nature. These models include layers of neural networks that learn the features and characteristics of images or data sets [4]. GANs embody discriminator models to differentiate between real and non-real data sets. Taking hippopotamus images as an example, the discriminator model acts as a classifier that determines whether the hippopotamus images generated by the generator model are images of hippopotamuses or not. The model can represent the classification on a scale of zero to one—i.e. a probability of zero identifies a wrong result, and a probability of one points to the correct value.

A generic implementation of a discriminator model using TensorFlow is as follows:

```
model = tf.keras.Sequential()
model.add(layers.Conv2D(64, (5, 5), strides=(2, 2),
padding='same', input_shape=[28, 28, 1]))
model.add(layers.LeakyReLU())
model.add(layers.Dropout(0.3))

model.add(layers.Conv2D(128, (5, 5), strides=(2, 2), padding
='same'))
model.add(layers.LeakyReLU())
model.add(layers.Dropout(0.3))

model.add(layers.Flatten())
model.add(layers.Dense(1))

return model
```

8.3 Major steps involved

GANs brings together two models, such as generative and descriptive models, to create newer images or data sets. From a broader perspective, GANs follow the steps mentioned below to create images or newer data sets.

8.3.1 Load and prepare

The load and prepare step keeps the relevant data that is useful for the analysis. For instance, learning images or generating a newer image using GANs require the algorithm to load relevant images or data sets. In addition, the raw images or data set might not be a viable data set for the algorithm to process. In such cases, algorithms have to preprocess the data before use. Notably, a GAN model utilized to generate new faces or digits expects the images to have certain dimensions, such as 24 x 24, 256 x 256, and so forth.

8.3.2 Modeling

In the GAN approach, as discussed above, two different models, the generative model and the discriminative model, are required for data sets. These models work with the given data sets to understand their underlying features. These models are organized as two independent neural network layers that have sufficient hidden layers to learn the data sets. These two different learning models uniquely contribute to the generation of new images/data sets.

8.3.3 Loss and optimizers

A loss function or optimizer, such as the adam optimizer, is required to assess the models. The loss and optimizer functions determine the quality of the predictions, as the training can be performed using tens of hundreds of iterations. The threshold of acceptance for the loss values can be set before starting the neural networks when they are used to generate newer images/data sets.

8.3.4 Training step

Having finalized the models and the loss functions required for the input data sets, they are used for training. The training step typically takes a long time. A few performance improvement mechanisms can be implemented if the training process needs to be handled more effectively. For instance, using the right set of computing infrastructure can speed up the training step of GANs.

8.3.5 Testing step

Following the creation of a training model for a GAN implementation, the algorithms is tested. The testing step of the GAN process creates newer images or data sets using training inferences.

8.4 GAN architecture

A GAN architecture consists of two major entities, the generator and the discriminator. The layers and the functionalities of these components are discussed in this section. The architecture of a GAN specifies the utilization of its components, such as its generators and discriminators.

8.4.1 Generators

As shown in figure 8.1, the generator component collects its input from some random input variables or parameters to create newer data sets. For instance, the generator component can create newer scripts of numbers from the Modified National Institute of Standards and Technology (MNIST) data set based on the features of numbers. In the meantime, the real data sets are sampled and their features are extracted. These two inputs are fed to the discriminator component, which analyzes the crucial differences. The discriminator is typically implemented using binary classifiers for the majority of image-based applications. The binary classifier determines whether a given input is real or not. Samples created by the generator are known as fake samples. This process continues until the model is stopped by some external agency or the specified number of loops has been completed.

The generator of a GAN gains the knowledge required to create a non-real data set, also termed the fake data set, with the assistance of the discriminator. The objective of the generator is to keep the discriminator accepting the data sets generated by the generator module as acceptable real data. Thus, we can observe

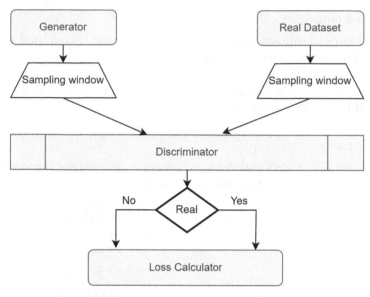

Figure 8.1. GAN architecture.

that the training part of the generator requires a close relationship with the discriminator part of the GAN.

The most commonly applied generative models, especially for image data sets, are as follows:

1. Explicit likelihood models—these likelihood models understand the data distributions of data sets such as Poisson, Gaussian, binary, and so forth; they generate a new set of distributions to frame the data. A few notable approaches in this category are listed below: (a) probabilistic principal component analysis (PPCA), (b) factor analysis, (c) mixture models, (d) PixelCNN/PixelRNN, (e) WaveNet, (f) autoregressive language models, (g) approximate maximum likelihood, (h) Boltzmann machines, and (i) variational autoencoders.

2. Implicit likelihood models—in implicit models, the statistical properties of the data are studied by the generators. This gives more clarity in learning the new instances of data provided the right amount of data is inspected for this purpose.

8.4.2 Discriminator

The discriminator of a GAN aims to point out the differences in given data set, including image data sets. When a `fake` sample is given to the discriminator as an input, the software module of the discriminator has to identify it as a fake one—i.e. the generator attempts to fool the discriminator by making it identify a fake thing as real.

The discriminator module of a GAN uses some computation and software modules to perform the difference calculations while attaining the objectives. The difference is often evaluated using a min–max optimization formulation in which the generator aims to minimize the objective function while, on the other hand, the discriminator aims to maximize the same objective function.

8.5 Types of GAN

GANs are often classified into six broad approaches depending on the methodology adopted to generate newer data sets, including images (see figure 8.2). The functionalities of these GANs and their objectives are discussed below:

8.5.1 DCGANs

Deep convolutional GANs (DCGANs), as the name indicates, utilize convolutional networks. In general, CNNs are considered to be black boxes due to the unavailability of specific information about learned data sets. However, CNN's achieve excellent results due to their robust modeling features.

In DCGANs, the generators and discriminators are supported by black-box implementations of CNNs. Black-box CNN implementations are specifically modified to create DCGANs. In general, DCGANs try not to connect all convolutional layers during the learning processes. Recently, efforts have been made to apply DCGANs to the restoration of images [8]. A few notable modifications incorporated in DCGANs, as compared to CNN's, are as follows:

1. The max-pooling component of traditional CNNs is replaced with more spatial components. As a result, the deterministic approach to the learning process is removed from the system. Obviously, the generators of DCGANs are able to independently learn from the larger spatial data sets.

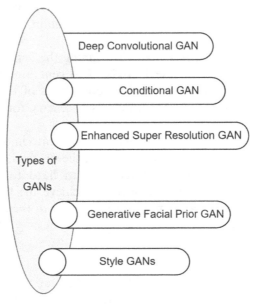

Figure 8.2. Types of GAN.

2. The second modification observed in DCGANs is the tendency to convert fully connected layers into partial ones. For example, increasing the use of average pooling across multiple layers supports a joint effort to calculate results across layers. Obviously, this approach can increase the accuracy achieved, but the expected convergence speed is reduced.

3. It is a known fact that adding batch normalization increases the stability of learning models. In DCGANs, newer insights are required. Accordingly, the generator and discriminator models attempt to avoid batch normalization, in contrast to other CNN's.

8.5.2 CGANs

Conditional GANs (CGANs) are a type of GAN that can generate a new data set using some additional inputs. Compared to the previous DCGAN approach, CGANs use some inputs or conditions to learn data sets. They are similar to DCGANs in that they also have generators and discriminators to generate newer data sets, including voice or video data sets. The authors of [6] authors applied conditional GANs to distill knowledge from input sources.

CGANs are typically considered to be an extension of the vanilla GAN approach. Conditions are provided to CGANs in the form of inputs or variables that influence the learning layers of convolutional networks. These conditions are fed not only to the generator model but also to the discriminator model of CGANs.

The key idea of incorporating specific conditions into CGANs is to specifically obtain a certain featured output based on the input data sets. For instance, if the user wants to print a specific number while generating numbers based on the MNIST handwritten data set, a CGAN will be able to provide it based on the conditions or preferences supplied to the generator and the discriminator of the CGAN. Clearly, a CGAN is a good fit when the user prefers to obtain deterministic generative solutions from a GAN.

The training phase of a CGAN involves training the generator component and the discriminator component of the CGAN. The generator component converts labels to sophisticated arrays that represent conditions of the input data sets. In addition, reshaping or preprocessing of data is necessary for the learning components of CGANs.

The objective of the generator component is to create images or data sets that keep the discriminator component unsure about the outputs, whereas the discriminator component of a CGAN attempts to learn hard to understand the real situations of the input images or data sets. To achieve the best from the training phase of the discriminator, CGANs minimize the losses of their training modules for a given batch of input data sets.

8.5.3 ESRGAN

The official implementation of Enhanced Super-Resolution GAN (ESRGAN) can be found at https://github.com/xinntao/ESRGAN. Executable versions of ESRGANs are available for Windows, Linux, and MacOS machines.

The super-resolution of image data sets has been extensively studied in the past [2]. The objective of this approach is to increase the quality of image restoration. There are a few approaches to restoring the quality of images, such as the bicubic downsampling approach. However, the traditional approaches fail to provide high-quality restoration processes.

A few processes are used to restore high-resolution images, such as filtering blur, removing noise, choosing a suitable resizing method, incorporating efficient compression techniques, and so forth.

Blurring is an important source of image quality degradation. Certain blur filters, such as isotropic filters, anisotropic filters, and so forth, have been implemented as kernels in the past to remove blurring from images.

Noise in an image is due to a random variation in the brightness or the color combinations of an image. The presence of a noise component in the image can lead to difficulties in restoring high-resolution images. The two most commonly found noises are additive Gaussian noise and Poisson noise, depending on the distribution of noise in the image—i.e. based on a Gaussian distribution or Poisson distribution.

Choosing an suitable image size can reduce the risk of restoring high-resolution images. In some cases, image reshaping is not properly performed by algorithms.

8.5.4 GFP GANs

Generative facial prior GANs (GFP GANs) focus on restoring old photos with a greater emphasis on facial detection. They apply some pretrained GAN models and spatial feature transforms to restore facial images. This approach is commonly called the blind face restoration process [2], because the method is capable of generating high-quality faces from degraded images.

Degradation is quite common in images, even newer images. It occurs due to noise, blur, camera misfocus, compression artifacts, and so forth. However, many sectors are keenly interested in overcoming these degradations.

In the past, efforts have been made to identify facial landmarks or the heat maps of facial primers to remove image defects from faces.

GFP GANs are not only utilized to restore facial images but also to enrich image color. They consist of a pretrained face, such as a StyleGAN, and a degradation removal module, namely U-NET. The network includes latent code mapping and channel split spatial feature transform layers. GFP GANs are designed to extract the latent features of faces in order to map them onto a facial image.

The core objectives of GFP GANs are to minimize i) reconstruction loss, ii) facial primer, and iii) adversarial loss.

8.6 StyleGAN

StyleGAN is a GAN variant based on style transfer research. It collects the facial primers of facial images and attempts to provide a larger change in them.

The resulting model provides newer views and outlooks on images in addition to traditional improvements such as blur removal, addressing compression artifacts, and so forth. The authors of [7] attempted to improve the performance of StyleGAN inversions.

8.7 A simple implementation of a GAN

This section describes a simple implementation of a generator and a discriminator that produces handwritten digits using the MNIST data set, a popular data set of handwritten digits.

The implementation of GANs is carried out in several stages as described below.

8.7.1 Importing libraries and data sets

The required libraries and MNIST data set are first loaded into the GAN architecture. The most important libraries utilized to implement GANs are listed below:

```
import tensorflow as tf
from tensorflow.keras.layers import Dense, LeakyReLU,
Dropout
from tensorflow.keras.models import Model
from tensorflow.keras.optimizers import SGD, Adam
```

The TensorFlow platform offers the `keras` libraries and the associated Python sublibrary packages, such as dense layers, activation functions, dropout layers, and optimization features using `Adam` or `Stochastic Gradient Descent (SGD)`. These packages are imported at the initial stage of GAN execution.

We now need to load the MNIST data set comprising handwritten digits, as shown below:

```
mnist = tf.keras.datasets.mnist
(x_train, y_train), (x_test, y_test) = mnist.load_data()
```

It is a known practice to load MNIST data sets directly into the training and testing data sets.

8.7.2 Generator models

As discussed earlier, generator models consist of a sequence of layers that include batch normalization enabled by TensorFlow platforms. Accordingly, the MNIST data set is subjected to a sequence of dense layering, batch normalization, and activations as per the requirement of the GAN model's principles:

```
input = Input(shape=(dimension,))
layer_x = Dense(256, activation=LeakyReLU(alpha=0.2))(input)
layer_x = BatchNormalization(momentum=0.7)(layer_x)

layer_x = Dense(512, activation=LeakyReLU(alpha=0.2))(layer_x)
layer_x = BatchNormalization(momentum=0.7)(layer_x)

layer_x = Dense(1024, activation=LeakyReLU(alpha=0.2))(layer_x)
layer_x = BatchNormalization(momentum=0.7)(layer_x)

layer_x = Dense(dimension, activation=âtanhâ)(layer_x)

gen_model = Model(input, layer_x)
```

8.7.3 Discriminator models

The discriminator model for the MNIST data set is created using dense layers of TensorFlow packages and specifying the activation functions, as shown below:

```
input = Input(shape=(sizeofImage,))
layer_x = Dense(512, activation=LeakyReLU(alpha=0.2))(input)
layer_xx = Dense(256, activation=LeakyReLU(alpha=0.2))(layer_x)
layer_x = Dense(1, activation='sigmoid')(layer_x)
des_model = Model(input, layer_x)
```

8.7.4 Compiling and optimizing

Once the generator and discriminator models are defined with respect to the MNIST data sets, the models are compiled and optimized using tools such as the Adam optimizer, as shown below:

```
des_model.compile (loss='binary_crossentropy',
optimizer=Adam(0.000 2, 0.5), metrics=['accuracy'])
gen_model.compile(loss='binary_crossentropy',
optimizer=Adam(0.000 2, 0.5)) #introducing noise
```

8.7.5 Generate images

The last step is to train both the generator model and the discriminator model to create a set of handwritten images. These handwritten images are cross-checked against each other to improve the accuracy of the models.

Thus, newly created handwritten images are developed using a GAN architecture and TensorFlow platforms.

8.8 Quality of GANs

Compared to other deep learning models, GANs do not have straightforward assessment methods to finalize the accuracy. For instance, in other methods, we can specify the loss function as an objective value. However, in GANs, both the generator model and discriminator model have to work together to improve the final objectives of the training models.

In this context, the quality of GANs depends on both the models and the design procedure that drives these models. For instance, assessing the quality of generated messages or images could performed by an objective function that evaluates the quality of a GAN rather than by objectively fixing the model accuracy.

8.9 Applications and challenges

GANs have been used in several applications in various domains ranging from academia to industry. This section lists a few notable applications and relevant domains that apply GANs.

8.9.1 Human face generation

There has been a keen interest among various users and mobile application developers in generating human faces or emojis of images using GANs. The amount of software development in this field of research and product development has increased in recent years.

8.9.2 Music generation

Music is an art. A few researchers have created initiatives to generate new music from input samples. In fact, considering the rhythm and the tone collected from tens of thousands of music samples, we can provide a perfect melody using GAN-based music software. This application could easily merge with several other comfort-related developments in future applications.

8.9.3 Translation

GANs can be applied to convert images to a certain posture, convert texts to paragraphs, and convert images to super-resolution images. A few pretrained GAN models exist that can perform these tasks in the cloud. In addition, these models can be offloaded to mobile nodes to create real-time conversion/translation.

8.9.4 Guided generation

GANs also have options that can generate images if certain input control steps are provided. For instance, a tourist who wants to view the image of a location as it was decades ago can apply GAN-based software to generate such images. In the last few decades, most tourist locations or cities will have made several changes, such as the locations of water bodies, buildings, trees, and so forth. This information could be generated from previous similar images or from features extracted from images found in other cities of the particular period. In such situations, GANs can receive guidance from the user in order to generate images or location pictures in real time.

References

[1] GANs using tensorflow libraries, May 2022 Page Version ID: 1088786364

[2] Andrei S S, Shapovalova N and Mayol-Cuevas W W 2021 SUPERVEGAN: super resolution video enhancement GAN for perceptually improving low bitrate streams *IEEE Access* **9** 91160–74

[3] Bhattacharya G 2021 From DNNs to GANs: review of efficient hardware architectures for deep learning arXiv:2107.00092

[4] Bianco M J, Gannot S, Fernandez-Grande E and Gerstoft P 2021 Semi-supervised source localization in reverberant environments with deep generative modeling *IEEE Access* **9** 84956–70

[5] Gan Z 2018 Deep generative models for vision and language intelligence *PhD Thesis* Duke University, Durham, NC, USA

[6] Kim S 2022 A virtual knowledge distillation via conditional GAN *IEEE Access* **10** 34766–78

[7] Wei T, Chen D, Zhou W, Liao J, Zhang W, Yuan L, Hua G and Yu N 2022 E2Style: improve the efficiency and effectiveness of StyleGAN inversion *IEEE Trans. Image Process.* **31** 3267–80

[8] Zhang F, Wang X, Sun T and Xu X 2021 SE-DCGAN: a new method of semantic image restoration *Cogn. Comput.* **13** 981–91

Chapter 9

Deep reinforcement learning architectures

Deep reinforcement learning (RL), in general, is a machine learning technique that learns contexts using rewards and punishments. It is considered to be a goal-oriented learning process. The techniques behind creating agent rewards and actions are discussed in this chapter.

9.1 Deep reinforcement learning—an introduction

The deep RL approach is a machine learning (ML) technique. When applied in a learning system, it takes actions such that the rewards are maximized and the failures are decreased in a strategic manner. This is achieved by agents that take a sequence of decisions, preferably remarkable ones, in a short time. This sequence of decisions becomes an outcome of the learning procedures adopted in the deep RL processes.

The concept of RL was first used decades ago [1, 9, 13]. However, the approach is still being utilized in several domains, including the transportation sector [11].

The RL approach has two broad entities that execute the intended objectives:

- agents
- environments

Agents are actors that perform autonomous learning processes with using inferences about environments; these entities are considered to be soft decision-makers. The environments are locations where agents perform actions.

The concept of applying RL to various sectors has become much more popular in recent years due to its applicability in various domains, including industrial Internet of things (IoT), for solving huge tasks while taking a sequence of decisions. The RL approach has manifested a remarkable rate of growth in the robotic world, especially in the form of in-home devices that automatically clean houses and assist elderly people. In fact, RL is observed in humans—i.e. the learning process used by

doi:10.1088/978-0-7503-4024-3ch9

humans is improved by rewards and positive environments. For instance, an employee with sufficient rewards could be forward-looking or optimistic in his/her duties.

9.2 The difference between deep reinforcement learning and machine learning

Deep RL is considered to take advantage of a simple RL approach. It is a known fact that artificial intelligence can be applied in two major ways:

- rule-based
- machine-based

In the rule-based approach, intelligence is applied based on human experience and knowledge transferred from experts in a learning domain [2]; by contrast, machine-based intelligence is based on learning processes incorporated into machines that learn a huge volume of data.

The main idea of the deep RL approach is to design policies that improve existing rewards in the long run.

Similarly to several other learning approaches such as deep learning, RL is a method in which machines learn in an automated fashion. The learning mechanism endeavors to suggest a better sequence of decisions for the agents of the RL system. Fundamentally, the RL approach attempts to develop a sequence of rules that maximizes the decision interests on its own. Of course, the learning accuracy and behavior must be improved after several trials are carried out in the domain of interest.

The RL technique is equivalent to the teaching of children in school or society. They learn several important facts and figures after experiencing a situation. At times, they fail or are penalized for poor memories. The case of RL processes is similar, in which wrong decisions taken due to uncertainties need to be penalized for efficient near-future learning or decision-making processes.

9.3 The difference between deep learning and reinforcement learning

There is a slight distinction between the deep learning and RL mechanism, although they both learn facts and figures without the involvement of human-specified rules—i.e. the deep learning approach aims to learn by splitting data sets into training, validation, and test portions. The deep learning mechanism enables automated learning, a much deeper learning process, within a bounded data set. In contrast, the RL approach does not require such data classification, as it proceeds with an independent learning process while obtaining feedback from the data. The deep RL process combines deep learning and RL mechanisms to achieve better production of the decision sequence.

The RL mechanism is divided into supervised and unsupervised learning algorithms. In the machine learning paradigm, many supervised and unsupervised algorithms have been implemented in the recent past. The supervised learning algorithms require training data that contains appropriate hints about the data. For instance, labeling training data is equivalent to providing keys for learning inferences. As an example, consider a few images of flowers and animals that are input into a machine with proper labels containing their names. In such cases, a machine can learn the characteristics of these images or their parameters. However, this approach is equivalent to a teacher–student model, which is a poor fit for some of the new learning domains. The RL mechanism does not need such keys or labels. In some cases, however, the performance of a supervised reinforcement solution may be higher than those of other bare solutions [6].

In the unsupervised learning process, no labels or complete labels, including training keys, are input to the learning algorithm [8]. Obviously, unsupervised learning algorithms must learn by themselves. To do this, most of these algorithms formulate a sort of association between the data and cluster them based on similarities or dissimilarities. The RL mechanism, on the other hand, applies agents to learn and perform a sequence of decisions. These agents learn from the unknown environment under consideration.

9.4 Reinforcement learning applications

Reinforcement learning has been applied in a few notable application domains such as autonomous vehicles, robotics, natural language processing systems, games, and so forth.

9.4.1 Autonomous driving

In general, autonomous driving is centered around learning from scenes and scenarios observed in environments. Understanding the scenes helps the RL agent to learn the environment, modify states among the preferable states, and maximize rewards or penalties so that the learning is self-contained in the application. The most important aspect of these algorithms is diligently collecting relevant information from the environment with alacrity. In some cases, there is a critical need for collaboration between instances of neighboring machines or sensor nodes. Safe driving and minimizing complexities are inherent objectives when RL algorithms are designed for these applications [7]. In addition, identifying driving locations, locating speed limit barriers or lanes, and avoiding collisions in various travel spots are crucial applications in which the RL mechanism is implemented.

9.4.2 Robotics

Robots were developed to mimic human actions with minimal intelligence. They use mechanical components, electronics, and artificial intelligence (AI) to perform actions. These robots are, in general, developed to help society or industry [4]. For example, a robot in the tire manufacturing industry can assemble and prepare tires without human intervention. As a result, humans are protected from several harmful diseases caused by industry. Robots implemented using RL attempt to use trial-and-error steps to learn their environments.

9.4.3 Natural language processing systems

Natural language processing (NLP) has become quite popular due to the increase in the numbers of voice assistive gadgets such as Alexa, Siri, and so forth. The learning processes of NLP-based systems have been more complex than traditional learning algorithms because of the increasing number of states in their machines. The application of RL techniques to NLP-based systems would improve the learning process due to the inherent nature of the multidimensional parameters involved in linguistics [12]. Obviously, traditional NLP tasks, such as word embeddings, part-of-speech tagging, stop-word removal, lemmatization and stemming, dependency parsing, constituency parsing, and so forth, could benefit from the application of the RL technique.

9.4.4 Games

For computer scientists, games have not only been ways to entertain users but also enrich computational optimization strategies. In the past, researchers from Google LLC and leading subsidiaries such as DeepMind Technologies have attempted to demonstrate the importance of applying deep RL mechanisms by playing Go board games. Their agents were able to defeat several champions by accomplishing their tasks using RL algorithms.

9.5 Components of RL frameworks

The major components of the agents that support the RL mechanism are listed below:

- Policy components
- Value function components
- Model-based components

9.5.1 Policy components

The policy-based components of RL define the required behavior of RL agents. As an example, if a machine-to-machine application has machines communicating with each other, if machine A decides to communicate with machine B, this can lead to a complex decision-making process, depending on various factors such as success rates and so forth. If any weak decisions are taken by the machine, there is a high possibility of failure.

In short, the policy components of RL are responsible for establishing equations with input and output states in which the output states depend on the policies specified by the components [3]. Each state of any problem domain specifies the current situation of the environment. The policies are generally either stochastic or deterministic, depending on the preferred action of the machine. For instance, if machine A chooses the machine that is most often communicated with in order to reach a target node, although the route to reach the machine is larger, the choice is determined by a deterministic policy; by contrast, if the machine makes a random choice based on an expectation of quick reachability, the choice is determined by a stochastic policy.

To improve the formation of policies, especially in deep RL frameworks, it is necessary to frame some generalizations for data sets. In practice, the generalization is achieved in two different fashions, as outlined below.

Implementation approach
Considering the real-time and real-world situations used to create policies, the use of agents is a quite common intuitive way for RL solutions to perform actions. However, it often fails because of the practice of performing the training process with limited data. Also, setting up the environment to collect such relevant data for training purposes is an expensive procedure in the majority of cases.

Simulation approach
Simulators may be used to overcome the difficulties of creating a real-world environmental setup and the non-availability of training data. Although a sufficient quantity of data might be obtained using this approach, the expected data quality is not available, which leads to inaccurate policies.

9.5.2 Value function components

These components of RL frameworks value the states of the RL agents while choosing one of the states. The states can be dynamic or static. However, the value functions define the importance of states for problems. For instance, in the previous example of a machine communicating with other machines, choosing the correct route among all possible combinations leads to value functions that define the state changes. These components typically assign rewards and penalties while choosing states. Rewards are positive notions that improve the choices made by decisions.

9.5.3 Model components

Reinforcement learning frameworks use modeling to predict the next state. A machines that is choosing an intermediate machine before sending data to a target machine depend on certain parameters. These parameters are often mathematically represented as models based on environmental variables. The models aim to predict the value functions of the RL problems.

The most generic modeling approach in RL frameworks involves the Markov decision process. The Markov decision process is a discrete-time stochastic control process based on a finite number of states and decisions. Figure 9.1 illustrates the three major components of RL that applies implementation or simulation approaches.

9.6 Reinforcement learning techniques

The broad concept of RL can be refined using the variation in the implementation steps—i.e. the RL techniques used—as given below:

- Associative RL
- Deep RL
- Adversarial deep RL

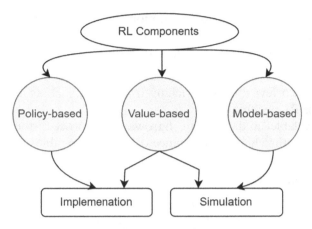

Figure 9.1. Reinforcement learning components.

- Inverse RL
- Safe RL

9.6.1 Associative RL

Associative RL mechanism is a technique that incorporates associative networks into RL frameworks [10]. Associative memory units are, in general, similar to brain networks in which massive data correlation is found. Our human brain is capable of analyzing environmental patterns with ease.

The application of associative properties to learning neural networks is subcategorized into two sectors:

- auto-associative
- hetero-associative

The auto-associative property in RL attempts to include numerous neurons of the same kind to autonomously create states. The hetero-associative nature of the learning process favors bidirectional associative memory units.

In associative RL, associative memory units are hosted by RL models to provide decisive steps or stages.

9.6.2 Deep RL

The traditional RL approach prepares new actions given a state. For each state and the given environment, the policy suggests new states. However, the complexities are immense, especially when the complex games or applications with tens of thousands of dynamic state changes are considered. This can lead to a situation in which the normal approaches to computation are not sufficient for the automated learning process. In such cases, a neural network-based learning process with deeper hidden layers is considered. The deep RL mechanism uses a learning approach with a large number of hidden layers to understand the next state based on a policy.

Although there are a few incorrect notions about the success of the deep RL mechanism, research work is in progress to increase the accuracy of this approach. A few research directions that adopt deep RL techniques are listed below:

1. Increase the rewards of agents if success is unanimously identified.
2. Incorporate a few reward-enriching techniques, such as applying imitations or reverse RL techniques.
3. Apply scalable and efficient hardware to process the algorithms and methods, so that high-performance delivery is possible.

9.6.3 Adversarial deep RL

Adversarial networks [14] are designed to guide learning networks while predicting certain objectives; they attempt to improve the learning accuracy and/or prediction accuracy by competing with learning models. One of the most commonly implemented adversarial networks in deep learning frameworks learn competitive themes in parallel to the intended learning mechanisms. For instance, deep learning algorithms that learn the societal impacts of utilizing mobile phones compete with the learning algorithms that study the benefits of mobile phones for the same set of users. The similarities and differences between these two competent learning frameworks work hand in hand to improve the learning accuracy of the system.

In a deep RL context, adversarial networks are implemented to quickly learn the near-impossible events by increasing the rewards/penalties. For instance, learning the unobstructed path of an autonomous car while considering several environmental factors requires a large number of failure cases so that the model can become a robust solution. To increase the path inferences learned by the RL agents, it is crucial to train another RL agent that introduces tougher learning scenarios to the original agents. In adversarial RL frameworks, therefore, two sets of RL agents work hand in hand to improve the learning accuracy of applications.

When two learning agents are incorporated in parallel to increase the learning accuracy, it is possible to implement this in two ways:

1. Sharable learning space—the sharable learning space is a common learning approach in which two RL agents attempt to explore the same learning space. For instance, a student and a teacher learn the same concept and reproduce the findings in either exams or lectures. The findings of both the actors and the agents can be refined to obtain a better knowledge of the intended topic.
2. Non-sharable learning space—by contrast, a non-sharable learning space provides different contexts for the two learning RL agents—i.e. one agent can study the electricity utilization of a smart city while the other agent observes the comfort zone of a smart city.

9.6.4 Inverse RL

Inverse RL is a technique that applies rewards, policies, and models [5]. This technique is oriented toward agents that complete actions—i.e. changing the states based on input behaviors. In general, the reinforcement learning approach attempts to suggest rewards based on the behavior or action taken by the agents. For instance, in an autonomous driving car, the RL agent is rewarded if it travels on roads according to the traffic signs or rules. Notably, rewards are bestowed to the RL agent:

1. if it travels through green traffic lights;
2. if it controls speed based on the speed control signage;
3. if it slows down when it observes pedestrian paths, and so forth.

In the inverse RL approach, the reverse process is followed—i.e. rewards are created based on behaviors. In this approach, autonomous learning is established by understanding the behaviors of human actions. For example, humans would not lower the speed of cars while observing the 30 km/h signage near schools during school holidays. There are situations in which it is necessary to violate the rules—i.e. blindly rewarding actions based on policies would not the right fit in a few use cases. Therefore, in the inverse RL approach, rewards are derived based on possible behaviors. This requires the collection of behaviors at varying locations and for various scenarios.

However, the inverse RL approach has a few drawbacks. It has to understand the possible choices of actions or behaviors. Therefore, this may not lead to the best solution—i.e. a set of tradeoffs is used to confirm that the mechanism has found the optimal solution.

9.6.5 Safe RL

The RL mechanism, due to its autonomous decisions or actions based on inherent policies, can lead to strange failures or issues. In a safe RL approach, the actions that take place as a result of policies are expected to improve the safety of actions. The safety measures not only involve safety considerations for the environment but also for the computational units involved in the learning process. For instance, decisions based on inferences and policies in RL might be delayed due to the huge computational demand of the algorithm. In addition, there are a few other associated performance bottlenecks due to memory usage. In some cases, these algorithms could lead to huge energy consumption and inefficiency. Safe RL processes attempt to reduce the computations used by of learning algorithms while maintaining near-optimal satisfaction compared to traditional RL algorithms. Figure 9.2 highlights the taxonomy of the different RL techniques discussed in this section.

9.7 Reinforcement learning algorithms

Reinforcement learning algorithms are classified based on the inclusion of statistical data, as follows:

- model-free RL
- model-based RL

9.7.1 Model-free RL

In model-based RL, previous historical information is not utilized to formulate the reward function or to define the state changes during the process of learning. The

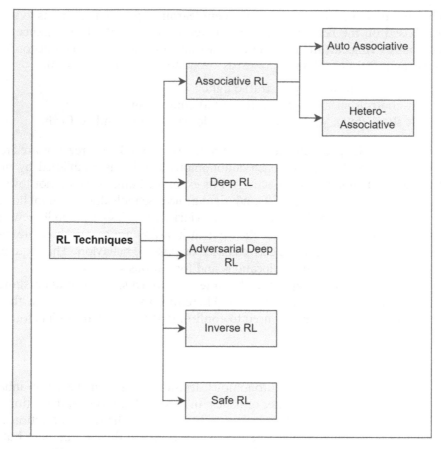

Figure 9.2. Reinforcement learning—most commonly applied techniques.

associated algorithms are less effective, as the output is barely dependent on the current state and the reward functions of the state.

The most popular model-free RL algorithms and their inherent features are classified into two broad categories, value oriented and policy oriented, as discussed below.

Value-oriented algorithms
Value-oriented RL algorithms attempt to increase the rewards while choosing a suitable action for any given state of the environment. A few algorithms that belong to this category are (i) hindsight experience replay and (ii) Deep Q-learning. Among these algorithms, the Deep Q RL algorithm is popularly applied in several applications.

Value-oriented learning algorithms typically have worse execution times, as the results can diverge between good and poor predictions.

Deep Q RL Algorithm
In general, Q-learning learns the environment by calculating Q values which represent the rewards of agents. For instance, a RL agent can understand the total possible

rewards based on the current state of the environment and can proceed to perform actions. Obviously, this algorithm expects the agent to understand the current state of the environment but to have no prior knowledge about previous instances. In addition, the algorithm has a set of policies to calculate reward points for the environment.

Let us consider an example in which a machine has the objective of cleaning cars. If an RL algorithm is designed based on the Q-learning approach, the RL agent can be introduced with options to maximize rewards based on cleaning more cars or the quality of the cleaning processes. The objectives of these algorithms would be to suggest possible reward points to the learning algorithms based on the current state of the environment. The importance of involving deep learning in the Q-learning processes is to improve the accuracy with which actions are chosen based on input states. Q-learning resembles the state–action pair in any working environment.

The deep Q-learning approach can suggest better action points if the numbers of states and action points are greater. This approach delves into the possible state–action pairs to maximize the Q value in a deep learning approach—i.e. the algorithm has to parse a possibly large list of action points based on the input states and reward options. Figure 9.3 pictorially represents the different types of RL technique.

The steps involved in observing the values of action–policy pairs in Q-based RL approaches are listed below:

1. Initialization—first, the Q-table consisting of actions and rewards is created in the initialization phase of the Q-based deep learning algorithm.
2. Iterations—a set of tasks is then performed in a repetitive manner to update the Q-table of the deep Q RL algorithm, as follows:

   (a) Select action—in the iterative step, one action is chosen from a pool of actions.
   (b) Evaluate reward—for this chosen action, the expected rewards are calculated considering the environmental conditions present when the action is attempted in the environment.
   (c) Update table—the evaluation and the Q value that results from performing the actions are recorded in the Q-table.

In the deep Q-learning approach, the agents cannot review a large range of probable choices that happened in the past. Obviously, the performance of the

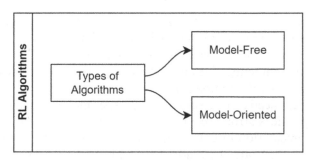

Figure 9.3. Types of RL.

Q-learning approach can be hampered because the previous states and the impacts of choosing actions are not known. However, this approach is useful if the device is memory limited or it does not have a way to handle a large volume of memory.

Policy-oriented algorithms

If reinforcement agents are asked to learn policies and suggest a suitable policy given the state of an environment, the respective algorithms are termed policy-oriented deep RL techniques. A few examples of this type of policy-based RL algorithm are the policy gradient algorithm, asynchronous advantage actor–critic (A3C), and so forth.

Policy-oriented deep RL algorithms typically converge comparatively better than the previously explained value-oriented deep RL approach.

9.7.2 Model-based RL

As mentioned earlier, a model-based RL approach applies models to choose favorable actions. These models are dependent on previous actions and the rewards they earned. In the model-based RL approach, models can be generated for specific problem domains, such as automatic driving, emotional inferences, and so forth.

The models generated using the model-based RL approach are restricted to specific domains. Accordingly, they have to be reinstated for all possible problems. This approach, therefore, has required more computation and space. Additionally, poor accuracy in the learned models increases the computational cost involved in deriving actions using the model-based RL mechanism.

9.8 Integration into real-world systems

Although models are learned and rewards are derived for specific actions, there is a need to transfer the learned actions into working environments. For instance, the actions identified by the deep Q RL approach have to be communicated to connected machines or real-world environments.

For example, if deep RL algorithms are adopted by a robotic environment where robots need to clean cars in a car workshop, each action and its associated reward need to be cleverly integrated into the machines/robots (see figure 9.4).

In general, we can observe three major procedures that realistically action the findings of algorithms based on the state information of environments:

1. Simulation-oriented—here, the actions and states of the environments are applied and used for experiments in a simulated environment. In general, simulation environments use several assumptions to calculate rewards and reshape environments. Although this approach is a low-cost option to attempt all possible combinations of available states in a RL approach, the algorithm needs to be subjected to experiments in real-world situations before it provides strong recommendations about the test scenario.
2. Real-implementation-oriented—the next approach to applying RL algorithms is to integrate the algorithms and findings into real environments. Real implementations of transferred learning outcomes can lead to risks and

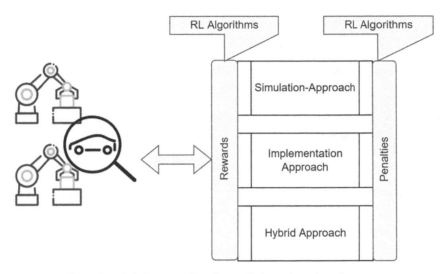

Figure 9.4. Reinforcement learning applied to robots that clean cars.

challenges due to integration issues. For instance, enabling robots to learn different states and perform actions as per the requirements of the deep Q RL approach mandates the flashing of action parameters to robot microcontrollers. Flashing code units, consequently, leads to several implementation challenges.

3. Hybrid-oriented—in most cases, simulators are applied to collect the states, actions, and rewards of RL algorithms. Accordingly, the states are imparted to real working environments. One example is modeling simulators based on the state information collected through sensors in real-time. Modeling them using actions activated through the actuators after performing deep learning algorithmic inferences is another use case in this category.

References

[1] Fang M, Li H and Zhang X 2012 A heuristic reinforcement learning based on state backtracking method *2012 IEEE/WIC/ACM International Conferences on Web Intelligence, WI 2012, Macau, China, December 4–7, 2012 (Macau, China)* (Piscataway, NJ: IEEE) pp 673–8

[2] Hirchoua B, Ouhbi B and Frikh B 2021 Deep reinforcement learning based trading agents: risk curiosity driven learning for financial rules-based policy *Expert Syst. Appl.* **170** 114553

[3] Jin Z, Wu J, Liu A, Zhang W A and Yu L 2022 Policy-based deep reinforcement learning for visual servoing control of mobile robots with visibility constraints *IEEE Trans. Ind. Electron.* **69** 1898–908

[4] Kobayashi T 2022 Adaptive and multiple time-scale eligibility traces for online deep reinforcement learning *Robot. Auton. Syst.* **151** 104019

[5] Lee K, Isele D, Theodorou E A and Bae S 2022 Spatiotemporal costmap inference for MPC via deep inverse reinforcement learning *IEEE Robot. Autom. Lett.* **7** 3194–201

[6] Li X, Wang X, Zheng X, Dai Y, Yu Z, Zhang J J, Bu G and Wang F-Y 2022 Supervised assisted deep reinforcement learning for emergency voltage control of power systems *Neurocomputing* **475** 69–79

[7] Muzahid A J M, Kamarulzaman S F, Rahman M A and Alenezi A H 2022 Deep reinforcement learning-based driving strategy for avoidance of chain collisions and its safety efficiency analysis in autonomous vehicles *IEEE Access* **10** 43303–19

[8] Siddique A B, Oymak S and Hristidis V 2020 Unsupervised paraphrasing via deep reinforcement learning *KDD '20: The 26th SIGKDD Conference on Knowledge Discovery and Data Mining, Virtual Event, CA, USA, August 23–27, ACM 2020* ed R Gupta, Y Liu, J Tang and B A Prakash (New York: ACM) pp 1800–9

[9] Skoulakis I E and Lagoudakis M G 2012 Efficient reinforcement learning in adversarial games *IEEE 24th International Conference on Tools with Artificial Intelligence, ICTAI 2012, Athens, Greece, November 7–9, 2012* (Los Alamitos, CA: IEEE Computer Society Press) pp 704–11

[10] Strehl A L 2017 Associative reinforcement learning *Encyclopedia of Machine Learning and Data Mining* ed C Sammut and G I Webb (Springer: Berlin) pp 71–3

[11] Wang K, Wang L, Pan C and Ren H 2022 Deep reinforcement learning-based resource management for flexible mobile edge computing: architectures, applications, and research issues *IEEE Veh. Technol. Mag.* **17** 85–93

[12] Wang W Y, Li J and He X 2018 Deep reinforcement learning for NLP *Proceedings of ACL 2018, Melbourne, Australia, July 15–20, 2018* ed Y Artzi and J Eisenstein (Stroudsburg, PA: Association for Computational Linguistics) Tutorial Abstracts pp 19–21

[13] Xie N, Hachiya H and Sugiyama M 2012 Artist agent: a reinforcement learning approach to automatic stroke generation in oriental ink painting *Proceedings of the 29th International Conference on Machine Learning, ICML 2012, Edinburgh, Scotland, UK, June 26–July 1, 2012* (icml.cc/Omnipress)

[14] Zhao J, Li H, Qu L, Zhang Q, Sun Q, Huo H and Gong M 2022 DCFGAN: an adversarial deep reinforcement learning framework with improved negative sampling for session-based recommender systems *Inf. Sci.* **596** 222–35

IOP Publishing

Deep Learning Technologies for Social Impact

Shajulin Benedict

Chapter 10

Facial recognition and applications

Facial recognition systems are attractive applications of deep learning models [5]. Facial recognition is considered to be a form of biometric authentication and is often combined with sensor-enabled systems. It falls into the computer vision and pattern recognition research domain.

This chapter discusses the prolific growth of this domain, the processes and techniques involved in recognizing faces, a few applications associated with facial recognition, and so forth. In addition, further details of emotion detection are presented and the importance of deep learning models is discussed.

10.1 Facial recognition—a historical view

In general, facial recognition is the process of identifying individuals in order to enable access to certain services. For instance, facial recognition is utilized to open doors in modern smart homes.

In the 1960s, facial recognition was studied by Goldstein, Harmon, and Lesk to identify the landmarks in the face. The landmarks in the face include the eyes, nose, mouth, eyelids, and so forth. They also identified hair color and the sizes of landmarks to distinguish patterns. The researchers developed the idea from Woodrow W Bledsoe, who wondered whether computers could recognize faces.

In fact, the majority of these works were carried out confidentially without much publication or publicity. A few other works were announced by some close contacts of the group, who developed pose orientation. To develop pose orientation tasks, some mathematical models were created to shift landmarks or orient them toward the region of interest.

Within a decade, several researchers, mostly mathematicians, joined hands with computer scientists to apply algebraic concepts to the manipulation of facial parts. Feature extraction using algebraic expressions also bolstered the importance of this approach at this time. One of the crucial challenges the researchers encountered at this time was the unavailability of sophisticated camera devices. Traditional cameras that picked up human faces were 2D cameras. These cameras were often fixed-focus cameras that could not sharpen faces at varying distances. In addition, the camera lenses were not adjustable, and the facial images were often captured in daylight.

With the advent of 3D cameras, the estimation of depths in images became a reality. Cameras had features that could locate the width, depth, and height of captured images. Obviously, a few options for focusing on faces and landmarks were made easier by technology. In addition, camera technology adopted digital solutions such that the recorded images could be transferred to compact discs (CDs), Digital Versatile Discs (DVDs), and other digital storage units.

10.2 Biometrics using faces

Facial recognition is one of the biometric approaches used in the security domain [16]. It can be observed that faces are unique creations in the world.

In general, biometrics are known to be physiological characteristics which remain unique among persons. Analyzing biometrics has been a constant topic used to promote authentication services [6] or similar security-related applications.

Several types of biometrics (see figure 10.1) are used to enable security in computing systems or information and communications technology (ICT) systems. The most common biometric solutions that have been widely utilized in the market are as follows:

1. Fingerprint biometrics—fingerprints are unique physical representations of humans. They can be scanned using various types of fingerprint scanner: optical sensors, thermal sensors, or capacitive sensors [10]. Optical sensors

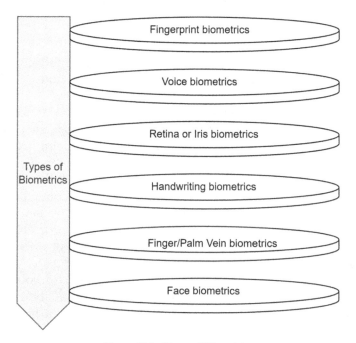

Figure 10.1. Types of biometric.

convert fingerprint images into electric signals, thermal sensors convert fingerprint images into thermal variations, and capacitive sensors convert the images into corresponding capacitances.

The major attraction of fingerprint biometrics is the availability of cheaper sensors and solutions; fingerprint biometrics avoids the necessity of utilizing passwords in machines. However, the drawback of this approach is that fingers are susceptible to problems—i.e. humans break and lose fingers. When this happens, the authentication mechanism fails due to the fingerprint biometric approach.

2. Voice biometrics—the voices of humans have unique characteristics that our brains can recognize. In fact, learning the voice features of our known family members or friends is much faster and more accurate using the neural networks of our human brains. Similarly, voice-biometrics-based authentication can serve as a better choice for modern applications [14]. The effort required for voice-biometrics-based devices to perform authentication is very small—i.e. there is nothing to type on computer keyboards if voice-enabled biometric systems are applied.

   The major advantages of the voice biometric approach are listed below:

   (a) it is a fast solution when compared to typing passwords on machines;
   (b) the voice is considered to be a natural medium of communication; and,
   (c) voice is unique in nature.

   However, there are a few challenges, as mentioned below: (i) a requirement for sophisticated learning algorithms, such as deep learning, to extract the learning steps; (ii) it requires quiet environments in order to collect authenticated voice messages; and so forth.

3. Retina or iris-based biometrics—utilizing the retina or iris for biometrics has been considered one of the most accurate biometric solutions. In this method, the structure of the iris is captured and its unique features are identified. To do this, the pupil of the eye is initially detected. The iris is later detected in the captured image. Although this approach offers a better authentication mechanism, the image capture camera needs to stay very near the eyes. Obviously, this approach is limited to some kinds of application.

4. Handwriting biometrics—this approach is useful to identify authors of writings. Humans naturally have different writing styles, including signatures. For instance, some people write texts in a left-slanting manner; a few write texts in a right-slanting manner; a few of them write drafts in bold characters, and so forth. The author can be determined using the writing style. This technique is also becoming popular in e-health applications [4].

   Handwriting biometrics can be detected using optoelectric sensors which capture handwritten scripts and process their features. In recent years, due to technical advancements, there has been a requirement to process handwritten scripts in real time. A few gadgets that support the real-time writing process include tablets, digital writing pads, and so forth. The major disadvantages of using the handwriting biometrics approach are (i) the non-availability of the required fingers and (ii) the variation in the handwritten scripts of authors over time.

5. Finger/palm vein biometrics—this approach identifies the unique patterns of veins located in the palms or fingers [11]. Some veins of individuals are structured uniquely, so that this technique remains one of the most promising biometric approaches for authentication. However, this method assumes that the scanning requires contact with optical devices.

6. Face biometrics—in line with the other available biometrics, face biometrics is a suitable approach for an authentication mechanism if a camera is available. With modern cameras, face recognition can be enabled from greater distances without much human intervention. Accordingly, several applications have emerged based on face biometrics in various locations. Notably, applications such as FaceID, which is used to unlock iPhone devices, have become more attractive utilities for many Apple customers.

10.3 Facial detection versus recognition

Deep learning is more commonly applied in facial-recognition-related applications than in facial-detection-related applications. Hence, it is important to understand the key relationships between these two terms that are often utilized in the literature.

Facial detection is a mechanism in which faces are identified in images or the surrounding locations of interest. The algorithms utilized for facial detection have little to compute, as facial parameters are quite popularly available in several datasets.

The concept of facial recognition, however, deals with the exploration of faces in the context of specific faces. For instance, this approach learns the features of certain faces and attempts to detect the same face among a set of pictures or faces. The processes involved in detecting faces are quite different from those involved in recognizing them.

10.4 Facial recognition—processes

The key processes involved in facial recognition systems are highlighted in figure 10.2 and detailed explanations are provided in the following subsections.

10.4.1 Face detection

Face detection is the process of searching for faces in images or videos. It is often considered to be a computer vision problem. As part of this process, all faces and their corresponding coordinates are collected from images. These faces are often very dynamic in nature, such that a static representation of facial coordinates is not possible. Several state-of-the-art deep learning algorithms can detect faces in images. However, practitioners traditionally applied cascade filters or similar filters to detect facial features in images.

In a few video streaming applications, frames are extracted from videos in real time for facial detection. A few Python packages based on OpenCV can detect faces from images or videos. These packages are implemented to utilize computing architectures such as graphics processing units (GPUs) for the fast processing of images.

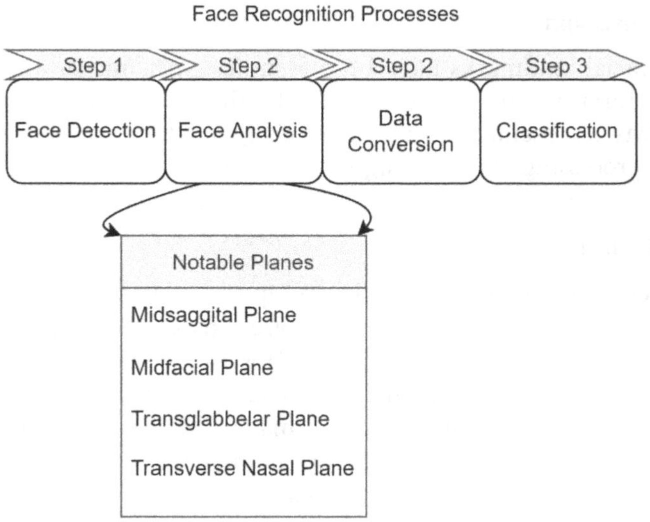

Face Recognition Processes

Step 1	Step 2	Step 2	Step 3
Face Detection	Face Analysis	Data Conversion	Classification

Notable Planes

Midsaggital Plane

Midfacial Plane

Transglabbelar Plane

Transverse Nasal Plane

Figure 10.2. Processes involved in facial recognition.

10.4.2 Face analysis via feature extraction

Once an array of faces has been detected in an image, facial analysis needs to be carried out using the facial geometry corresponding to any given facial image from the database. During this process, facial features based on facial geometries are captured. The facial features include skin color, the presence/absence of beard, eyebrows, the thickness of the lips, the shape of the chin, and so forth. Typically, human faces include ridges, crests, slopes, projections, and so forth that occur irregularly and create uniqueness among faces. Although several variations occur in faces, there are a few notable landmarks that are common to all of them. For instance, the locations of the eyes, nose, and mouth are particularly common in most faces. Understanding the commonalities and the differences helps us to extract features and to analyze them.

The four notable planes observed in human faces are as follows:

1. Midsagittal plane—this plane vertically divides a face such that each division holds one eye and one ear.
2. Midfacial plane—this plane horizontally divides a face such that the mid-portion of the nose is connected to the plane.
3. Transglabellar plane—this plane horizontally divides a face while running in parallel to the midfacial plane. It is found above the midfacial plane; it contains the eyebrows and the complete ears.
4. Transverse nasal plane—this plane also horizontally divides a face and is located parallel to the midfacial plane. However, this plane is below the midfacial plane and contains the nasal portion of the face.

The authors of [7] introduced eigenplanes for robust face detection.

10.4.3 Data conversion

Once the key facial landmarks have been identified, it is important to convert the findings into a form of data understandable by the associated learning algorithms. Facial blueprints represented in the form of digital data are beneficial for image storage or the processing stages of algorithms.

10.4.4 Classification

The final process of the facial recognition setup is to classify a specific facial image from the available list of databases. There are tens of thousands of facial image databases connected with applications. For instance, employee and student lists contained in university databases include facial images that can be linked to an algorithm to recognize the intended facial image. The best known example of the facial recognition problem is the face detection process handled by Facebook, Twitter, Instagram, and similar social media sites.

10.5 Applications

Facial recognition technology has been widely applied in several contexts and situations, as illustrated in figure 10.3.

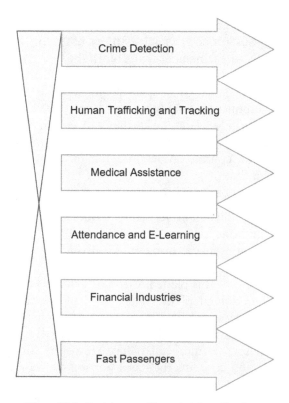

Figure 10.3. Facial-recognition-related applications.

Depending on their utilization, the face-recognition-related applications and their advantages are highlighted in the following subsections.

10.5.1 Crime detection

Criminals may be drastically reduced if machines are allowed to recognize them. Humans have a limited knowledge of the large set of criminal databases that exist in cities. In addition, police investigation teams it difficult to recognize criminals if they change costume or gestures. There is an obvious need for deep-learning-based facial recognition systems such that the faces of criminals loaded from various cities can be captured in a short period [3].

A few popular applications that have been introduced for police officers, such as FaceFirst [1], have been utilized by various government sectors to protect against criminal activities.

10.5.2 Human trafficking and tracking

Human trafficking by mafias or certain criminal sectors must be diligently tracked by learning mechanisms. For instance, a schoolchild missing from a city can be identified by capturing video footprints from closed-circuit televisions (CCTVs) dedicated to different street locations. If the image of the lost schoolchild is included in the database, all connected surveillance units can use facial recognition patterns to clearly identify the child among camera-attached locations in a city.

10.5.3 Medical assistance

Facial recognition software helps doctors or medical practitioners to identify the underlying health-related issues of patients. In most cases, patients find it difficult to guess the right answers to the questionnaires prepared by doctors. However, while they answering the questions, the inner consciences of patients provide answers which are considered to be almost 95 percent accurate in most cases. Additionally, applications that provide medicines based on facial recognition systems have been used in the past [2].

In addition, emotion-related applications have marked importance for several modern applications spanning from the educational domain to the financial domain.

10.5.4 Attendance and e-learning platforms

The number of enrollments in schools and engineering institutes has grown drastically in many countries. Teachers or faculty of institutions find it difficult to mark attendance for each session [17]. With the incorporation of a facial recognition system into the attendance portal, teachers or faculty can automatically detect the presence of students with ease. Also, parents can benefit from this approach, as they can be apprised of their child's up-to-date attendance percentage for subjects. In addition, there are solutions that evaluate the interest of students in particular subjects based on the number of attended hours compared to their attendance of other subjects. For instance, a school student attending all the lecture hours of the mathematical subjects reveals his/her keen interest in pursuing engineering-related subjects in the future.

Detecting emotions in an online education system is important in order to analyze the behavior of students. In this way, they become productive in the teaching–learning processes. In addition, it keeps them up to date by maintaining materials, delivering content and study topics, and so forth. With the involvement of true facial responses, student engagement levels can be determined by teachers. In addition, the teachers can guide them if they feel uncomfortable with some of the topics.

10.5.5 Financial industry

Facial recognition systems have been installed in many banking and financial/industrial sectors to increase security. For instance, a person entering the national bank buildings is monitored by facial recognition software. In this way, security violations, if any, are immediately notified to the relevant authorities.

10.5.6 Fast-moving passengers

Travelers waiting for tickets or boarding public transportation such as airplanes or trains wish to move fast. They cannot miss the vehicle or delay their travel due to their committed agendas. In earlier decades, airplane travelers had to show their passports to the controlling authorities to verify their identities. Travelers' faces are generally verified using photo identity cards. In the modern world, this process is automated, and facial identification is verified by the monitoring robots installed in airports.

10.6 Emotional intelligence—a facial recognition application

Humans are often emotional in nature in addition to their natural intelligence. Some people are highly intelligent but have a limited emotional quotient. Such people are often tempted by suicidal thoughts as a result of the difficulties caused by experiencing failure. In contrast, some people are highly emotional without sufficient intelligence. There is a need to balance both components to achieve better results.

Emotions are fundamental to human beings. They play an integral role in how humans perceive and understand things [13]. A person's emotional state has a significant impact on his learning, decision-making, and communication abilities. In some situations, emotions prevent us from taking the right decisions. Therefore, we are often told not to take decisions if we are emotionally tied up with a subject. The term 'emotional intelligence' is connected with deep learning and allied algorithms.

10.6.1 Emotional intelligence

Emotional intelligence is the ability to recognize, interpret, understand, and establish relationships for better living. In the modern world, emotional intelligence is described using four key attributes:

1. Self-management—self-management is the quality of being able to control oneself without any third-party or second-party interpretations. For instance, a person without a sufficient budget to run the family should control spending money so that sufficient funds are available for unexpected

needs. This is also a quality that must be practiced over long years for perfection.

2. Self-awareness—self-awareness describes the capability to know oneself. It is indeed a challenging task, as many of us do not know the purpose of life. Self-awareness enables people to know the depths of their best and worst wishes; they are able to live stress-free lives, as they are choosing the right options.

3. Empathy—empathy is a quality that promotes good relationships with others, especially when they are distressed. It keeps us feeling the feelings of others when they are experiencing sorrow or happiness. For instance, a fresh deep learning engineer who succeeded in coding an artificial intelligence (AI)-assisted engine will feel happy about it. As an empathic person, you could share his/her happiness, which improves emotional intelligence and relationships.

4. Socialism—socialism is a skill set required for both leaders and common people. It enables everyone to develop relationships in order to relieve stress and achieve goals. For instance, an entrepreneur or startup enthusiast could particularly share the previous experiences of bringing together a small group of team members. In this way, the startup could earn lots of profit/revenue.

Industries are developing systems and solutions that incorporate emotional intelligence, as machines could lead a large number of application developments.

10.6.2 Types of emotion

Emotions are categorized into over 25 types. These emotions are as follows: admiration, adoration, appreciation of beauty, amusement, anger, anxiety, awe, awkwardness, boredom, calmness, confusion, craving, disgust, empathic pain, entrancement, excitement, fear, horror, interest, joy, nostalgia, relief, sadness, satisfaction, and surprise.

Among these different types of emotion, the most commonly applied emotions include happiness, surprise, disgust, anger, and boredom.

A few notable gestures (see figure 10.4) that correspond to these different types of emotions are listed below:

1. Happiness—when a person feels happy, the shoulders are raised and the face expresses happiness.

2. Surprise—if a person is surprised to see some objects or a winning situation, he expresses surprise with raised eyes. In addition, the other parts of the body show signs of surprise. For instance, the majority of people hold their hands together and close their mouths to show their surprised feelings.

3. Disgust—a feeling of disgust is expressed by people when they dislike an activity. The facial expressions reveal this emotion in the form of wrinkled faces, mouths tilted, or dropped shoulders. This feeling is conveyed in several fashions with limited uniqueness.

4. Anger—anger is a very common emotion exhibited by people experiencing discomfort with another party. This emotion can be expressed by clenched teeth, squared shoulders, and/or sharpened eyes.

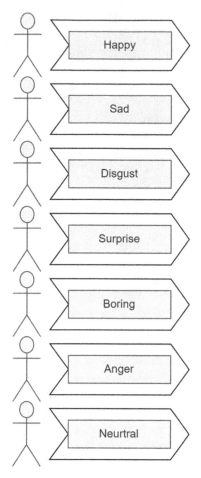

Figure 10.4. Facial gestures.

5. Sadness—sadness expresses the inherent worry-feeling in a person.
6. Neutral—at times, faces do not indicate any sort of response or emotion. This could be due to not listening to the other person or for several other reasons.
7. Boredom—reading or studying lengthy documents, listening to certain talks, and so forth, can provoke this emotion. The inability to cope with certain agendas can also convey boredom to the public. Usually, it is expressed in the form of partially closed eyes, lips pointing downwards, face resting on hands, and so forth.

10.6.3 Emotion detection approaches

If machines are going to exhibit emotional intelligence, they have to comprehend the emotions of human beings. Detecting human emotions can be carried out using diverse approaches.

Depending on the input provided to emotion detection systems, the classification methods are categorized as: (i) text-based, (ii) speech-based, and (iii) facial expression-based approaches (see figure 10.5).

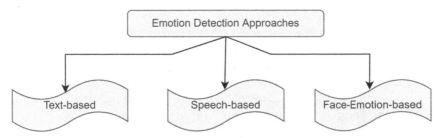

Figure 10.5. Input-based emotion detection classifications.

10.6.3.1 Text-based emotion detection

Identifying emotions in texts [18] is crucial for web-related applications. Bots and chatbots are becoming viral not only in enterprise-based web applications but also in governmental organizations where there is less manpower to answer questions. Handling emotions based on texts requires sophisticated deep learning techniques, such as the sentiment analysis discussed in previous chapters (see chapter 6).

Bare sentiment analysis is slightly removed from the interpretation of emotion in texts. For instance, sentiment analysis uses deep learning methods to focus on providing opinions on business deals or provoking newer thoughts using a list of ideas. More specifically, sentiment analysis attempts to find positive, neutral, and negative feelings in texts. However, emotion recognition in text must look at more detailed information to infer feelings such as happiness, sorrow, disgust, and so forth.

NLP plays an inherently vital role in text-based emotion detection systems. The emotion recognition process is a content-based classification problem in which emotional keywords are identified in texts. These keywords may or may not appear in the documents where the search is performed. A few datasets exist that can be used to detect emotions in texts. Notably, the ISEAR dataset, Emobank, dailydialog, and so forth have been utilized for detecting emotions in texts.

10.6.3.2 Speech-based emotion detection

Speech-based emotion detection is becoming quite popular [8], especially when robots are involved in answering telephone calls. In most business establishments, handling customers' queries or orders is initiated using robots. These robots ask the clients/customers multiple questions before the call is handled by a human. In the meantime, if the customer becomes annoyed by too much waiting or answering, the robots can understand the customer's emotions using an underlying deep learning solution.

Speech emotion recognition (SER) is basically performed using two steps—(i) feature extraction and (ii) classification. These steps are common to the methods described for the previous emotion recognition techniques. Traditional SER approaches were based on old learning models such as Markov chain models, Gaussian models, and support vector machine models. However, these traditional learning models are not convenient for speech emotion recognition approaches due to their poor feature engineering techniques. The use of deep learning methods for SER clearly improves the quality of emotional reasoning. For instance, long short-term memory (LSTM) networks, autoencoders, and generative adversarial networks (GANs) have achieved better results for these applications.

10.6.3.3 Face-based emotion recognition

The most effective and widely utilized emotion recognition method is based on facial expressions. In fact, the face offers several expressions that do not require active communication—i.e. emotions are clearly expressed in the form of body language. Generally, facial expressions combine the inherent feelings of our mind, physique, and personal opinions [12]. Accordingly, facial expressions can be captured by automated machines, such as cameras, to visualize emotions without many difficulties.

10.7 Emotion detection—database creation

One of the major topics of interest for human-to-computer interactions and vice versa is to empower computers to understand human emotions. Human emotions differ across regions or boundaries, as they are bound to cultural influences and other social factors.

To capture the emotions of humans or living beings, emotions need to be absorbed and learned from various use-case scenarios. Although there are several ways to capture emotions, their effectiveness can be limited if they do not follow certain well-organized procedures.

The most common procedures used to create emotion-related databases are as follows:

- Questionnaire preparation
- Capturing videos
- Processing images
- Annotating emotions

10.7.1 Questionnaire preparation

The study of emotions is based on psycho-physical experiences inherent in humans. These experiences vary between one person and another due to their previous routine practices. To capture the most common human emotions, such as anger, fear, sorrow, disgust, and so forth, appropriate questions or screenplays must to be displayed to them. For instance, some sort of stimulating videos could be played to the defaulters for expressing their emotions.

10.7.2 Capturing videos

A few volunteers may be needed to take the specified questionnaire so that their emotions can be captured by cameras for the subsequent processing stages. These volunteers should not know when they have to show emotions. For this reason, they may have to be exposed to an environment where hidden cameras are located and stimulating videos are played.

The capture of emotions depends on quality cameras and the background lighting conditions of the environments where the emotions are to be captured. Modifying the camera angle based on the directions of the lighting sources, such as sunlight or room lights, can drastically impact the capture of emotions. Additionally, some low-resolution cameras can hardly capture the distinction between emotions. Obviously, a camera that has good resolution is needed to capture the emotions expressed by the volunteers.

10.7.3 Processing images

Deep learning models, such as convolutional neural networks (CNNs) or residual neural networks (ResNets), require preprocessed images to perform better classification. In this problem domain, the images need to be classified as expressing one of the few emotions that were categorized earlier.

To obtain and preprocess the images, a few steps need to be followed:

1. First, the captured videos need to be split into video clips based on the emotions found. As emotions are only found in certain portions of the video clips, they are divided into smaller video clips. For instance, a volunteer could have started the questionnaire by only exhibiting emotions three minutes after entering the environment. Hence, the first few video portions are not informative and could actually waste computational power that could be used to categorize emotions.

2. The video clips are then converted into frames that contain potential emotions. In this way, the emotions can be fed to deep learning algorithms that categorize the emotions in the frames. To do this, tools such as `opencv` provide libraries and programming APIs that are suitable for converting video clips into frames.

   The conversion of video clips into frames is often organized in stages, as described below:

   (a) Removing unwanted frames—even though the frames are captured such that the video clips contain proper emotions, they are sometimes blurry and shaky in nature. These frames, even if they were used for detecting emotions, could cause the categorization of emotions to fail. Hence, such frames can be removed at this stage of execution.

      In fact, there are a few techniques, such as fast Fourier transform or Laplacian transform techniques, which have been found quite popular for removing blurry or shaky frames from selected video clips.

   (b) Collecting selected frames—quality frames that have the potential scope to be used in processing emotions must be collected either in a database or as image objects so that they can be applied for the subsequent processing steps.

10.7.4 Feature extraction

Features of images from the selected frames need to be extracted using capable toolsets, such as OpenCV. The most common features that can be extracted from the images include facial landmarks in 2D and/or 3D, head pose, eye gaze movement, and so forth. This information can be collected in CSV format so that appropriate emotion datasets can be developed by labeling it.

10.7.5 Annotations

Having found the right features for the given preprocessed images, the images can be annotated in several ways. The most common approaches that are followed to annotate emotions in images [15] are as follows:

1. By volunteers—volunteers who have experienced questions asked by video stimulators are important sources of image annotation. They have the correct information to point out their own emotions and can suggest whether they felt sad, happy, angry, or so forth. This labeling information could be crucial for learning algorithms to train themselves for future emotion detection.
2. By psychologists—psychologists have a special way of observing people and emotions. If the questions and the corresponding emotions are given to them, they have the ability to judge whether a person of interest has presented the expected emotions. In fact, the quality of the annotations used by this method is highly dependent on the expertise of psychologists.
3. By machines—it is also possible that learning algorithms or deep reinforcement learning (DRL) methods can be applied as unsupervised learning methods that enable machines to annotate emotions. However, high-quality annotations require a large volume of data and the capability of algorithms to perform the annotation task well.

Figure 10.6 represents all of the components involved in collecting emotions from volunteers using cameras and deep learning algorithms.

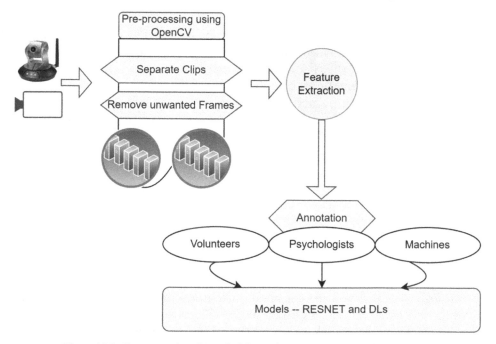

Figure 10.6. System used to detect facial emotions using deep learning methods.

10.8 Challenges and future work

Although face recognition and emotion detection mechanisms have several known applications in the market, a few known challenges require researchers to work on them soon. Some notable challenges and associated suggestions are listed in the following subsections.

10.8.1 Face detection—environmental conditions

A common issue is that faces are not exposed as expected for the learning algorithm to quickly obtain the features or landmarks of faces. For instance, during the COVID-19 pandemic, people wore masks that partially exposed their faces. Learning algorithms find it difficult to identify unique faces under such conditions.

Another environmental condition that impacts facial detection procedures is related to lighting conditions. If faces are not exposed to light in the required manner, the detection mechanism fails.

10.8.2 Pose variations

The pose can vary from person to person and from time to time. Even though a person is supposed to view the camera while images are captured, the viewing angle of the person varies. For instance, a few people have a common practice of showcasing their faces with tilted shoulders. These modifications create challenges for emotion detection software, particularly automated software.

10.8.3 Occlusion

Occlusion is a condition in which the whole facial image is not fed to the learning algorithm as an input. Obviously, some facial landmarks are then skipped, resulting in a failure to identify a person or detect the emotions in images. There are several possible reasons for occlusion. For instance, unpredictable growth of a mustache or beard, wearing a mask or cap, hiding behind a wall, and so forth, are a few notable reasons for occlusion in facial images. The authors of [9] attempted to improve facial recognition despite several conditions related to occlusion.

10.8.4 Ageing

Another notable challenge in facial recognition systems is the aging problem. Aging relates to the non-coherence between the images available in a database and the the corresponding reality. People belonging to the younger or elderly age groups show abrupt changes in faces within a few years or months. If the images available in databases are not updated frequently, there is a high chance that facial recognition software will abruptly fail.

References

[1] Facefirst project, May 2022 Page Version ID: 1088786364
[2] Chaiyarab L, Mopung C and Charoenpong T 2021 Authentication system by using HOG face recognition technique and web-based for medical dispenser machine *2021 IEEE 4th*

International Conference on Knowledge Innovation and Invention (ICKII) (Piscataway, NJ: IEEE) pp 97–100

[3] Cui W and Yan W Q 2016 A scheme for face recognition in complex environments *Int. J. Digit. Crime Forensics* **8** 26–36

[4] Faúndez-Zanuy M, Fiérrez J, Ferrer M A, Díaz M, Tolosana R and Plamondon R 2020 Handwriting Biometrics: Applications and Future Trends in e-Security and e-Health *Cogn. Comput.* **12** 940–53

[5] Ge H, Zhu Z, Dai Y, Wang B and Wu X 2022 Facial expression recognition based on deep learning *Comput. Methods Programs Biomed.* **215** 106621

[6] Huang H 2022 Travellers' intentions to use facial recognition systems for authentication in hotels *Int. J. Inf. Syst. Serv. Sect.* **14** 1–15

[7] Lei L and Kim S 2014 Eigen directional bit-planes for robust face recognition *IEEE Trans. Consum. Electron.* **60** 702–9

[8] Manohar K and Logashanmugam E 2022 Hybrid deep learning with optimal feature selection for speech emotion recognition using improved meta-heuristic algorithm Knowl *Based Syst* **246** 108659

[9] Mills I and Cleary F 2022 Facial emotion recognition analysis using deep learning through RGB-D imagery of VR participants through partially occluded facial types *2022 IEEE Conference on Virtual Reality and 3D User Interfaces Abstracts and Workshops (VRW)* (Piscataway, NJ: IEEE) pp 862–3

[10] Moolla Y and De Kock A 2021 Biometric recognition of infants using fingerprint, iris, and ear biometrics *IEEE Access* **9** 38269–86

[11] Nayar G R, Thomas T and Emmanuel S 2021 Graph based secure cancelable palm vein biometrics *J. Inf. Secur. Appl* **62** 102991

[12] Pester A and Galler K 2018 Demonstration: face emotion recognition (FER) with deep learning—web based interface *15th Int. Conf. on Remote Engineering and Virtual Instrumentation, REV 2018* vol 47M E Auer and R Langman (Cham: Springer) pp 466–70

[13] Retnamony J R K, Muniasamy S and Stanley B F 2022 Enhanced global and local face feature extraction for effective recognition of facial emotions *Concurr. Comput. Pract. Exp.* **34** e6701

[14] Sholokhov A, Kinnunen T, Vestman V and Lee K A 2020 Voice biometrics security: extrapolating false alarm rate via hierarchical Bayesian modeling of speaker verification scores *Comput. Speech Lang.* **60** 101024

[15] Singh S and Benedict S 2020 Indian Semi-Acted Facial Expression (iSAFE) Dataset for Human Emotions Recognition *Advances in Signal Processing and Intelligent Recognition Systems* ed S M Thampi, R M Hegde, S Krishnan, J Mukhopadhyay, V Chaudhary, O Marques, S Piramuthu and J M Corchado (Singapore: Springer) pp 150–62

[16] Smith M and Miller S 2022 The ethical application of biometric facial recognition technology *AI Soc.* **37** 167–75

[17] Tamilkodi R 2021 Automation system software assisting educational institutes for attendance, fee dues, report generation through email and mobile phone using face recognition *Wirel. Pers. Commun.* **119** 1093–110

[18] Yang H, Alsadoon A and Prasad P W C 2022 Deep learning neural networks for emotion classification from text: enhanced leaky rectified linear unit activation and weighted loss *Multim. Tools Appl.* **81** 15439–68

Part III

Security, performance, and future directions

Chapter 11

Data security and platforms

Artificial intelligence (AI), including deep learning techniques, has strengthened the information security practices of the past. Various security attacks have been robustly addressed by augmenting novel technologies with deep learning concepts. This chapter discusses security concepts from two broader perspectives:

1. security challenges and techniques/methods adapted for deep learning algorithms or deep-learning-based applications, and
2. the application of deep learning algorithms to addressing the security challenges of other applications.

11.1 Security breaches

Security is typically an important feature or step for computing machines. It is a human tendency to protect resources from invaders. This tendency has been found not only in personal lives but also within national borders. For instance, there are always reasons to fight with the neighbors or neighboring countries, which highlights security vulnerabilities.

The tendency to protect resources has also been an enduring objective in the informatics domain. Several methods have been practiced in the past to protect private or public computing or data resources from invaders. Deep learning has been an excellent learning mechanism that automatically understands the attacking behaviors of these potential hackers.

Many industries and volunteers, including academicians, choose to address the security concerns of existing computing systems for the following reasons: (i) to prevent potential data breaches or data-related attacks; (ii) to prevent unauthorized access to confidential data or compute resources; (iii) to continue to offer services without involuntary disruption; (iv) to protect networks from the unnecessary utilization of computing instances; etc. These reasons are respectively discussed below:

1. Potential data breaches—a leak in medical data over the Internet due to a weak Internet of things (IoT)-enabled sensor could lead to potential threats for several employees in an organization.
2. Unauthorized access—the data, if stolen, could have a serious impact on business establishments or financial proceedings.
3. Avoiding involuntary disruption—for instance, a mobile node connected using the Message Queue Telemetry Transport (MQTT) protocol may use brokers to transfer packets between senders and receivers. If the broker refuses to serve the data or falls prey to denial-of-service attacks, the entire IoT-enabled application is prevented from operating.

11.2 Security attacks

Since deep learning-related applications are diverse and have proliferated in numbers, they encounter various security attacks and threats. The security threats are based on computer networking threats, as deep learning applications are often applied in distributed or data-centric environments.

Traditionally, security attacks that appear in computing machines occur for several reasons—both intentional and unintentional. These security attacks are often countered by robust security features enabled in machines. The capabilities of security threats and the difficulty of solving them increase day by day. However, the birth of novel security attacks and countermeasures to the attacks has been an unavoidable part of the history of information security.

A few security attacks (see figure 11.1) that have targeted deep learning-related applications, especially during the post-COVID period, are as follows:

1. Malware attack—security attacks due to viruses, worms, Trojans, ransomware, or software that causes malfunctions in computing hardware or

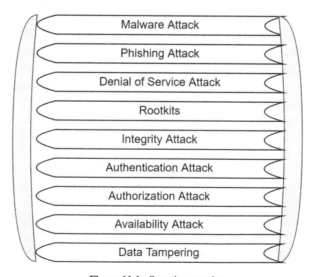

Figure 11.1. Security attacks.

software components have frequently used various patterns and methods for many years. Although security-enabling software attempt to address these attacks, the creation of novel approaches for invading computing resources is constant in the computer world. These attacks are commonly activated through external links, email attachments, or flash drives. A few researchers have developed approaches to identify these malware attacks [8].

2. Phishing attack—this security attack attempts to deliver a lot of information or many messages to a targeted recipient with scripts attached to the information. In this way, the recipients are directed to fall prey to malicious scripts that gain access to personal data or resources without prior permission. The authors of [6] developed a framework to detect such phishing attacks.

3. Denial-of-service attack—even though services are running, the denial-of-service attack causes refusals when users inquire about service instances. The authors of [7] developed approaches to counter this attack.

4. Rootkits—attacks that compromise the root credentials of machines or sensor nodes are often termed rootkits. This attack is commonly found in virtual machines (VMs) that do not have sufficient isolation. Rootkit attacks in cloud services can reduce the capacity of computing machines that host deep learning applications.

5. Integrity attack—an integrity attack is an attack that modifies the contents of data or features (most often in an intentional manner). Here, an attacker gets access to files or commands and can modify them without prior permission. Accordingly, integrity attacks degrade trust between the involved participants.

6. Authentication attack—this attack attempts to challenge the authentication processes of deep learning-related services hosted on computing machines. Typically, these attacks enable attackers to discover usernames, passwords, authentication keys, and so forth, that are compromised (often using scripts), which are then used to access resources. The authors of [9] developed protection approaches to handle authentication attacks in physically unclonable function (PUF)-based authentication systems. In some cases, deep learning services hosted on third-party compute machines are accessed by attackers who use password recovery validation approaches.

7. Authorization attacks—in general, authorization describes the process of gaining access to resources or services, whereas authentication describes the process of verifying who has access—i.e. authentication relates to the people involved in the attacking processes. Authorization attacks are observed in computing services, including deep learning services, in which file access is granted to unknown parties.

   Typically, decoding the passwords or passphrases used for communications between nodes has been challenging for computing nodes. A common problem is that passwords are hacked using various methods, such as password-generating software and so forth.

8. Availability attack—this attack relates to the non-availability of data or a model during learning processes. In modern IoT-enabled applications, machines can automatically preprocess data and create models using input

datasets. If the data or model becomes unavailable, the learning outcome might be compromised. Availability attacks are introduced by attackers to prevent users or machines from accessing data. In fact, the availability attacks can also be treated as unintentional threats.

9. Data tampering—data is often a crucial ingredient for deep learning applications. However, if the data is tampered with by malicious software or intended users, the modeling fails. It is better to protect data using technologies such as blockchains. In blockchain technologies, the data become immutable due to the involvement of multiple parties and the establishment of hashes in a Merkle tree approach. The involvement of disparate parties prevents one party from modifying the document found in the blockchain databases.

11.3 Deep-learning-related security attacks

Apart from various traditional security-related vulnerabilities, deep learning applications and learning mechanisms can encounter novel security attacks. The most common security attacks that are unique to deep-learning-related applications (see figure 11.2) and their crucial features/characteristics are listed below:

1. Model invasion attack—in this scenario, the hacker attempts to learn the feature sets of trained models that are created using private data and deep learning algorithms. The model invasion attack can give hackers a clue about future events or potential forecasts made by the system based on the data.

2. Inference hacking—in general, inferences are provided to specific machines or restricted communities of a learning system [5]. However, in machine-to-machine (M2M) communications, faulty machines or intentional attackers can obtain the contents of deep learning model parameters. This issue remains a challenge in MQTT-based protocol communications.

   For instance, if the deep learning predicted topic submitted by a faulty machine or an attacking machine to an MQTT broker is as follows, the receiving actuator node of a door could open for any stranger to enter the house.

   ```
   \houseNo1\frontdoor\open
   ```

3. Privacy attack—there is a strong chance that attackers can learn the private information inherently found in data. Attackers can utilize these data for

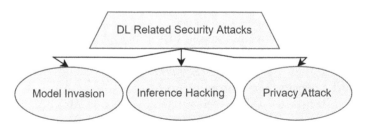

Figure 11.2. Deep-learning-related security attacks.

monetary gain. For instance, a poorly exposed deep learning model that reveals the business flow or customer interests of certain countries, especially developed countries, could distract investors or business traders while planning future investments. Similarly, exposing sensitive data such as facial emotions due to any weakly protected DL models could challenge users' privacies.

Deep learning adversaries are one of the security challenges that have been thoroughly studied by several researchers/practitioners [4] in the past. The adversarial attacks that are possible for deep learning models are classified by methodology, as described below (see figure 11.3):

1. Perturbations—learning the perturbation patterns of deep learning models that are used in the hidden layers of deep learning models could become a potential attack for deep learning-based applications.
2. Challenging adversarial samples—attackers can provide adversarial samples to deep learning models so that the outcome of the model changes in the normal course of the learning process. In this way, attackers can create confusion about the existing deep learning architecture. Typically, adversarial sample modification is carried out in several ways:
   (a) Applying patches—attackers can create a code snippet that integrates with the deep learning modeling algorithm and develops newer data sequences. These code snippets are derived from randomness or matrices.

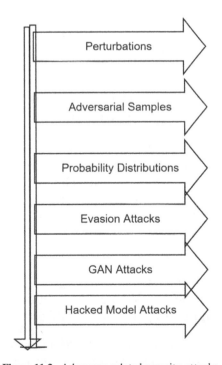

Figure 11.3. Adversary-related security attacks.

(b) Augmenting data—the attackers inject skewness or use a few augmentation methods on the existing data sequences. Accordingly, the modeling varies, satisfying the intentions of potential hackers.

3. Challenging probability distributions—deep learning models function using the data features or the probability distributions of data. The attacker can modify the distribution of probability distributions in a decentralized manner by varying the code portion of the deep learning model. Accordingly, the evolving model and its associated predictions will be surprisingly different.

4. Evasion attacks—in deep learning, evasion attacks are attacks that modify the decisions of deep learning-enabled machines [3]. These attacks happen due to the inclusion of adversarial samples that are too small and have intended variations at the initial stage of the learning process. The sample magnifies to such an extent that it reaches a state that creates wrong decisions. Evasion attacks are often studied in self-driving car applications that utilize deep learning algorithms. Compared to data augmentation or patching approaches, evasion attacks are more specific to inducing the intended adversarial samples during the learning processes.

5. Generative adversarial network (GAN) attacks—in general, GAN has two components, the generator and the discriminator. The generator component of GAN tries to learn about its adversaries by reducing GAN losses. As GANs are purely unsupervised learning models, attackers can attack such learning models by inducing wrong adversaries or misleading the GAN learning programs. Attackers can provide malformed inputs that deviate adversaries from the expected delivery of learning inferences. Typically, GAN attacks impair outcomes considerably. In addition, they have a detrimental impact on the computational time, which indirectly affects the underlying computing machines or increases the cost of hosted services, especially when they are executed on cloud services. The authors of [2] studied the impact of GAN attacks for IoT-enabled applications.

6. Hosted model attack—in several use cases, deep learning algorithms use pre-trained models for inferences. For instance, to classify flowers, a pretrained You Only Look Once (YOLO) model that has been modeled using flowers may be considered. However, an attacker could host similar pre-trained models which produce the wrong results and poor efficiency. As a result of such an attack, users may have to bear additional computational costs if the application is executed on cloud services or they may have to waste time applying the wrong pretrained model to their datasets.

Threats are situations or circumstances that often create unusual attacks in an unintentional manner. By contrast, the attacks discussed in the previous section describe intentional approaches to creating risks to learning models. The potential threats that are often found in deep learning scenarios are listed below:

1. Software crashes—crashes and software failures are common in deep learning-related applications. These situations are considered potential

threats to completing the assigned learning tasks. Software crashes happen due to software version mismatches or hardware failures. However, if the software crashes are induced by intruders or potential hackers of machines, then the situation is called a crashing attack.

2. Undefined termination—code that requires continuous iterations in the hidden layers of deep learning algorithms, such as convolutional neural networks (CNNs), YOLOv5, GANs, and so forth, create risky situations for computational nodes, especially constrained nodes that are often battery operated. The algorithm does not terminate and deliver its findings or observations. This is often known as an undefined termination threat to deep learning models. This threat can also be converted into an attack if an attacker introduces code into the learning model.

3. Memory leaks—it is possible for deep learning algorithm to have with memory leaks. Memory leaks in deep learning algorithms occur due to errors in programming. For instance, memory dynamically allocated by an algorithm can turn into a memory leakage problem if it is not linked to the program throughout the execution. Deep learning algorithms have several operations based on arrays or tensors. If these algorithms cause memory leakage issues, unlinked memory units with large amounts of data could become a potential threat for deep-learning-related applications.

4. Memory unavailability—deep learning algorithms are typically considered to be memory-intensive algorithms. It is common for these algorithms to have lengthy execution times. For instance, training facial emotions in a data set consisting of 10 000 images using modern deep learning algorithms could take over 14 hours. The corresponding memory units used by the running software will reach from megabytes to gigabytes. After long hours of waiting to obtain the trained model, the program could abruptly stop functioning due to the unavailability of memory in devices such as edge nodes or battery-operated devices. Such situations are considered threats to deep learning applications.

5. Computational overload—computational overload is a huge risk for deep learning-related applications, as the machine can halt without prior notification. Deep learning applications hosted by Docker containers (lightweight virtual machines) can lead to failures owing to the default killer processes of kernels. These kernels kill overloaded processes without issuing prior warnings to users.

11.4 Metrics

The strength of attacks or threats is measured using metrics. Such metrics enable users or application developers to gauge the pros and cons of the underlying algorithms. Figure 11.4 illustrates the list of metrics that are utilized to measure security-oriented impacts on deep learning applications.

The potential attacks that are evolving in deep learning models can be measured and monitored using metrics so that the attackers may be penalized. A few

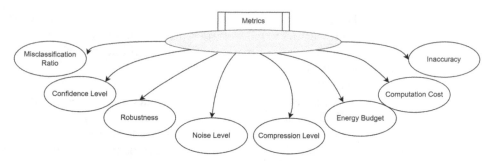

Figure 11.4. Metrics utilized to measure security risks.

notable metrics that are applied to measure the security features of deep learning applications are listed below:

1. Misclassification ratio—an attacker can modify data or use any method to hamper the predictive ability of deep learning applications. Image-processing applications often require image classification steps. The metric known as the misclassification ratio defines the number of classification misses observed when these compromised deep learning systems are used for experiments.

2. Confidence level—learning models are characterized using a confidence level. If the generated model is utilized to predict samples, the confidence of the predictions can be impacted by several factors, including the attackers' impact. Confidences compromised due to attacks are represented by specific levels. This metric represents the confidence level using numbers varying between zero and one to denote the impact of attacks.

3. Robustness—images or data are compromised by blurriness, noise, or compression methods.

   Blurriness occurs in images when they are captured or after they are captured. The major reasons that lead to blurriness when images are captured are as follows:

   (a) the camera does not have a sufficient shutter speed. Obviously, shaking cameras lead to blurriness;

   (b) exposing cameras to a low-light environment can reduce the sharpness of images; and,

   (c) In some cases, people avoid carrying tripods or camera support equipment, which reduces image sharpness.

4. Noise level—similarly, noise can be induced by an attacker in several image-based machine learning models, especially for GANs. Introducing noise into facial images deteriorates the quality of learning models. For instance, GANs have difficulty in distinguishing faces in the input images. Attackers have also made efforts to introduce Gaussian noise into watermarked images. Attackers who work with watermarked images typically perform the following actions:

    (a) The attackers attempt to remove the watermarks from images. This technique is called a removal attack.

    (b) The attackers apply brute-force methods to identify the security keys of watermarked images.

    (c) The attackers can modify the geometry of images. Typically, the geometry of images is modified by flipping, cropping, rotating, and so forth. Accordingly, if this takes place, classification becomes more challenging.

5. Compression levels—varying the compression levels of images can confuse receivers or intended recipients, including machines, when they decode the images or learn the features of images.

6. Computation cost—the overhead of compensating for attacks is high. For instance, large computational instances are required to repeat the learning process if images are affected by noise or blurriness. Thus, the computation cost is considered to be one of the key metrics used to judge the activity of attackers. The computation cost is taken more seriously if the learning algorithm is hosted by cloud services, especially public cloud infrastructures such as Amazon Web Services (AWS) or Google.

7. Energy budget—the energy budget is a metric that is tightly connected to computation and environmental issues. In fact, energy is a limited resource in the majority of countries, and is carefully spent in computational data-centers. The energy consumption of learning algorithms, if not diligently handled, can lead to carbon emissions and increased machine costs. The energy budget is, therefore, considered to be a metric that can be used to evaluate the impact of attackers while analyzing deep learning algorithms.

8. Inaccuracy—attackers tend to modify the images and influence the learning inferences, which often has a substantial impact on accuracy.

11.5 Execution environments

The security issues depend on the environments where deep learning algorithms are implemented and processed. Algorithms are typically hosted in IoT environments, cloud instances, edge nodes, mobile nodes, and hybrid infrastructures.

Depending on the location where deep learning algorithms are executed, the security features vary accordingly.

11.5.1 IoT environment

Not all the training and testing phases of deep learning algorithms can generally be executed on IoT-enabled sensor nodes. These algorithms require large computational capabilities and storage spaces. IoT-enabled devices are battery operated and have minimal memory storage spaces.

Obviously, we cannot include more robust security features or sophisticated algorithms on these devices. This leads to several security challenges, as follows:

1. Unauthorized access—as strong username and password mechanisms are not included on sensor-enabled devices, unauthorized access to deep learning machines is quite common in such situations.

2. Heterogeneous devices—if deep learning algorithms are implemented on IoT-enabled microcontrollers or microprocessors, the implementation steps might need wider support for data formats and protocols. Obviously, due to the limitations of sensor nodes, the support for heterogeneous devices is limited.

3. Software failures—hackers typically aim at the application layer of networked systems. They can inject incorrect data into the connected databases or repositories of IoT systems. Consequently, security is challenged on these nodes.

4. Middleware failures—most of the IoT-enabled devices that are operated in virtual environments use Docker or middleware software components. If any hacker attempts to modify the structure of the middleware layers, the whole group of Docker instances or VM instances running on top of the hardware is compromised.

5. Enabling access control—faulty system-level software components can impose strict access control mechanisms on sensor devices. The sensor nodes that are responsible for delivering images or data are not granted access to submit the data to the underlying deep learning algorithms. This leads to poor learning accuracy in IoT-enabled applications.

6. Network intrusion—the IoT is considered to be the future Internet, where millions of computing nodes and trillions of objects are connected. In such environments, unauthorized access to networked devices and resources leads to poor security.

The authors of [1] revealed a few possible security features that could be adopted by IoT-enabled systems.

Security concerns in IoT environments can be addressed by enabling the following methods in deep learning systems or their frameworks:

1. Offloading—as IoT-enabled nodes cannot provide robust security, the security-related tasks are offloaded to powerful devices, including cloud instances or fog nodes.

2. Privacy preservation—privacy is crucial in order to enable freedom of movement and respect between individuals. A person can have unusual behaviors which should not be visible to the public in future interactions, i.e. failure to preserve privacy can lead to destruction.

3. Anomaly detection—any abnormalities found in the layers of the IoT networking stack can be detected and reported to the associated cloud services. Accordingly, security failures in constrained devices can be detected. The concept of anomaly detection is quite often used in industrial IoT systems or frameworks.

11.5.2 Cloud instances

Most deep learning algorithms are hosted on cloud environments as Dockers, VM templates, or services. These cloud instances are prone to several security challenges that are specific to cloud environments. A few notable cloud-based security challenges that remain challenging for deep learning-related applications are as follows:

1. Service overloading—hackers consume a large number of computational connectivity services, including deep learning services. Accordingly, the computational cost of deep learning-based cloud services is magnified unless controls are present.
2. DevOps failures—today, deep learning-based applications are often implemented using DevOps technologies. When the DevOps approach is used, the coupling between the application development team and the operational team is very high—i.e. the services are developed and hosted in near real time with limited down time. Failures in such DevOps systems can cause delayed hosting or significant down time for the deep learning machine or system.
3. Vendor lock-in situations—vendor lock-in is a common problem for cloud solutions. In clouds, the services, including the data storage services, hosted by third-party providers are vulnerable to potential vendor lock-in issues— i.e. the providers cannot offer the specified service level agreements (SLAs) or vary the service terms without affecting the connectivity between the services and the customers.
4. Multicloud failures—to avoid vendor lock-in issues, most cloud developers, including deep-learning-solution-based cloud developers, prefer hosting the solutions in multicloud environments. The multicloud environments include many third-party providers, such as Google, AWS, Azure, and so forth. However, due to poor service policies or integration strategies, deep learning-based cloud services can fail despite these mitigating circumstances.

11.5.3 Edge nodes

Edge devices are often constrained nodes that have more limited computational power than fog or cloud nodes. Deep learning applications and parts of deep learning intelligence incorporated into edge nodes experience security issues in several ways. The security issues most commonly encountered while implementing deep-learning-related applications on edge nodes are described below:

1. Flooding attacks—edge nodes experience flooding attacks, which keep the devices busy with unwanted work/tasks. In general, edge nodes attempt to collect sensor data and apply a little intelligence before the gists are forwarded to cloud services. As these devices are computationally less powerful, engaging more sensors that submit several sets of sensor data within a limited time frame could become a challenging risk/threat to the devices. In most cases, filtering those data to obtain the wanted data is very difficult for edge nodes.
2. Protocol-oriented attacks—various sensors are connected to edge nodes using the User Datagram Protocol (UDP) instead of the traditional Transport Control Protocol (TCP) as utilized in Internet connections. For instance, the Constrained Application Protocol (CoAP), which provides a request–response model for connectivity between nodes, combines the UDP protocol with reliable messaging concepts to transfer messages. In general, the UDP is a connectionless transport-layer protocol in networks. This protocol, although faster in sending messages across nodes, fails to provide

reliable communications. Depending on the protocol applied, the security of the connections is challenged in most cases.

3. Side-channel attacks—edge nodes heavily suffer from side-channel attacks. In side channels, the communication signals are traced to study the patterns of communication, such as energy utilization patterns. Later, user behaviors can be tracked, or the utilization of the devices can be hacked by entering the edge device system information.

11.5.4 Mobile networks and deep learning

Mobile applications have increased tremendously due to the utilization of smartphones and 5G connectivity systems. In fact, many web applications have been moved to mobile-assisted solutions in addition to existing services, due to their larger bandwidth availability and increasing computational power. Mobile networks also continue to be a part of IoT systems.

IoT technology has driven the improvement of traditional wireless technologies. For instance, the birth of 5G technology is based on the demands/requirements of IoT-enabled applications, such as smart city applications, smart transportation applications, smart logistics applications, and so forth.

A few security challenges that impact deep learning applications when they augment mobile networks are described below:

1. Key exchange failures—mobile networks are vulnerable while exchanging keys in order to establish connections or share information. Although a few lightweight key-sharing protocols exist for IoT situations, these protocols are still vulnerable to attackers.

2. Bandwidth unavailability—mobile networks are designed as smaller units of hexagonal footprints. Typically, a broad spectrum of bandwidth is shared among a group of mobile cell networks, such that the mobile range has a hexagonal footprint. Each cell of a mobile network has a base station that captures the information from the mobile nodes. The frequencies of mobile networks can be reused by other mobile towers such that interference between towers is minimized.

    The designers of 5G networks attempt to reduce the signal footprint, i.e. the connectivity range. In this way, more customers can be accommodated; the power required to transmit from base stations is reduced; and interference between base stations is minimized.

    As the bandwidth is comparatively smaller than that required by the number of customers, the bandwidth is reused by multiple mobile towers. However, this bandwidth is sometimes not served to potential customers. In the case of deep learning applications, if the data does not reach deep learning services due to the unavailability of mobile networks, the learning processes may be inaccurate. Attackers can try to keep the mobile networks busy all the time without allowing the nodes to easily develop the intelligence—a security challenge.

11.6 Using deep learning to enhance security

In the second part of this chapter, we will learn how deep learning is applied to enhance the security aspects of applications. This chapter focuses on the application of deep learning algorithms and their associated techniques or frameworks.

In general, there are multiple applications (see figure 11.5) that can apply deep learning algorithms to improve their security features. In this context, the most commonly available applications that perfectly fit the incorporation of deep learning algorithms are as follows:

- cybersecurity applications
- IoT applications
- network applications
- campus security monitoring applications
- healthcare applications
- botnet applications
- energy monitoring applications

11.6.1 Cybersecurity applications

Cybersecurity problems have started to increase exponentially in the post-COVID-19 era, as the majority of operations involve online operations. Organizations that

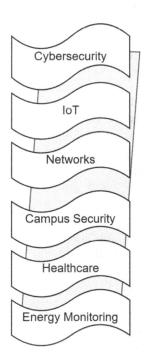

Figure 11.5. The use of deep learning applications to enhance security features.

are not prepared to withstand security breaches have become targets of choice for attackers/hackers.

To overcome this problem, solutions that aim to improve insecure environments have proliferated using various approaches. Among these approaches, deep-learning-based solutions have been the most attractive out-of-the-box solutions for the majority of organizations.

The most common cybersecurity problems that impact normal societal living conditions, especially in the Internet/cyber world, are described below:

1. Non-awareness—being aware that competitors will reach us to compete with us is the first step in developing cybersecurity measures. Organizations and industries often attempt to keep track of their competitors or knowledge forums. As information can be collected from various sources in an automated fashion, organizations might have to be cautious in dealing with these situations. In such contexts, deep learning algorithms can play a major role in automatically learning about the attackers from various sites. Cybersecurity problems in organizations can often be solved if employees are aware of the initial causes, i.e., deep learning-enabled solutions can suggest possible addressing methods directly to concerned officers.

2. Untrusted networks—the online mode of working, especially during the COVID-19 period, has considerably compromised the security features of internetworks. Organizations that have to handle data confidentially also have to be flexible in dealing with their employees. Consequently, organizations have had to weaken the security features across internetworks.

3. Ransom using bitcoins—collecting a ransom amount from organizations, which denotes success in the intended attack, is becoming popular in the cybersecurity domain. The attackers carefully inject scripts or programs to compress documents or folders without the knowledge of their users. The ransom amount collected often amounts to several bitcoins before the data are decrypted by the attacker. Deep learning-enabled solutions can find such potential hackers based on parameters that impact the attacks.

4. Automated attacks—most cybersecurity problems are due to automated real-time attacks. Attacks such as ransomware attacks, intrusion attacks, phishing attacks, and so forth, are automated using scripts or hidden programs in web services. Since they are automated, the solution used to find the attacks must be more powerful than the attacks themselves. Obviously, only deep-learning-based or traditional machine learning algorithms can fit this problem domain.

11.6.2 Deep learning for cybersecurity problems

Deep learning algorithms serve as a candidate solutions for solving cybersecurity problems. Supervised and unsupervised algorithms are applied in various use cases. The following subsections describe how supervised and unsupervised deep learning algorithms are applied to cybersecurity problems.

11.6.2.1 Supervised learning-based deep learning

Deep learning algorithms that input labeled datasets in order to train and create models are known as supervised learning algorithms. These algorithms are utilized to predict malformed Internet Protocol (IP) addresses, network failures, resource contamination issues, and so forth. For instance, a few network packets can be sniffed, and their properties may be labeled as secured or unsecured packets. After a few such packets have been sampled and labeled, future network packets can be automatically guessed or predicted by deep learning algorithms.

11.6.2.2 Unsupervised learning-based deep learning

In most cases, labeling the data set is a tedious task. For instance, inspecting networking packets and labeling them can be a time-consuming task, even though the learning model can be derived from the data set.

In fact, unsupervised deep learning algorithms, such as reinforcement learning algorithms, would be perfect candidates for such situations. Reinforcement learning algorithms have the ability to assign rewards and penalties based on intermediate learning-based actions. Accordingly, it is possible to improve learning mechanisms and solve cybersecurity attacks in an automated fashion.

11.6.3 Deep learning for the IoT

IoT-enabled applications involve battery-operated constrained nodes. As discussed earlier, these nodes are not computationally powerful and do not have sufficient storage units. Obviously, demanding applications such as deep learning algorithms cannot be processed by these machines. Additionally, these tiny devices might not have the required security components to handle recent software issues related to security features.

Considering the need of the moment, establishing deep learning algorithms, mostly lightweight programs, has become an important agenda for various researchers and practitioners. For instance, TensorFlow Lite has been introduced by Google to support the use of demanding deep learning algorithms on battery-operated mobile devices or edge nodes.

Deep learning is applied for IoT-enabled solutions in various ways, as described below:

1. Botnet applications—deep learning algorithms have been applied in the past to investigate forensic issues relating to botnets. In general, botnets are software components hosted on web services or websites to automatically answer queries raised by customers. These bots are employed throughout the lifetime of an application. In this way, customers are assisted 24/7 without major limitations.

   However, botnets are prone to various forensic issues, depending on the programs involved. In such cases, learning algorithms can assist officials to chase the defaulters or confirm the causes of forensic problems.

   As a case study, a voice-assisted IoT device or application such as Siri could automatically open the user's bank account and transfer money to e-shops. Obviously, a faulty device could listen to the attackers' commands, leading to an attack. Deep learning-enabled applications could serve as a candidate to address such situations.

2. Phishing detection—deep learning algorithms are quite popularly used to detect phishing attacks. These attacks are considered to be societal problems. They undermine the social impact of a person. For instance, phishing attacks could present users with unwanted links from legitimate websites. These attacks try to make users trust untrustworthy links. If the attackers win by luring the users, they can claim a ransom or extract monetary benefits from the users.

    Clearly, phishing attacks are considered non-social-good applications which need to be analyzed using robust learning algorithms, such as deep learning algorithms. In fact, in this scenario, the attackers often target college students, most preferably women.

    Several learning algorithms based on deep learning or machine learning could be applied to quickly identify phishers. For instance, support vector machines, random forests, classifiers, and so forth, from the machine learning domain; regression-based CNNs, classifier-based CNNs, their variants, and a few unsupervised learning algorithms are considered to be potential algorithms that could be used to understand the phishers. A few researchers have collected a considerable list of potential phishers who have sent threats to email users in the past.

3. Campus security monitoring—deep learning algorithms have been widely applied on campuses to provide security while protecting their wards. Campuses contain many cameras for video surveillance, voice assistants to support disabled students, gadgets for computational assistance, assets, and so forth. Providing security to all these campus components is a challenging task if human interventions are required. In constrast, deep-learning-assisted solutions could be a perfect fit for such situations.

    For instance, detecting anomalies in videos captured over months/years is not an easy task for a human workforce. Deep learning algorithms supported by framing tools such as OpenCV can process videos in parallel to quickly detect anomalies, if any.

4. Energy observations/auditing—energy monitoring and the auditing of energy sources and their associated utilization are considered to be social-good applications. Insecurity of energy sources can lead to national issues, especially in border countries. For instance, energy drawn from border countries without prior intimation or permission from the host countries can lead to nation-level skirmishes, which in turn lead to hatred. Observations of the level of utilization, the energy drawing pattern, and energy sources together with anomaly detection etc. are possible with the application of deep learning algorithms.

    (a) Energy sources—the top energy sources are wind, water, solar, nuclear, coal, and so forth. All energy sources, including renewable and non-renewable energy sources, are generally connected to one national power grid so that the power can be shared across regions. Unfortunately, these power sources follow a typical pattern of energy generation. For instance, windmills cannot produce energy during the winter season when the airflow is very small. Deep learning algorithms can identify the power generation pattern based on previous data.

(b) Energy utilization—finding the utilization pattern of energy over years for different locations undoubtedly increases the energy auditing capability of nations. In short, energy consumption during the night hours is higher than during daytime hours; also, the energy consumption in the US has a different timing pattern when compared to Eastern countries. Data can be generated to support the analysis of the utilization patterns of energy sources so that future energy demands can be predicted or proper planning can be devised.

(c) Anomaly detection—energy consumption in a smart city may have a specific pattern. However, it could be interesting for energy auditing officials to figure out the reason for a surge in energy requirements. Predicting the anomalies in datasets could definitely engender the necessary support to plan for violations.

References

[1] Abdel-Basset M, Moustafa N, Hawash H and Ding W 2022 *Deep Learning Techniques for IoT Security and Privacy Studies in Computational Intelligence* vol 997 (Berlin: Springer)

[2] Chen Z, Fu A, Zhang Y, Liu Z, Zeng F and Deng R H 2021 Secure collaborative deep learning against GAN attacks in the internet of things *IEEE Internet Things J.* **8** 5839–49

[3] Herath J D, Yang P and Yan G 2021 Real-time evasion attacks against deep learning-based anomaly detection from distributed system logs *CODASPY '21: Proceedings of the Eleventh ACM Conference on Data and Application Security and Privacy* A Joshi, B Carminati and R M Verma (New York: ACM) pp 29–40

[4] Ren K, Zheng T, Qin Z and Liu X 2020 Adversarial attacks and defenses in deep learning *Engineering* **6** 346–60

[5] Song L, Shokri R and Mittal P 2019 Membership inference attacks against adversarially robust deep learning models *2019 IEEE Security and Privacy Workshops, SP Workshops 2019, San Francisco, CA, USA, May 19–23, 2019* (Piscataway, NJ: IEEE) pp 50–6

[6] Tang L and Mahmoud Q H 2022 Deep reinforcement learning for building honeypots against runtime DoS attack *IEEE Access* **10** 1509–21

[7] Veluchamy S and Kathavarayan R S 2022 Deep reinforcement learning for building honeypots against runtime DoS attack *Int. J. Intell. Syst.* **37** 3981–4007

[8] Xing X, Jin X, Elahi H, Jiang H and Wang G 2022 A malware detection approach using autoencoder in deep learning *IEEE Access* **10** 25696–706

[9] Yashiro R, Hori Y, Katashita T and Sakiyama K 2019 A Deep Learning Attack Countermeasure with Intentional Noise for a PUF-Based Authentication Scheme *Innovative Security Solutions for Information Technology and Communications—12th Int. Conf., SecITC 2019, Bucharest, Romania, November 14–15, 2019, Revised Selected Papers* ed E Simion and R Géraud-Stewart vol 12001 (Berlin: Springer) pp 78–94

Chapter 12

Performance monitoring and analysis

This chapter describes the evolving performance issues that occur when deep-learning-based algorithms are executed by various computing machines, such as servers, cloud instances, edge nodes, mobile devices, and so forth. It pinpoints the most commonly applied performance monitoring tools, metrics, algorithm-specific parameters, and so forth, for deep learning-related applications.

12.1 Performance monitoring

Deep learning is designed to learn the patterns of data and provide predictions, which can consume a lot of compute resource or energy if it is not carefully designed.

In general, deep-learning-based applications must be monitored to improve their performance and reduce energy consumption. Application developers are often uninterested in looking into performance issues or underlying hardware issues. They engage themselves in developing logic that is a good fit for their anticipated working domains, such as transportation, smart logistics, smart factories, and so forth.

12.2 The need for performance monitoring

Performance monitoring is considered to be an important step in improving deep learning applications. Figure 12.1 highlights the reasons for implementing performance monitoring tools.

Most commonly, deep learning application developers prefer to have performance monitoring mechanisms for the following reasons:

1. Best resources—performance monitoring enables application developers or users to choose the right combination of computing resources. For instance, certain implementations of deep learning are effectively executed on tensor processing units (TPUs), as they are not considered to be the best candidates for central processing units (CPUs).

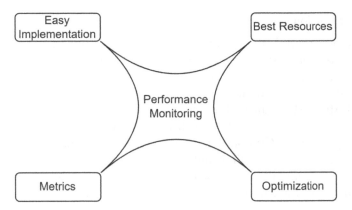

Figure 12.1. Reasons for monitoring the performance of DL applications.

An application developer might not be interested in learning about the performance impacts caused by applying TPUs, graphics processing units (GPUs), or CPUs. However, they would be happy if a tool or an integrated development environment (IDE) were to do the job for them.

2. Optimization strategies—deep learning algorithms can utilize maximum memory footprints or CPU/GPUs, especially for real-world applications. However, optimization strategies can be developed to improve the efficiency of applications running on various hardware nodes. For instance, the authors of [6] studied the performance of deep learning applications while inferring data; the authors of [10] evaluated the scalable performance of deep learning models, and so forth.

3. Easy implementation—in some cases, tools can assist application developers to choose the best set of packages when implementing deep-learning-related applications. In fact, if the application capabilities and associated packages are not known, users might not be effective in writing code. For instance, if a tool highlights memory leakage problems while selecting certain deep learning-related packages, the developer could automatically modify them.

4. Metrics—tools assist users or application developers to easily find the performance metrics of deep learning algorithms. In general, algorithms are bound to space and time complexities. These components are quite difficult for users or developers to write. Additionally, the situation is worsened if the users want to understand various software or hardware-related performance metrics. The most important feature of a deep learning monitoring tool is to capture a few performance-related metrics for applications executed on hardware architectures, including heterogeneous architectures.

12.3 Performance analysis methods/approaches

Performance analysis of deep learning-related applications is carried out in several ways, depending on the hardware utilized and the needs of the users. The most common approaches to monitoring application performance are described below:

12.3.1 Expert opinion

The performance of applications can be manually monitored, although this method is not an advisable one. In this approach, the quality of the application performance monitoring depends on the expertise of the person tasked with gauging the performance of an application.

In general, the performance of applications, such as memory usage, CPU usage, energy consumption, scalability measure, and so forth, can be theoretically formulated by experts. Computing, which is the combination of software and hardware units, depends on a thorough knowledge of software and hardware units. Such expertise is unavailable in most cases. Obviously, this approach is not a scalable solution for determining application performance.

12.3.2 Characterizing workloads

The performance of deep learning-related applications can be studied if their workloads are characterized [11]. In this approach, the major modules of the applications are captured and assessed in relation to the underlying machines. By characterizing workloads, users can obtain:

1. the requirements imposed on hardware components by software modules;
2. a proper plan and the level of parallelism, if any.

The characterization of workloads also enables scheduling, pipelines, or capacity planning features, and it allows the development of robust prediction models. Additionally, workloads have been characterizing using their concurrency levels in the past. The authors of [9] studied the efficiency of GPU-based concurrent deep learning tasks.

12.3.3 Characterizing I/O

Learning the input/output (I/O) behavior of applications can demonstrate the relationship between parallel processors of an algorithm. Typically, deep learning algorithms involve several parallel computing machines or clusters combined with networked I/O components. Executing these applications on a high-performance computing (HPC) cluster offers better performance than executing the same application on a cloud instance. Most of difficulties with cloud instances are due to virtual machine (VM) instances.

Characterizing the I/O of deep learning algorithms that execute on CPUs, GPUs, or TPUs enables users to complete the following related tasks:

1. it is possible to efficiently handle deep learning algorithms, as the underlying application performance can be estimated;
2. the number of nodes that need to be clustered may be predicted or selected;
3. it documents the affinity to CPU, GPU, TPU, or VM instances; and,
4. it helps performance monitoring tools to be executed with a small overhead when they are implemented along with the deep learning applications.

12.3.4 Applying benchmarks

Benchmarks are software components that enable processes to measure the performance of the underlying hardware or software components. They have known customized computing units that can be related to real-world deep-learning-algorithm-based applications.

For instance, if a benchmark code snippet performs efficiently on TPU machines, users or application developers can consider the code snippet to be a yardstick that can be used to measure newer algorithms or applications. The authors of [2] developed benchmarks to understand the behavior of Internet of things (IoT)-enabled deep learning tasks.

The major goals of implementing benchmarks in deep learning-related applications are as follows:

1. Assessment—newer algorithms can be assessed on different hardware units. For instance, if an algorithm is developed to detect objects in video frames, its performance on TPU-based machines, CPU-based machines, Docker-enabled containers, and so forth, can be assessed using benchmarks.
2. Tuning algorithms—these help users to tune their deep learning algorithms by selecting suitable parameters. In fact, several performance tuning tools or optimization engines can apply benchmarks to fine-tune parameters while executing algorithms on hardware clusters or machines.
3. Theoretical analysis—benchmarking paves the way for theoretical scientists to innovate and bolsters the impact of theoretical studies of algorithms. In fact, benchmarks remain an intermediary source of knowledge between pure theoretical study and unadulterated production-ready applications.
4. Validation—developing benchmarks for deep learning applications allows proofs of concept to be carried out while executing these applications on different machines.

Typically, researchers and practitioners have designed deep learning benchmarks which can be utilized to develop efficient algorithms—i.e. a few variants of existing deep learning algorithms. For instance, distributed deep learning benchmarks were developed to study the impact of spreading deep learning jobs/tasks across distributed machines; similarly, the authors of [4] developed Bayesian deep learning benchmarks to study the performance of e-health-related applications.

12.3.5 Applying microbenchmarks

In addition to benchmarks, microbenchmarks are also widely utilized to study the performance of deep learning algorithms. Users prefer microbenchmarks in certain situations in which they need to assess the value of a single function or one GPU kernel call routine.

Coarse-grained benchmarks yield limited insights into the impact of individual instructions or the performance of system calls. By developing microbenchmarks, application developers gain the following benefits, compared to those obtained from benchmarks:

1. they learn about the impact caused by the application of certain functions in developing deep learning algorithms;
2. they obtain finer-grained insights about applications;
3. they become intuitive developers, as they learn about the combination of both the software and hardware components of deep learning algorithms; and so forth.

12.3.6 Top-down performance analysis

In top-down performance analysis approach, deep learning applications are monitored from the higher levels of intuition to the lower levels. The levels most commonly observed (see figure 12.2) by performance monitoring in deep learning application domain are described below:

1. User level—the performance obtained by submitting deep learning-related jobs to corresponding IDEs or services varies depending on the active participation of users. If the user does not submit jobs on time or does not deliver jobs to clusters in the appropriate slots, the applications are not executed on time. This is a serious issue when deep learning algorithms are executed on third-party servers/clusters or batch-processing computational clusters, such as supercomputers.
2. Communication level—deep learning tasks submitted to cluster instances or cloud services such as machine-learning-as-a-service units typically follow the request–response model for submitting tasks. Obviously, performance gaps can occur when these tasks are communicated to the computing machines.
3. Cluster level—delving deeper into the performances of deep learning algorithms needs a strong understanding of the clusters or distributed machines. Distributed machines consist of tens of thousands of computing nodes that are tightly coupled using high-speed networking cables. It is important to understand the performance gaps that exist in these machines at a broader level.
4. Computational instance level—going even further down the levels used to understand the performance issues of deep learning applications, we need to discover the reasons for the performance impacts caused by individual

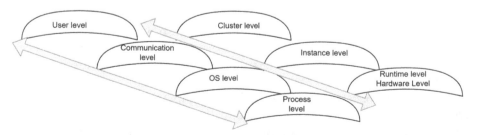

Figure 12.2. Performance observation levels.

compute instances. Cluster units can have tens of thousands of computer instances that are either dedicated servers or container-level nodes.

5. Operating system (OS) level—the next level in discovering the performance problems of deep learning algorithms is the OS level. The OS instances can be bare-metal OSs, hosted OSs, or guest OSs as found in cloud domains. Deep learning algorithms that are executed on cloud instances or HPC cluster instances need to be monitored at the OS level.

6. Process level—we next need to monitor the performances of individual deep learning processes that are executed on OSs or guest OSs. The processes of deep learning models can stall due to process failures or the unavailability of data. In DevOps cloud-native environments, application developers of deep learning applications must develop strategies that pinpoint those processes immediately before or after failures so that applications are executed with good performance.

   In most container-level deep learning applications, processes are killed by the 'out of memory' killer processes of kernels. Obviously, a deeper insight at this level of executing a deep learning application is a mandatory step for ensuring better performance.

7. Run time or hardware level—moving further into the details of executing deep learning applications, application developers or users are interested in discovering the run time behavior of these applications on machines. The run time behavior of these applications depends on hardware-level measurements that are found in processors or architectures. For instance, an Intel-based processor provides over 64 hardware counters to support the performance monitoring tasks of processes.

Learning about performance at this level leads to the following conclusions:

1. performance analysis requires a deeper hardware knowledge;
2. analysis at this level can lead to a big data problem;
3. in addition, the complexity level of this analysis is very high.

The top-down approach to performance analysis is useful:

1. when it is necessary to learn the tuning parameters of deep learning applications;
2. when it is necessary to develop optimization strategies for hardware resources; and,
3. when it is necessary to understand issues caused by hardware subsystems.

12.3.7 Bottom-up analysis

Bottom-up performance analysis is a key performance monitoring method that is used by several application developers. This analysis method is useful when users wish to conduct performance analysis for a specific application or algorithm. In this approach, the performance analysis is carried out at the lowest level of the application handling processes—i.e. the hardware metric level.

Obviously, the bottom-up approach to performance analysis manifests a strong relationship between an algorithm and the underlying hardware. The most common situations in which the bottom-up approach to performance analysis is used are listed below:

1. Resource selection—the bottom-up approach to performance analysis improves the resource selection process. For instance, the user of an algorithm could opt for field programmable gate array (FPGA) accelerators if it is not performing well. Since this approach deals with individual algorithms, it is very useful for selecting the right resources. The authors of [5] designed a resource selection mechanism that considered the constrained situations of compute nodes.
2. Optimization parameters—several optimization parameters are specific to applications. For instance, a deep learning algorithm executed on multiple CPU units might vary the CPU frequencies to fine-tune its performance. Similarly, the memory requirement of an algorithm can be modified for individual processes. The authors of [8] studied the impact of CPUs and memory utilization patterns on deep learning applications; the authors of [1] revealed the performance issues of deep-learning-based speech emotion tasks. The bottom-up performance analysis approach is the best strategy to use in order to learn these optimization parameters.
3. Execution environmental variables—typically, deep learning algorithms are executed with specific environment variables. Varying the environment variables could have an impact on performance. The bottom-up approach enables users or application developers to study the impact on performance caused by varying the values of execution environment variables.
4. Static applications—the bottom-up approach to performance analysis is a candidate solution if deep learning applications cannot be modified while improving their performance. As everyone agrees, there are several ways to alter the performance of deep learning applications. However, some solutions expect to be able to modify running applications.

   For instance, while improving the execution time of deep learning applications that are executed on commodity tiny devices or edge nodes, one approach to optimizing the number of iterations used by an application is to compromise the quality of the outputs. However, there are several other parameters or strategies that can improve the performance of these applications by varying hardware-related tuning parameters. Hence, the bottom-up approach to performance monitoring is quite beneficial for applications that generally cannot be modified.

12.3.8 Tool-based

Performance analysis tools remain a widely utilized method for monitoring the performance of deep learning applications. These tools are typically standalone software components that measure the performance of deep learning applications.

In general, performance analysis tools are classified into two broad categories. These are described below.

12.3.8.1 Profiling method

In profiling methods, performance analysis tools execute applications and then use the measured properties to throw light on what happened to the applications. This profiling method is busy collecting measurements at run time and preparing the collected measurements after run time.

This profiling method of performance analysis is useful if users wish to review the performance problems in future events. For instance, it is possible to perform a statistical study of the performance problems of applications using the profiling approach.

The major drawbacks of the profiling method of monitoring applications are listed below:

1. The analysis is not performed online—i.e. the performance analysis is performed only after the execution of an application. As this approach needs to wait for the completion of an executing application, the users have to wait a long time before they can understand the underlying performance problems. In general, deep learning applications have to be executed for hours when the data sets are larger or the algorithms have more epochs. Obviously, users are encouraged to wait for the completion of the algorithm so that they can understand the performance problems.
2. The analysis can generate a large volume of performance data. The performance data often exceed many megabytes for deep learning applications executed on parallel or distributed machines. Handling such performance data that are represented in different data formats, such as Extensible Markup Language (XML), comma-separated values (CSV), JavaScript Object Notation (JSON), and so forth, can generate additional computational requirements for tools that need to be executed.

12.3.8.2 Instrumentation method

An instrumentation-based performance monitoring approach increases the flexibility with which the performance of applications can be identified. It is a method in which programs are modified using specified function calls while undergoing analysis. Typically, these functions are instrumented using code snippets so that the measurement libraries can capture the performance properties of applications.

12.3.9 Prediction-based

Additionally, the prediction-assisted performance modeling approach has seen remarkable growth in the recent past. In the prediction-assisted approach, mathematical models are derived using several independent parameters. The major reasons for using prediction models to predict the performances of deep learning applications are as follows:

1. Avoid implementation—deep learning-based applications that are executed using DevOps or cloud services may require continuous integration of newer services on different hardware components. Obviously, implementations can become performance inefficient if the programs are not carefully written to take account of the hardware details.

   Rather than implementing the programs, it might be a better choice to perform predictions—i.e. the anticipated performance of deep learning-based applications could be predicted instead of executing the compute/memory-intensive applications.

2. Performance tuning—tuning the performance attributes that provide a better implementation of deep learning algorithms is a core topic of interest for many researchers or practitioners. In this regard, attempts are practiced at the research or production levels. In most cases, tuning an application's performance can lead to several computations.

   To avoid such computations while tuning the performance of applications, a widely accepted approach is to develop performance models that can provide mathematical derivations that highlight the performance.

3. Deep learning alternatives—there are hundreds of deep learning models that fit specific applications. For instance, object detection can be handled using deep learning algorithms such as a residual neural network (ResNet), YOLOv3, YOLOv5, MobileNET, Visual Geometry Group (VGG), and so forth. If a user has limited computation time, especially when experimenting in cloud environments, it is better to decide on the most suitable algorithm by considering performance features such as the memory consumed, energy consumed, CPU utilization, and so forth.

   Using performance prediction models, it is possible to evaluate the computing needs of these algorithms without implementing them.

Figure 12.3 illustrates the performance monitoring techniques/methods used for deep learning applications.

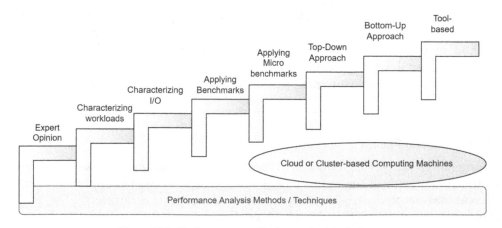

Figure 12.3. Performance monitoring methods/techniques.

12.4 Performance metrics

Performance metrics are crucial for observing the improvement of deep learning algorithms executed on computing machines or clusters. These metrics remain a yardstick for algorithms when experimenting with them on machines.

Some of the reasons for using performance metrics when executing deep learning applications on machines/clusters are as follows:

1. Analyzing applications—performance metrics are quite often utilized to analyze the functionality of deep learning algorithms or associated hardware characteristics, such as CPU usage patterns, memory access patterns, and so forth.
2. Learning about complexity—metrics are important to study the complexities of algorithms executed on single machines or cluster-based distributed machines. The complexities that represent time and space components can be observed using performance metrics.
3. Tool efficiency—performance analysis tools utilize metrics to assess algorithms, including various deep learning algorithms. If the metrics are predefined, the tools can focus on evaluating algorithms. In this way, application developers or users can orient their findings accordingly.

   For instance, an application developer focusing on minimizing the energy consumption of deep learning applications has to measure their energy consumption. If this is not done, the objective of minimizing energy consumption values cannot be fulfilled.

Typically, the users of deep learning algorithms are more focused on certain performance metrics used to improve or tune the algorithms. The most commonly available performance metrics for deep learning algorithms or associated hardware units are listed and described below:

12.4.1 Hardware-specific metrics

Deep learning algorithms can be monitored by observing hardware information or evaluating the necessity for hardware components. Metrics that involve hardware components to measure the performance values are classified as hardware-specific performance metrics. Figure 12.4 reveals the crucial hardware-level performance monitoring metrics used for deep learning applications.

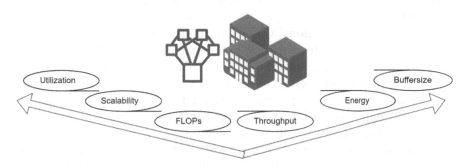

Figure 12.4. Hardware-level performance metrics used to monitor deep learning applications.

A few common hardware performance metrics are listed below:

1. Hardware utilization—in general, utilization-related metrics describe the utility of hardware components. Algorithms, both sequential and distributed, involve hardware components that need to be effectively utilized. Metrics that relate to hardware components are called hardware utilization metrics.

   For instance, the utilization of CPUs, memory, network, TPUs, GPUs, and so forth, falls into this category. Performance analysis tools that focus on hardware utilization metrics are used with the aim of increasing the utilization factor of the underlying hardware components used for deep learning algorithms.

2. Scalability—hardware units are hardly more scalable than software components. As various researchers would agree, scaling the number of deep learning services is easier than increasing the memory/CPU/GPU requirements.

   To some extent, hardware components can be increased by applying virtualization concepts. However, the software approach to scaling algorithms is easier than scaling the hardware-level components. The metric that captures the scaling capability of computing nodes when they are used to experiment with deep learning algorithms is called a hardware-level scalability measure.

3. FLOPS—the floating point operations per second (FLOPS) is a performance metric that represents the number of floating point operations used by a deep learning algorithm. The FLOPs represents the number of operations required by a training model or a test model. This metric provides hints about the number of iterations the inner phases of algorithms need to perform while running applications. In short, this metric is useful in the following ways:

   (a) to represent the unit of speed of an algorithm; and,
   (b) to represent the number of instructions that is processed by a computing platform.

4. Throughput—in deep learning contexts, the throughput metric is a measure of the number of classifications or regressions performed within a specified time. In most cases, deep learning algorithms require GPUs in order to perform object inferences. The throughput metric provides a way of expressing the number of inferences that occur in deep learning algorithms.

5. Energy metric—it may be important to focus on energy-related utilities in the context of deep learning algorithms. The energy consumption metric captures the energy used by an application. In general, the energy consumption of applications varies depending on the CPU frequencies or networking delays. Increasing CPU frequencies can enhance the speed of applications. On the other hand, increasing the frequencies could have a negative impact on energy consumption values.

   A few researchers or practitioners, especially those who are environmentally cautious, wish to reduce the energy consumption of applications by reducing the execution time of applications.

6. Network buffer size—networks are widely applied in deep learning tasks, as input data from various locations are collected and processed. Depending on

the network buffer size, the performance of the deep learning algorithms can be affected. For instance, increasing the buffer size can reduce the latency involved in algorithms.

12.4.2 Algorithm-specific metrics

Several performance metrics enhance the operations of deep learning applications. These metrics are often utilized while creating models or performing inferences. For instance, metrics such as the root-mean-square error guide the training models in deep learning applications. Figure 12.5 reveals the crucial software-level performance monitoring metrics used for deep learning applications. The authors of [3] described a few performance analysis metrics used for differential deep learning tasks.

The following paragraphs describe the different performance metrics that can be applied in deep learning algorithms or applications.

1. Time-accuracy—execution time is a common performance metric that is applied by users. The execution time of algorithms can be measured using wall-clock units or CPU cycles. Wall-clock units represent the time in the usual seconds or minutes for algorithms, whereas the CPU clock cycles correspond to the number of CPU cycles. If the time measurement is not accurate, the evaluation cannot be performed precisely. Obviously, the consequences are repeated over a long run of algorithms with several iterations and/or hidden layers.
2. Communication overhead—communication between computing nodes in a cluster or between processes within a single node is one of the metrics that influences the performance of algorithms. The overhead may be reduced by applying several approaches, as follows:

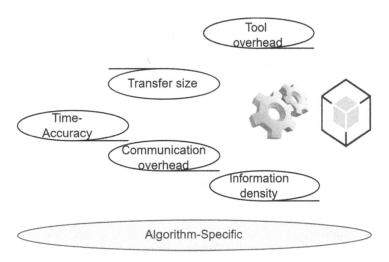

Figure 12.5. Software-level performance metrics used to monitor deep learning applications.

(a) increasing the affinity of CPUs involved in processing deep learning algorithms;

(b) improving the communication channels between connected nodes. For instance, the performance of connected machines with high-speed networks, such as Infiniband networks, is better than those of other clusters with low-speed networks;

(c) locating the required data nearer to the computing instances; and so forth.

3. Tool overhead—performance analysis tools can cause overheads if the tools are not diligently programmed to capture performance issues. For instance, tools that are developed to instrument the code portions of deep learning applications can have instructions that need to collect the performance values from hardware components. These tools execute lengthy code sections from their respective monitoring libraries. Obviously, these tools could be a performance bottleneck for bare deep learning applications or algorithms.

4. Information density—the increase in the amount of information that must be processed during the training or testing phases of deep learning applications is another bottleneck. A favorite choice for deep learning application developers is to reduce the amount of data or information required to create deep learning models. However, in most of the existing deep learning algorithms, the training data size is very large. In addition, developers tend to increase the density of the information fed to these algorithms to improve the prediction accuracy of applications.

5. Transfer size—deep learning applications can have poor performances if applications have to transfer data across nodes or services hosted in geographically dispersed locations. The transfer size can obviously become a bottleneck to increasing the performance of applications.

In particular, the importance of handling the transfer of training or test data of deep learning applications is a fundamental task when deep learning applications are hosted in federated environments. Additionally, implementing federated learning-based deep learning applications is considered to be a huge risk to increasing application performance.

12.4.3 Prediction-related metrics

Performance metrics that are specific to the training or testing of deep learning applications can be fine-tuned to improve the performance of such applications. These metrics are often integrated into traditional deep learning training models or test software components of applications. For instance, metrics such as the confusion matrix, accuracy, precision, recall, sensitivity, specificity, F1 score, and so forth, are called the prediction-related performance metrics of deep learning algorithms or applications. Improving the prediction level of applications could impact their performance.

The performances of several deep learning applications that utilize training and testing models from diverse learning domains, such as sentiment analysis, video analytics, and so forth, can be improved by varying prediction-related metrics.

12.4.4 Security-related metrics

Deep learning applications or algorithms that cause security challenges may be tuned using specialized yardsticks or measurement properties. Such measurement properties, which influence the security aspects of applications, are termed security-related metrics. A few notable security-related performance metrics are as follows:

(a) Misclassification—misclassification in deep learning models, especially in generative adversarial network (GAN)-related models, can increase the computation requirements and have severe performance impacts on applications. Generally, GANs are strongly dependent on the input data and varying image feature sets. These features are induced in compromised systems by hackers. Accordingly, users will have to pay the costs associated with these issues.

(b) Misprediction ratio—failures to predict values that iteratively modify real-world situations or connected machines can become a security challenge. Metrics such as the misprediction ratio are considered security challenges to IoT-enabled deep learning systems. This metric defines the number of missed predictions for either classification or regression problems that modify real-world situations. A few more security-oriented metrics are discussed in chapter 11.

12.4.5 Error-related metrics

Error is an important feature of learning newer things or subjects. Deep learning, especially in the unsupervised domain, is subject to errors.

The calculation of error functions in deep learning models uses two important terms while calculating the associated errors:

(1) the training model's output value; and,
(2) the real or expected value.

Error functions are centered around these two input parameters—i.e. they are calculated by taking the difference between these values.

Controlling the the occurrence of errors in trained models can invite performance challenges—i.e. the computation time or energy consumption of algorithms drastically increases when strict control measures are imposed. Accordingly, in deep learning models, a few tuning probes are organized, as follows:

(a) Mean squared error (MSE)—MSE is often utilized in learning algorithms, including deep learning algorithms. Typically, the MSE calculates the difference between the two input fields of error functions. The difference value is the averaged after the square of the difference has been calculated.

(b) Mean absolute percentage error (MAPE)—MAPE is an error function that calculates the error between the model output value and the real value of a learning algorithm as a percentage. To do so, the difference value is divided by the actual value. The difference values of all the findings in a data set are later averaged to form the metric.

(c) Mean bias error (MBE)—assumptions made during learning can lead to biased situations. This is also common in everyday human life. For instance, if a person makes prejudgements, the decisions related to the situation could be biased. Similar situations arise in deep learning algorithms if the input data are trained with prior assumptions.

Bias modifies the training model with assumptions that vary from real-world use cases. MBE is a metric that is used to represent the bias level of deep learning algorithms. The metric collects the mean value of the bias occurring in the training models of algorithms.

(d) Root-mean-square error (RMSE)—this metric is similar to MSE, in which the average of the squared error between the model and the real values is calculated. However, in RMSE, the root of the MSE is considered in evaluating the error function. The RMSE value typically falls between zero and one, although there are not many strict rules to be followed in this area.

12.4.6 Economic metrics

Metrics that describe the economic conditions caused by executing deep learning algorithms are categorized as economic metrics. These metrics relate to the costs involved in performing actions. A few notable economic performance metrics that are commonly applied in deep-learning-related applications or programs are described below:

1. Costs—cost is a metric that directly reflects the performance overhead of deep learning algorithms. This metric is important in situations in which algorithms are executed on third-party servers in a paid fashion. For example, deep learning algorithms hosted on cloud infrastructures can highlight the severity of the associated costs.

   However, training models can incorporate scalability features provided by clouds—for instance, the autoscaling feature in Amazon Web Service (AWS) solutions. The performance of algorithms can be increased through the use of modern architectures and scalable environments, but this increases the costs involved in the learning processes.

2. Cost-improvement ratio—the cost-improvement ratio is a metric that calculates the improvement that occurs in different iterations of the learning model. Notably, a learning model developed for the first time can take a long time or consume more computational power. Over recurrent learning stages, the cost of the learning process may be reduced due to the availability of the previous history of data. Accordingly, the associated costs are improved in deep learning algorithms. The amount of improvement is specified in ratio form in this metric named cost-improvement ratio.

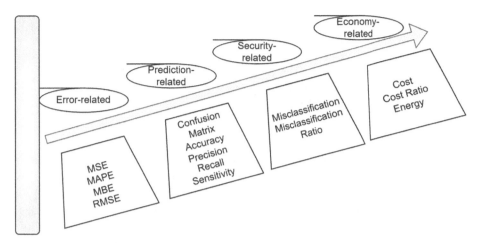

Figure 12.6. Error-, economy-, prediction-, and security-related performance monitoring.

3. Energy budget—energy consumption is often limited in some computing centers due to the scarcity of available energy sources. Accordingly, several techniques have emerged to control the energy utilization of algorithms. For instance, the cgroup feature of Linux kernels enables the energy of permitted processes in a container to be audited.

On a larger scale, data centers have a fixed energy budget for executing algorithms on their machines. The energy budget is a metric that determines the utilization of energy sources for deep learning-related applications or algorithms.

The energy budget of deep learning algorithms can be improved in the following ways:

(a) by decreasing the frequencies of the CPUs in a machine using the dynamic voltage and frequency scaling (DVFS) technique;
(b) by switching off certain containers, VMs, physical machines, or GPUs of a deep learning algorithm;
(c) by delivering data sets using optimal cache coherence mechanisms;
(d) by choosing appropriate compiler flags or energy-efficient Python packages when executing algorithms; and so forth.

Figure 12.6 lists the performance monitoring metrics related to errors. It details the economic situations, predictive options, and security aspects of deep learning applications.

12.5 Evaluation platforms

Depending on the monitoring locations in which performance metrics of deep learning applications were evaluated, the following different evaluation platforms and monitoring techniques are used:

- single-node performance
- cluster-level performance
- datacenter-level performance
- edge-node evaluation
- federated learning environment performance
- serverless function-level performance

12.5.1 Single-node performance

Performance metrics can be utilized to evaluate the performance of deep learning models on various computing nodes. These compute machines can be servers, laptops, Raspberry pi machines, workstations, etc.

The performances of deep learning algorithms executed on different nodes can provide varying acceleration- or performance-related findings. It is interesting for various researchers or users to understand the differences in execution times or performance metrics on different machines, including tiny compute machines such as the Raspberry Pi or Jetson Nanodevices.

12.5.2 Cluster-level performance

Depending on whether deep learning algorithms are hosted on clustered nodes, their performances differ. Metrics such as scalability, reliability, replica levels, snapshot requirements, volume requirements, networking capabilities, and so forth are crucial components that describe the cluster-level performances of deep learning applications.

1. Scalability—this metric defines the number of servers or compute units that are responsible for executing a deep learning algorithm. In some cases, it is also considered to be a Boolean metric that highlights the involvement of scalability features in the execution of deep learning applications.
2. Reliability—when deep learning applications are executed on distributed clusters, they can fail due to network connection issues or availability issues. This metric describes the need for reliable communications or reliable sources to drive the connected machines that execute deep learning algorithms.
3. Replica levels—deep learning algorithms that are executed in containers are often hosted using an orchestration tool such as Kubernetes or Docker swarm engines. These containers are replicated across clustering nodes to ensure a higher level of availability of services. Thus, the reliability metric is utilized in deep learning platforms that are executed on clusters.
4. Snapshots—creating snapshots or backups is one of the unique features of a cluster-level deep learning execution strategy. This metric suggests the necessity for snapshots and the associated memory requirements. In addition, the performances of creating snapshots, writing snapshots, and querying snapshots are predominantly studied in this level of performance monitoring.
5. Volume requirements—the number of volumes and the status of volumes are other metrics used in relation to cluster-level deep learning platforms. Each

node can augment several volumes, depending on the associated data and the costs involved in the deep learning algorithm. In addition, the volumes need to be numbered using logical unit numbers (LUNs). Creating LUNs can lead to performance issues in some cluster-level deep learning implementations. Hence, understanding the requirements of volumes and handling these volumes while executing deep learning-related algorithms or applications are considered to be important components.

12.5.3 Edge-node performance

Often, deep learning applications include edge-level computation to improve the security features and network bandwidth. As several applications have started to apply edge-level computation in addition to cloud services, studying the performance of deep learning applications on edge nodes has become a crucial task for several developers.

As a result of their power constraints, edge nodes are typically diligently designed to achieve maximum performance. Not only are execution time and latency fundamental metrics, but also other metrics, such as battery utilization, memory footprint, carbon emissions, and so forth, are important metrics for these edge platforms.

Edge nodes may be implemented using CPUs, GPUs, FPGAs, or system-on-a-chip (SoC) concepts. Additionally, these nodes can have connectivity via multiple communication protocols, such as LoRAWAN, WIFI, Bluetooth, PANs, and so forth. The performance of edge nodes differs, depending on the connectivity.

Measuring the performance of deep learning applications on edge nodes is considered to be a complex task for the following reasons:

1. Edge nodes are power-constrained nodes, such that using them for complicated measurements is hardly possible.
2. Edge nodes cannot handle the more robust data formats that are required to connect to heterogeneous nodes or autonomous machines.
3. Edge nodes have limited memory space. Obviously, storing performance measurement values in these nodes could be a tiresome activity, especially when memory-intensive deep learning algorithms are executed by them.

12.5.4 Federated learning environment performance

Deep learning algorithms can be hosted in federated environments that contain heterogeneous computing machines. In modern computing approaches, deep learning algorithms are split into layers of computing units in which certain portions of hidden layers are executed on different computing machines.

For instance, there is a possibility of executing the hidden layers of GANs on multiple edge computing nodes—i.e. computationally intensive layers could be executed by Jetson Nano boards, whereas a few of the other hidden layers could be executed on battery-operated Xtensa cores of ESP32 boards.

With such flexible split computing models, federated environments of deep learning algorithms raise a few novel performance concerns compared to the traditional performance issues of computing nodes.

12.5.5 Serverless function-level performance

In addition to observing the performance of deep learning applications at a coarse-grained level, monitoring the performance of deep learning applications at the function levels is attractive. However, it is not an easy task to observe the performance of applications at the functional level, for the following reasons:

1. The amount of performance data can grow exponentially due to the fine-grained performance monitoring approach.
2. The overheads of the associated monitoring tools can dramatically increase when this approach is used.
3. The resolution used to monitor the performance metrics of function-level deep learning applications cannot be as precise as those of the other monitoring mechanisms.

The serverless function-based cloud execution model has increased the visibility of deep learning implementation styles that use serverless functions [7]. Serverless functions are fine-grained functions that are mostly hosted on lightweight Docker containers. The function-level serverless implementation model of deep learning algorithms increases the fuzziness in the monitoring of application performance due to the higher level of randomness in the measurements.

References

[1] Agarwal G and Om H 2021 Performance of deer hunting optimization based deep learning algorithm for speech emotion recognition *Multim. Tools Appl.* **80** 9961–92
[2] Ahmad R, Alsmadi I, Alhamdani W and Tawalbeh L 2022 A comprehensive deep learning benchmark for IoT IDS *Comput. Secur.* **114** 102588
[3] Bae D and Ha J-C 2021 Performance metric for differential deep learning analysis *J. Internet Serv. Inf. Secur.* **11** 22–33
[4] Band N, Rudner T G J, Feng Q, Filos A, Nado Z, Dusenberry M, Jerfel G, Tran D and Gal Y 2021 Benchmarking Bayesian deep learning on diabetic retinopathy detection tasks *Proc. of the Neural Information Processing Systems Track on Datasets and Benchmarks 1, NeurIPS Datasets and Benchmarks 2021, December 2021, virtual* ed J Vanschoren and S-K Yeung (Berlin: Springer)
[5] Banerjee S and Chakraborty S 2020 Budgeted subset selection for fine-tuning deep learning architectures in resource-constrained applications *2020 Int. Joint Conf. on Neural Networks, IJCNN 2020* (Piscataway, NJ: IEEE) pp 1–10
[6] Castelló A, Barrachina S and Dolz M F 2022 High performance and energy efficient inference for deep learning on multicore ARM processors using general optimization techniques and BLIS *J. Syst. Archit.* **125** 102459
[7] Chahal D, Ramesh M, Ojha R and Singhal R 2021 High performance serverless architecture for deep learning workflows *2021 IEEE/ACM 21st International Symposium on Cluster,*

Cloud and Internet Computing (CCGrid) L Lefèvre, S Patterson, Y C Lee, H Shen, S Ilager, M Goudarzi, A N Toosi and R Buyya (Piscataway, NJ: IEEE) pp 790–6

[8] Daghaghi S, Meisburger N, Zhao M and Shrivastava A 2021 Accelerating SLIDE deep learning on modern CPUs: vectorization, quantizations, memory optimizations, and more *Machine Learning and Systems 3 (MLSys 2021)* A Smola, A Dimakis and I Stoica (mlsys.org)

[9] Gilman G and Walls R J 2021 Characterizing concurrency mechanisms for NVIDIA GPUs under deep learning workloads *Perform. Eval.* **151** 102234

[10] Kurte K R, Sanyal J, Berres A, Lunga D D, Coletti M, Yang H L, Graves D, Liebersohn B and Rose A N 2019 Performance analysis and optimization for scalable deployment of deep learning models for country-scale settlement mapping on titan supercomputer *Concurr. Comput. Pract. Exp.* **31** e5305

[11] Wang M, Meng C, Long G, Wu C, Yang J, Lin W and Jia Y 2019 *Characterizing deep learning training workloads on Alibaba—PAI 2019 IEEE Int. Symp. on Workload Characterization (IISWC), Orlando, FL, USA* (Piscataway, NJ: IEEE) pp 189–202

Chapter 13

Deep learning—future perspectives

Deep learning has undoubtedly developed across various sectors such as finance, agriculture, transportation, and so forth. The technique has raised interest at various levels, including researchers, artificial intelligence (AI) developers, entrepreneurs, and startup enthusiasts. Improved accuracy and utility factors have been the major sources of deep learning's popularity.

A few possible growth sectors for deep learning include:

- data diversity and generalization
- applications—healthcare, transportation, financial, agriculture, emotions, social improvements
- security and features
- AI methods and procedures
- performance features, etc.

This chapter discusses the future perspectives of deep learning and applications in the abovementioned categories.

13.1 Data diversity and generalization

Deep learning, due to the involvement of unsupervised learning concepts, can lead to the expected reasoning and generalizations. However, this technique is not mature enough to handle several broader applications, including societal applications. Deep learning algorithms must continually collect data from various sources in order to incorporate a continual learning processes. For instance, machines in industrial Internet of things (IIoT) scenarios need to continually learn based on the inferences obtained from nearby machines.

In addition, deep learning algorithms must be open to diverse data, including data formats—i.e. when data from different sources is added, the system must prefer to collect data received from diverse geographical locations, races, and age groups and data that represents diverse critical reviews from users. In this way, the algorithm can continually learn without any focused bias and can generalize its learning inferences.

13.2 Applications

As discussed earlier, tens of thousands of applications implement deep learning algorithms. However, these applications will continue to increase due to emerging innovations and proliferating research.

Concerning the applications, the most notable developments that can be incorporated in the near future are being studied in diverse sectors:

- healthcare
- education
- agriculture
- the environment
- finance
- energy
- security
- transportation, etc.

13.2.1 Healthcare sector

In the healthcare sector, several tasks could be implemented and utilized for the benefit of society. The following subsections list a few points for further reference.

13.2.1.1 Websites and materials
The majority of healthcare-related applications have worked by learning health data, including patient data, and the corresponding treatment methods. However, these methods have no approach to uploading data and/or creating awareness for newcomers. Often, medical data needs to be protected. However, the data that can be generalized or kept open must be accessible to the public. A procedure that automatically identifies the relevant data and processes the data to provide high visibility to a large number of groups is missing in the existing healthcare market. For instance, the development of an online database that represents a large group of like-minded diabetes or cancer patients can be beneficial for their quick healing. Similarly, quality datasets for brain imaging and tumor prediction are rarely found in the healthcare market. In fact, such focused databases could enable researchers, entrepreneurs, and doctors to make fundamental decisions based on their findings.

13.2.1.2 Focused ailments
Deep learning techniques are often applied in focused healthcare domains, such as care of the elderly or age prediction. It is important to identify suitable deep learning algorithms for these problems. Significantly, many researchers have proven that it is hard to identify one generic deep learning model that fits multiple problem domains,

because the collection methods vary. Similarly, the data processing approaches are dependent on the incoming sensor data, which has differing temporal resolutions.

13.2.1.3 Drug discovery

Deep learning could contribute to discovering newer drugs while utilizing scalable computational units. However, practitioners are still reluctant to suggest a suitable deep learning algorithm that will discover new drugs. Obviously, there is a dire need for newer techniques and mechanisms to enable drug discovery to overcome its existing challenges.

13.2.2 Education sector

Deep learning has played a crucial role in the education sector. The most commonly available applications, such as language assistants, voice assistants, teaching assistants, and so forth, have remarkably increased the visibility of deep learning. In addition, a few other applications that could be implemented or enhanced in the future are listed below:

1. Emotion-based learning—in general, classroom learning should involve several senses, such as speech, sight, touch, smell, and hearing. To increase the learning capabilities of students, teachers attempt to involve almost all these senses in classrooms and labs. In addition to the five senses, emotion-oriented teaching and learning processes increase the learning capacity of students. In this regard, several researchers in the informatics domain have proposed novel ideas for improving emotional expression in their lectures and student dealings.

2. Recommendation systems—several universities provide better teaching and learning methods for students. In general, many universities are established throughout the world to provide a better education to students in various fields such as engineering, medicine, law, and so forth. Students are often confused about how to choose the best university while considering several underlying trade-offs. A deep-learning-assisted solution that recommends the best university for higher studies while considering various factors such as budget, quality of education, geographical preferences, and so forth clearly needs to be developed.

3. Precision education—the education sector could apply a precision education system in the regular teaching–learning process. In general, precision education refers to increasing the performance of the learning methodology used by students. To do so, students must be automatically assessed at regular intervals, monitored using sensor-oriented systems, certified with sufficient credit points, and so forth, based on the suggestions and findings of deep learning techniques. To maximize student learning of students, precision education systems that apply deep learning techniques should not only consider the performance of the student but also the family and environmental situations.

13.2.3 Agricultural sector

The application of deep learning in the agricultural sector will soon become unavoidable. In fact, several applications have been practiced in the past, such as yield prediction, crop failure prediction, moisture content prediction, weed growth prediction, and so forth. Weed growth, which shrinks the yield obtained from cultivation, occurs in different ways: deep weeds and shallow weeds. It is reasonable to predict weed growth using sophisticated deep learning algorithms. Similarly, predicting the ripeness of fruits in a mango orchard or apple orchard requires modern deep learning algorithms equipped with power-efficient sensor nodes.

13.2.4 Environmental sector

The deep learning technique is widely applied to improve environmental conditions such as air quality, water quality, pollution control, and so forth. Society and research groups benefit from the deep learning-based implementations due to their proactive decisions and intrinsic intelligence. Several research topics that could be developed in this subcategory are listed below:

1. Air/water quality prediction—novel solutions could be developed while solving environmental issues such as predicting the air or water quality of environments. The prediction accuracy of such societal problems needs to be improved by the inclusion of better-combined technologies.
2. Use of renewable sources—it is often interesting to use renewable energy sources to reduce the potential carbon footprint of the globe. Many of us have a good understanding of the global warming issues that occur in nature. Diligently planning the utilization of edge/fog/cloud resources, while learning the domain problems, could dramatically reduce the upcoming environmental hazards.
3. Waste disposal—deep learning approaches have not yet become a common solution for categorizing and disposing of waste in cities and other locations. In fact, several object detection or learning algorithms could be incorporated into deep learning-based Internet of things (IoT) solutions to classify wastes. Notably, bio-wastes and plastic wastes must be separated into waste bins so that appropriate waste treatments can be applied by the relevant authorities or automated machines.

13.2.5 Financial sector

Deep learning could generally be improved in the financial sector. In the modern world, many people are engaged in stock marketing, financing, and so forth. Although deep learning has been introduced into the financial markets, its learnings are not particularly accurate. In addition, diverse applications such as stock purchase prediction, liquidity prediction, market prediction, failure analysis, brokering prediction, repayment prediction, loan waiving prediction, profit prediction, stock market prediction, and so forth, could be established in companies through the use of novel deep learning algorithms to achieve better process improvements in the financial industry.

13.2.6 Energy sector

The energy sector is focusing on renewable sources and predictive methods to diligently utilize scarce resources. The attention that is being paid to utilizing clean energy has drastically shifted the necessity for machine learning mechanisms. In most countries, including the USA, the traditional energy generation mechanisms are causing tons of carbon emissions. A few deep learning models based on probabilistic forecasting models could provide support while managing the resources related to carbon emissions. However, there are challenges in realizing the crucial phenomenon of energy management systems. For instance, integrating the sensors located in multiple energy measurement locations into deep learning models is a challenging aspect; similarly, collecting long-term historical data from geographically diverse locations leads to a big data problem.

Many other possible future directions relating to security and performance features are discussed in chapters 11 and 12.